W9-CHP-636

AFRICAN ISSUES

Series Editors Alex de Waal & Stephen Ellis
Published in the US & Canada by Indiana University Press

'Letting them Die' Why HIV/AIDS Prevention Programmes Fail
CATHERINE CAMPBELL

Somalia Economy without State*
PETER D. LITTLE

The Root Causes of Sudan's Civil Wars
DOUGLAS H. JOHNSON

Asbestos Blues Labour, Capital, Physicians & the State in South Africa
JOCK McCULLOCH

Fortress Conservation The Preservation of the Mkomazi Game Reserve, Tanzania
DAN BROCKINGTON

Killing for Conservation Wildlife Policy in Zimbabwe
ROSALEEN DUFFY

Mozambique & the Great Flood of 2000
FRANCES CHRISTIE & JOSEPH HANLON

Angola: Anatomy of an Oil State*
TONY HODGES

Congo-Paris Transnational Traders on the Margins of the Law
JANET MACGAFFEY & REMY BAZENGUISSA-GANGA

Africa Works Disorder as Political Instrument
PATRICK CHABAL & JEAN-PASCAL DALOZ

The Criminalization of the State in Africa
JEAN-FRANÇOIS BAYART, STEPHEN ELLIS & BEATRICE HIBOU

Famine Crimes Politics & the Disaster Relief Industry in Africa
ALEX DE WAAL

Published in the US & Canada by Heinemann (N.H.)

Peace without Profit How the IMF Blocks Rebuilding in Mozambique
JOSEPH HANLON

The Lie of the Land Challenging the Received Wisdom on the African Environment
MELISSA LEACH & ROBIN MEARNS (EDS)

Fighting for the Rainforest War, Youth & Resources in Sierra Leone
PAUL RICHARDS

*forthcoming

Reviews of *Congo-Paris*

'This fascinating book explores a neglected topic in African studies: petty transnational illegal trade between central Africa and Europe. *Congo-Paris* is unusual in at least three ways. First, it is concerned with the informal sector, focused as it is on the commercial activities of young traders who seek their "fortune" by setting up links between France and Africa. Second it discusses in some detail the question of African identity as it evolves in the course of such a long bi-continental roving existence. Finally it examines the relationship between seemingly insignificant trading activities and the evolution of globalization – as it applies to Africa...based on a relatively new form of anthropological research...' – Patrick Chabal in *International Affairs*

'An impressive illustration of the vigour of coping in the most daunting conditions of economic and political collapse' – Nigel Harris in *Development Policy Review*

'The strength of the work is in ethnographic detail and argument.' – *ASAAP*

AFRICAN ISSUES

Congo-Paris   Transnational
Traders on the
Margins of the Law

AFRICAN ISSUES

Congo-Paris

JANET MACGAFFEY
RÉMY BAZENGUISSA-GANGA

Transnational
Traders on the
Margins of the Law

The International
African Institute

in association with

JAMES CURREY
Oxford

INDIANA UNIVERSITY PRESS
Bloomington & Indianapolis

The International
African Institute
in association with

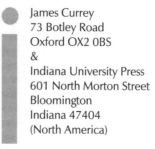

James Currey
73 Botley Road
Oxford OX2 0BS
&
Indiana University Press
601 North Morton Street
Bloomington
Indiana 47404
(North America)

British Library Cataloguing in Publication Data available
MacGaffey, Janet
   Congo-paris : transnational traders on the margins of the
   law. - (African issues)
   1. Commerce - Corrupt practices - Congo 2.Congo - Commerce -
   France 3. France - Commerce - Congo 4. Congo - Economic
   conditions - 20th century
   I.Title II.Bazenguissa, Remy III.International African
   Institute
   364.1'33'096724

   ISBN 0-85255-260-2 (James Currey Paper)
        0-85255-261-0 (James Currey Cloth)

Library of Congress Cataloging-in-Publication Data available
A catalog record for this book is available from the Library of Congress
                    ISBN 0-253-21402-5 (paper)
                    ISBN 0-253-33770-4 (cloth)

Typeset by
Saxon Graphics Ltd, Derby
in 9/11 Melior with Optima display
Printed in Great Britain by
Woolnoughs
Irthlingborough

CONTENTS

ACKNOWLEDGEMENTS

The authors wish to express their gratitude for the assistance of a grant from the Joint Committee on African Studies of the US Social Science Research Council and the American Council of Learned Societies, with funds provided by the National Endowment for the Humanities of the US and the Ford Foundation. Also for a grant from the Dean's Travel Budget of Bucknell University, Lewisburg, Pennsylvania, to Janet MacGaffey, and for funding from the Library of the African Studies Centre, EHESS, Paris, for Rémy Bazenguissa.

We are deeply grateful to all our informants for their time, their patience and their trust, and acknowledge most particularly the assistance of Bitsindou Simplice Mory, our essential contact with the milieu of the traders.

We wish especially to thank Jean La Fontaine for a detailed critique and helpful suggestions for Chapters 4 and 5; Keith Hart for reading and commenting on early drafts of several chapters; Claudine Vidal and Marc Le Pape for a critique of early drafts of sections of Chapters 3 and 6; and Cyril Musila for discussions on the organization of Zaïreans in France. We also acknowledge our debt to the late François Manchuelle for his comments on an earlier version of Chapter 2 and of some of the case histories.

We thank Kate Crehan, Sandra Barnes, Steve Feierman, T. K. Biaya, René DeVisch, Carl Milofsky and George Gerstein for stimulating discussion, comment or helpful criticism; and Véronique Walu Engundu, Didier de Lannoy and Ana Lanzas, Chizungu Rudahindwa and Honorate, Aubert Mukendi, Pius Ngandu, and Tamar Golan, variously for their valuable discussions of Congo-Kinshasa, assistance with research, or kind hospitality. We are also grateful to the following institutions and individuals for making resources available to us or for facilitating research: EHESS, Paris; Gauthier de Villers and CEDAF, Brussels; Stephen Ellis, Rijk van Dijk and the African Studies Centre, Leiden University; Eric Tollens, Frans Goossens and Godelieve van Zavelberg of the Catholic University-Louvain; and Stefan Marysse and Tom de Herdt of UFSIA, Antwerp.

Participants in seminars at the African Studies Centre, Cambridge University, 1994, Department of Anthropology workshop at the University of Pennysylvania, 1995, STANDD and the Department of Anthropology, McGill University, 1995, the Department of Social Anthropology, Manchester University, 1997, and the Northeast Africa Seminar, Oxford University, 1997, offered valuable comments and criticism on presentations on the research by Janet MacGaffey. Rémy Bazenguissa particularly thanks Laurent Monnier for an invitation to a discussion of the text at a seminar at IUED in Geneva, and the student participants for their valuable comments. Janet MacGaffey would like to express her appreciation of Bucknell University's excellent library and its always helpful staff, and to thank Jennifer Markewich, Lisa Toccafondi and Megan Langford for research assistance at different times, Mary Wyeth for helping to prepare the manuscript for the press, and Sara Abraham for her able assistance in translating from French drafts of some sections. Otherwise translations from French are by Janet MacGaffey. We are grateful to Cécile Vigouroux and Tila Andrevon for help in checking translations.

Finally, our especial thanks to Catherine Boutet and George Gerstein for their invaluable help in facilitating our emails and thus maintaining the connection between us, and for their patience with the process of this whole project. Without their assistance it would have taken much longer.

Earlier versions of parts of two chapters appeared in publications co-authored by us as follows. Ch. 2: 'Personal Networks and Trans-Frontier Trade Zaïrian and Congolese Migrants' in *Regionalisation in Africa: Integration and Disintegration* (Ed. D. Bach. James Currey, Oxford, Indiana University Press, Bloomington.) Ch. 6: 'Ostentation in a Clandestine Setting: Young Congolese and Zairian Migrants in Nganda Bars in Paris', *Mondes en Développement* 23 (91): 105–111, 1995.

GLOSSARY

aventure/ *aventurier*	going to France to acquire designer-name clothes
bizness	enterprises outside the law
bougeur	one who shifts things (referring to theft)
Château Rouge	station on the Paris metro
les circuits	trade and other activities outside the law
confiance	trust
la débrouillardise	fending for oneself
se débrouiller	to fend for oneself (also *on se débrouille, débrouillez-vous*)
descente	return of a *sapeur* to the home country
douanier	literally 'customs official', meaning one who sells because he has a clientele
la gamme	range of designer-name clothes of a *sapeur*
Grand	Great Man
kundu	witchcraft (Congo-Brazzaville)
Lari	Kongo language in Congo-Brazzaville
Lingala	trade language of the Zaire river; lingua franca of western Congo-Kinshasa
lusolo	inherited gift making one a successful trader
lutteur	one who struggles (literally: who bears heavy loads)
malaki	Kongo traditional ceremony to mark the end of mourning
mfumbu/ *fumbwa*	green leafy vegetable gathered wild
mikiliste	one who has travelled around and lived in Europe
miner	to mine
ndoki	witchcraft (in KiKongo and Lingala in both countries)
ndumba	independent woman in town; courtesan
nganda	unlicensed bar selling food as well as drinks
nganga	ritual specialist
NiBoLek	collective name for Niari, Bouenza and Lekoumou ethnic groups in Congo-Brazzaville
pagne	six-metre length of cloth sold to make a woman's costume

Parisien	one who returns to Brazzaville wearing designer-name clothes
radio-trottoir	gossip, rumour, informal channel of information
relations	personal connections
sachiste	one who carries bags of goods for clandestine trade/one who gets goods and gives them to a *douanier* to sell
safu/nsafu	purple fruit with a large pip
saka-saka	manioc greens
la Sape	*Société des Ambianceurs et Personnes Elégantes*
sapeur	one who dresses and practises the lifestyle of *la Sape*

ACRONYMS

GECAMINES	*Générales des Carrières et des Mines*
IMF	International Monetary Fund
INSEE	*Institut National des Statistiques et des Etudes Economiques*
MCDDI	*Mouvement Congolais pour la Démocratie et le Développement Intégral*
MEC	*Maison des Etudiants Congolais*
MIBA	*Société Minière de Bakwanga*
MPR	*Mouvement Populaire de la Révolution*
PCT	*Parti Congolais du Travail*
UJSC	*Union de la Jeunesse Socialiste Congolaise*
UPADS	*Union Pan-Africaine pour la Démocratie Sociale*

Rates of Exchange in 1994

5.68 FF (French francs)	US$ 1.00 (April)
34.29 BF (Belgian francs)	US$ 1.00 (March)
500 CFAF (CFA francs)	US$ 1.00
1.97 DF (Netherlands guilders)	US$ 1.00 (March)
£1.40 (British sterling)	US$ 1.00 (May)

THE AUTHORS

Janet MacGaffey is Professor of Anthropology, Bucknell University and is author of *The Real Economy of Zaire* (1991)

Rémy Bazenguissa-Ganga is Maître de Conference, Université de Lille I; Chercheur, Centre Lillois d'Etudes et de Recherches Sociologiques et Economiques, Lille I; Chercheur, Centre d'Etudes Africaines, Ecole des Hautes Etudes en Science Sociale, Paris.

INTRODUCTION

We open with a scene which encapsulates the cultural complexities and juxtapositions of the world today. The place is an empty corner in the vast lobby of a large, ultra-modern hotel in a Paris suburb, a meeting place selected by our informant. He is a prosperous Congolese wholesaler, an importer of African foodstuffs for the immigrant African community in Paris. He frequents the hotel, and is well known there, because airline flight attendants who import his goods in their free baggage allowance use the hotel when they stay over between flights. We sink into comfortable uphol-stered chairs and Jerome launches into the details of his life history and of his trading enterprise. Urbane and well dressed, he is at ease talking into our tape recorder. His fluent French gradually becomes more rapid and voluble as he gets carried away by recounting the problems he has had with his brothers back in Brazzaville. They are jealous of his success and he details the ill-health he has suffered because of the witchcraft they practise against him. He gives a vivid account of his consultation with a *nganga* (ritual expert) who, by magical means, extracted a viper's tooth and a small snail called *ngiumi* from his arm and two stones from his kidneys.

In the middle of this tale, a flock of Japanese tourists suddenly arrives and settles down in the chairs around us. Clearly they are about to get on to a bus to the airport: they are laden with large shopping bags and chatter away, exclaiming at one another's purchases from the luxury department stores of Paris. It becomes difficult to record the *nganga*'s activities, but suddenly the bus arrives and the whole flock takes off as precipitately as they came. We continue with details of Jerome's search for remedies. He proceeds to tell us of consultations at the hospital, X-rays and scans, all of which showed nothing and the doctors all said there was nothing wrong. The pain, however, continued. He next consulted a Malian woman in Paris, who gave a diagnosis of witchcraft, as did a clairvoyant back home in Congo to whom he sent a tape cassette recounting his sufferings. She told him he would recover. He continues with a detailed description of a *nganga* in Congo communicating with a dead uncle, attempts by another *nganga* to cure his illness caused by witchcraft, and his intentions to bring his sister and her husband, who have so far been unable to have children, to France to try *in vitro* fertilization.

In this luxury urban setting, international trade, international tourism, a multiplicity of languages and cultures, and traditional and modern medicine mingle, as Jerome's history ranges across cultural divides, geographical and temporal space, and simple and sophisticated technologies. Here we see the global mingling of cultures in the late twentieth century as they are juxtaposed in one individual's life.

How do anthropologists and other writers view people such as Jerome? Some would separate elements of his account into various dichotomous categories: traditional and modern activities, Western and non-Western sectors, beliefs from indigenous religion and Western science. Some would describe him as a man caught between two worlds, suffering the accompanying stresses. We believe that it is best to avoid these dichotomies. The polarization of the notions of tradition and modernity in relation to which actions are defined does not clarify the situation because, from the point of view of experience, the actors live only one social reality even if they sometimes speak of it in dichotomous terms. Jerome appears to notice no such divisions, no inconsistencies; all these elements form the whole that is his life. His existence ranges effortlessly between different continents and countries by means of jet travel; he builds up an international trading enterprise; he uses both modern forms of communication and a ritual expert's conversation with one long dead; he avails himself of both the latest medical technology and traditional African expertise. All of these phenomena figure prominently and equally in his discourse; he appears not to privilege any of them particularly. The stress from which he is clearly suffering comes not from this cultural intermingling but from the difficulties he faces in his family relationships.

Such intermingling of cultures and spatial transitions are commonplace in today's cities, a part of the globalization of the world culture and economy. They are very evident in the personal histories of traders like Jerome, who are the focus of this study. Throughout history, traders have travelled vast distances, or have sent commodities along trade networks; there is nothing new in this movement through cultures or in the exchange of cultural things around the world (Wolf, 1982). 'Trading communities of merchants living among aliens in associated networks are to be found on every continent and back through time to the beginning of urban life', some formally organized, others linked only by common culture (Curtin, 1984: 3). What has drastically altered such trade is the age of jet travel and the revolution in communications technology: the greatly increased rapidity of movement; the opening up of the range of places to which individuals can travel; the possibility of much more rapid shifting of far larger quantities of goods, in much greater variety, across greater distances than

rethinking dichotomous categories

was possible in the past. These developments have followed the emergence of a global economy into which all nations and peoples have been drawn: 'We have entered into an altogether new condition of neighborliness, even with those most distant from ourselves' (Appadurai, 1990: 2). The jet age has increased the rapidity of the process of globalization, and has radically transformed cultural interactions and the flow of resources between culturally and spatially separated peoples.

Globalization is generally thought of in terms of multinational companies and the changing relations between nation states and peoples as they become enmeshed in the world economy. Our study of the transnational trade of second-economy traders from Congo-Kinshasa (the former Zaïre, now the Democratic Republic of the Congo) and Congo-Brazzaville focuses instead on individuals operating in the interstices of these larger entities, and on how they manage to take advantage of the way the world economy now works. We examine the ways in which these traders organize their trade, the cultural factors on which it depends, and the part the commodities of the trade play in structuring identity among West Central African migrants in Europe. To avoid any confusion, we emphasize that there are now two countries called Congo, and that the traders of our study come from both.

The traders of our study come from the ranks of those who are excluded from social and economic opportunities. Half of the traders who were our informants were *sapeurs.* The movement of *la Sape* emerged among unemployed youth in Brazzaville in the 1970s. They competed for status by acquiring French designer clothing and wearing it as part of an ostentatious lifestyle. This movement brought young people into trade in the 1970s, as they sought the means to go to Paris and buy the expensive clothing that identifies them. This cult of appearance soon spread to the youth of Kinshasa and has become part of popular culture in both Central African countries. Through their trade and other activities, the traders protest and struggle against exclusion. In their search for profitable opportunities, we find them contesting boundaries of various kinds: legal, spatial, and institutional, and also the bounds of co-operative behaviour. They are individuals who refuse to abide by the constraints of the global power structure and its alliances between multinational capitalism, Western governments and African dictators. They contest the institutions and norms of both African and European society which frustrate their aspirations for wealth and status. They resist the hegemony and control of the large-scale entities dominating the global scene. We offer, therefore, a new perspective on a little known and altogether different facet of relations between the local and the global, one focused on individuals and their counter-hegemonic activities rather than on nation states and large companies.

The nation states of both Congo-Kinshasa and Congo-Brazzaville have been beset by civil violence and economic crisis. What happens in such a society as the formal institutional structure collapses, as 'disordered violence becomes a way of being' (Desjarlais and Kleinman, 1994: 11)? Despite prolonged periods of civil unrest in many countries, we know remarkably little about the social results of that unrest and economic crisis, about those who survive in a brutal 'ethos of predation' (Ibid.: 10–11). In 1987, a Zaïrean academic said despairingly: 'If things go on in this way in Zaïre, there will be no morality left.' They have gone on; and they have got worse. How have individuals responded to a situation of chronic repression and violence and the disintegration of social and economic institutions?

In confronting such chaos, we find people relying on the trust of personal relationships to compensate for the absence of a functioning legal and judicial apparatus to sanction contracts; creating their own system of values and status, their own order amidst disorder; and evading a venal bureaucracy and an oppressive state by operating in the second economy to find opportunities to better their lives.

The second economy consists of activities that are unmeasured, unrecorded and, in varying degrees, outside or on the margins of the law, and which deprive the state of revenue. Some of these activities break the law, others are legitimate in themselves but are carried out in a manner that avoids taxation.[1] As state personnel use the state to further their own interests, its revenues decline still further and its apparatus becomes more and more dysfunctional for the purposes it would normally be expected to serve. A vicious circle comes into being: as the official system collapses, more people turn to unofficial activities, and society and economy become more violent and chaotic. Yet, in the chaos, life still goes on: somehow, sometimes, somewhere, things work, though in unexpected and extraordinarily ingenious ways. The accounts of the traders of this study show how some forms of the second-economy trade, which to some degree, keep the economy functioning, are carried out and organized.

This study is based on the life histories of traders involved in second-economy international trade from these two West Central African countries. It builds on earlier studies of the second economy in the former country of Zaïre and across its borders, which emphasized the political and economic significance of the trade (MacGaffey, 1987: chaps 5 and 6; MacGaffey et al., 1991; MacGaffey, 1992), and on studies of politics and violence in Congo-Brazzaville (Bazenguissa-Ganga, 1996a and b, 1997). The focus here is on the organization of the trade, how it is able to function in the absence of a supportive legal system, and how opportunities can be found to avoid oppressive constraints by operating outside state laws.

Our analysis adds a new perspective to the literature on the everyday resistance practised by the poor and the politically powerless, using what James Scott calls the 'weapons of the weak' (Scott, 1985, 1990). This study

---

[1] For the reasons for using 'second economy' rather than 'informal economy' see MacGaffey et al., 1991: 8–10.

non-violent resistance of urban dwellers in the 2nd economy.

of traders shows that such non-violent resistance occurs not only in the lives of rural peasants as described by Scott, but also among middle- and lower-middle-class urban dwellers who likewise feel themselves to be subordinated and oppressed. The traders are explicit about their resistance to this subordination through their second-economy activities. When referring to these activities, we avoid using the terms 'illegal' and 'legal', since the boundary between legal and illegal is a political one, established by the dominant to maintain their power and control. This boundary is continually subject to challenge as those who are subordinated resist the control of the powerful by refusing to abide by regulations and those who are in power seek to enforce them. This is part of a dynamic process. A key exercise of power, and a point at which it can be contested, occurs when those who dominate choose, if they are able, whether or not to enforce their regulations. We wish to remain neutral and do not want to use this categorization of activities.

Our collaborative research was conducted primarily in Paris for six months in the spring and summer of 1994. The traders of our study had all begun their lives in Kinshasa or Brazzaville. They had traded first in these cities, then between their two countries, and thereafter with other African countries, with Europe and, in some cases, South-East Asia, the United States and other parts of the world. In 1994, at the time of our research, they were based in Paris (in one case just passing through). They all engaged in second-economy activity of some kind in carrying out their trading enterprises or related businesses.

The mobile individuals of our study make up ramifying networks extending through time, space and different cultures as they circulate commodities between countries. They present a challenge to traditional anthropological research and analysis, which focus on holistic studies of local communities. Our respondents could not be encompassed by the unit of study of any neat spatial and temporal locality. But, as Bruno Latour asks:

> Why would we no longer be capable of following the thousand paths, with their strange topology, that lead from the local to the global and return to the local? Is anthropology forever condemned to be reduced to territories, unable to follow networks? (Latour, 1991: 116)

Eric Wolf's eloquent statements on the need to understand the interconnectedness of peoples throughout history emphasize the futility of looking for bounded systems. He asks that we see human societies as open, not closed, systems, inextricably enmeshed with other aggregates in networks of connections (Wolf, 1982: 19). Such a global context requires that we move from intensively focused single-site ethnographic observation and participation, to a multi-sited ethnography that examines 'the circulation of cultural meanings, objects, and identities in diffuse time-space ...

tracing a cultural formation across and within multiple sites of activity'
(Marcus, 1995: 96). The narrated experiences of individuals reveal the
juxtapositions of social contexts. They are 'potential guides to the delin-
eation of ethnographic spaces shaped by categorical distinctions that may
make these spaces otherwise invisible' (Ibid.: 110). These histories reveal,
and enable us to examine, the ethnographic space of second-economy
activity, a phenomenon that is of increasing significance and scale in the
world economy, but which is often left out of studies of economics and
politics because it eludes their categorizations and cannot be enumerated.

The first two chapters of the book provide the framework for our data
and their analysis. The first describes the traders and their trade and
contrasts the kinds of networks through which they operate with those of
well-known Muslim long-distance traders from West Africa. It then
explores the methodological problems of a study of traders who are not
only highly mobile and thus difficult to locate, but who are also engaged in
clandestine activities, or to varying degrees operating outside or on the
margins of the law.

These traders are people who have suffered the consequences of the
political and economic crises of both countries, whose opportunities have
been constrained by repression and discrimination, and who have found
their opportunities to lie in operating in the second economy outside the
official regulated channels of trade. The second chapter gives the
historical background of each of the two Congo Republics in order to
provide details of the events and circumstances that have disrupted and
restricted the traders' lives in the tyranny of the post-independence period
of the two states. We outline the chronic economic and political crisis, the
consequences of civil violence and social disorder, and the drastic disintegration of social institutions and economic infrastructure in both these
nations. We show that the wealthy and powerful have amassed huge
fortunes at the expense of the rest of the population, and have excluded
those whom they dominate from opportunities for improving their lives. In
both countries, traders have confronted social life that has been marked by
violence and civil disorder, widespread violation of human rights, the
virtual disappearance of public health and welfare systems, and the
chronic breakdown of infrastructure. The chapter then outlines the history
of migration from these West Central African countries to France, which
was the primary location for our research. Finally, it relates individual
traders' reasons for leaving home and the ways in which they manage to
surmount the difficulties of getting to Europe, and describes the fluctuating fortunes and changing flows that are characteristic of their trade.

The commodities imported from Africa by these traders contribute to
the construction of an African urban identity for West Central African
immigrants in Paris. Chapter 3 details the goods and services for which the
traders find a market in this population. Material goods are a part of
selfhood, and defining identity is thus related to the practice of
consumption. The situation of rapid travel and communication in today's

world has permitted the construction of identity from multiple cultural sources and from many different contexts. The chapter sets out the basic data on the trade, including the terms used for trading and other activities, and how they are carried out.

A striking feature of the traders' life histories is that their strategies for survival and success involve contesting and transgressing boundaries of various kinds, as noted earlier. Boundaries are liminal areas. They are contested spaces and, as such, are areas of potential opportunity and ambiguity because one never quite knows what will happen. As Victor Turner observes 'liminality is full of potency and potentiality' (Turner, 1977: 33). Boundaries of all kinds therefore have potential significance in social and economic life. Chapter 4 describes the ways these traders transgress and thus contest the boundaries of the law by evading taxes, licensing requirements, and other commercial regulations. It relates the ways they evade the regulations governing spatial boundaries by refusing to abide by the visa regulations and payment of customs duties required for crossing national frontiers. It gives details of how they cross institutional boundaries by creatively finding ways to stretch institutional participation beyond its normal limits. Finally, it shows how some of them transgress the norms and bounds of co-operative behaviour by cheating each other in the pursuit of profit.

The organization of the trade depends heavily on personal relations because of the importance of trust for activities that are often outside the law and which therefore lack its sanctions. Chapter 5 shows how these relations work: their basis in kinship, ethnicity, religion, or friendship from neighbourhood or workplace; the reciprocity for favours rendered; the kinds of sanctions that can be invoked; and the pressures on the traders for redistribution of the wealth they accumulate.

Chapter 6 shows how the *sapeurs* demonstrate an oppositional counter-hegemonic culture in the ostentatious, competitive consumption of their lifestyle. They search for the excitement of pulling off a coup in risky anti-social activities, such as theft, drug dealing or setting up unlicensed bars (*nganda*). They spend conspicuously on fashionable clothes, and on the consumption of alcohol and rounds of free drinks in these bars. We find these activities to be examples of the tournaments of value identified by Arjun Appadurai, and to be comparable to other oppositional cultures in which those excluded from socially acceptable paths to ascendancy assert their own forms of identity and status. In their marginal existence, these people are fashioning a society outside society, a world of their own. In it they survive, live life to the full on their own terms, improve the conditions of their existence, and achieve status through the ostentatious consumption of *la Sape* and *nganda*. Society has excluded these people from opportunities to better their lives or fulfil their ambitions. In response they, in turn, reject both the activities and the value system of mainstream society. This rejection is made evident in ostentatious behaviour and in frequenting *nganda*.

For traders who aspire to move into the official economy, it is generally the case that, if they manage to overcome the difficulties of making this move, they still find they have to participate in second-economy activity in order to survive. The concluding chapter addresses the wider context of these traders' activities and locates their everyday resistance to the exclusion from opportunity and their social marginality in the broader class struggle at the national and international level. It offers some explanation of the unfavourable political circumstances in which they strive to protect and preserve their assets, and the nature of the odds they confront. In our analysis, we particularly emphasize human agency as we observe the indomitable efforts of individuals who strive against, rather than passively accept, the structural conditions that present them with such formidable obstacles.

1
Traders, Trade Networks & Research Methods

The traders we are investigating do not in any way constitute a bounded group or community. In this study, we are following the experimental trend of some recent works of anthropology: we combine political economy and interpretative anthropology by situating detailed texts on the lives of individuals in the context of trade between countries and continents in the global capitalist economy. Approaches to the African official or unofficial commercial and entrepreneurial spheres have shifted between those where historical structural factors determine individual actions, and those which stress the effect of human agency and individual choice in economic and social affairs; we find it most fruitful to combine them both.

These traders operate on the margins of the law: studying them is a challenge for anthropological research, not only because the activities in which they are engaged may be clandestine, but also because of the mobile nature of their operations. This chapter shows how we surmounted the problems confronting such research. We first lay out the dimensions of our subject, describing the traders of the study and their various activities, and then situating them in a broader context by examining the nature of trade networks, and their differences in particular regions and particular circumstances. We then proceed to detail the methods we used to surmount the difficulties of establishing relations of trust with informants that were sufficiently solid to allow us to gather data for an ethnographic study of activities which were often outside the law.

The Traders and Their Trade

The traders of our study do not constitute a homogeneous group. We can disaggregate them into three categories: undocumented immigrants, students who have failed academically, and former government employees. There is a commonality among their differences, however:

their life stories reveal that they are united in the experience of being excluded by the state from the opportunity to improve their lifestyle, fulfil their ambitions or even to survive. The response of some people to this exclusion has been to create, in turn, a world of their own in which they reject both legal economic activity and the value system of the society in which they carry out their extra-legal activities. They come from this type of experience in Africa to Europe, where they find themselves again excluded and respond once more in the same way.

This perception of the common exclusion experienced by the traders raises the question of their attitudes towards trading as an occupation. Among the cases we studied, those workers excluded from the administrative sphere in both Congo-Kinshasa and Congo-Brazzaville seem to have turned quickly to commerce. Why they make this choice, and the relation between commerce and other non-administrative activity in general, is an important question, because another tendency among second-economy traders is that they move out of second-economy enterprise as soon as they can find work in the official sector. We need to look at the wider context of state and educational institutions and their dysfunctionality to see why a switch to trade is the primary means of coping with the crises they have caused in people's lives, and why second-economy trade has so greatly expanded. Chapter 2 will give details of the situation in these two African nations.

Congolese from both countries are aware that colonization, which based local politics on the assimilation of elites into colonial society through education, made trade a dishonourable occupation. The valued profession was the civil service. This attitude has changed during successive crises, but our research shows that the conversion of the educated into traders is always a difficult experience which is often represented as temporary. One shopkeeper told us: 'My friends say to me disdainfully: "So you are just a manioc seller?" For me, this is a temporary situation on the way to doing what I have always wanted to do, that is to be a commercial lawyer.' A woman with a university degree who owned a dressmaking business had a similar comment: 'For myself, I am not a trader. I am rather an innovator, a creator of style. I must always be creative.' Another woman from Brazzaville emphasized to us that she did not enter trade from necessity, and in fact had artistic leanings that she would have liked to develop into a career.

> I did not go into trade because I had failed in school. My father wanted me to become a doctor, but I have an independent nature. I would have liked to become an interior decorator. I do, in fact, do something of that from my own home: I work as a sub-contractor to a white man making curtains. I go to Kinshasa, find a tailoring workshop, give them the measurements and they make up the curtains. When I have a customer, I also put together a team who will decorate a room. This is what I would have done if my parents had listened to me.

The traders of our study were living in circumstances of educational failure or in extended training programmes, were unemployed, or were living clandestinely. Some had been in such circumstances before they left their country, others only since they arrived in France.

In the precolonial period, the status of commerce was different. For the Republic of Congo, Georges Balandier shows that trade was a highly valued activity for local people at the beginning of the century (Balandier, 1985: 63–9). As time went on, traders entered the political arena. But, later, trade began to be devalued compared with the public service. The denigration of trade increased in direct relation to the level of education. Taking up commerce was considered an indication of academic and social failure, as Althabe and Devauges demonstrate in their analyses of unemployment during the 1950s (Althabe, 1963: 20–2; Devauges, 1963: 57–8, 61–2). Then, in the 1980s, trading acquired higher status as the political and economic crisis intensified. It was the common opinion that the state could no longer be counted on. This history of attitudes to commerce shows us, however, why large-scale traders in Congo were a rarity.

In Congo-Kinshasa a similar process occurred, although well before colonization trade was looked down upon. It was carried out by itinerant traders and people preferred farming. The Belgians downgraded petty trade but exerted influence through traders. They favoured people of mixed race, and Portuguese and Pakistanis, who formed an intermediate class between colonizers and colonized. There were more Portuguese than Belgians in the early years of the colony, and they dominated commerce in this period (Vellut, 1991).

For Africans, before 1970, being a trader was ridiculed; everyone wanted to be in the public service. Thereafter, it was the reverse, as the purchasing power of civil servants was gradually eroded. During Zaïreanization (indigenization of businesses), traders became wealthy, as did their clients, through a process of redistribution; they are now considered to be the people with wealth.[1]

Some of the traders of our study imported African foods and other goods for the African immigrant communities of Paris, Brussels and other European cities and in turn exported electronic and other manufactured goods and appliances, second-hand cars and spare parts, and clothing and accessories to Africa. Others accumulated wealth in enterprises outside the law in Paris, and then travelled to different European countries to buy clothing and other goods more cheaply than they could in Paris and profited from selling them to Central Africans in the city. Some travelled worldwide to obtain goods that they sold in Paris or in Kinshasa or Brazzaville. Their life histories provide details of earlier activities as travelling traders in Congo-Brazzaville or Congo-Kinshasa, of trading between the two countries, or with other African countries, and also of going on

---

[1]We are indebted to Cyril Musila for this information.

trading trips to Europe to import goods that were scarce in their own countries. These individuals engaged in an extraordinarily wide-ranging trade, and some were extremely mobile as the direction of trade shifted continually in response to changing market opportunities. They were not part of any structured trade diaspora but operated as individuals.

The immediate and intriguing question arises: how do these individuals organize their worldwide trading enterprises? We found that they relied heavily on personal ties based on kinship, ethnicity, nationality, and friendship from workplace and locality. Such ties are mobilized at all stages of trade. They may be used in assembling venture capital and for credit, in obtaining goods in foreign countries and transporting them home and, finally, in the process of finding customers and selling the goods. Traders rely on personal connections to help find their way around strange cities and locate sources of cheap goods, to get assistance with language problems, to find board and lodging, or to arrange vital assistance in shipping goods or evading regulations for crossing frontiers. The next question to address is: does the use of these ties, and the relationships on which they are based, constitute any sort of network organization?

The Nature of Trade Networks

Historically, trade diasporas appeared where the communities involved in trade were characterized by ethnic heterogeneity, where there was an absence of effective central institutions to guarantee respect of contract, and where regular services for communication and transportation were lacking. Such problems were often overcome when members of one ethnic group controlled all or most stages of the trade (Cohen, 1971: 266). Such a trade diaspora was made up of an interrelated net of commercial communities forming a trade network (Curtin, 1984: 2).

The trade we investigated between the two Congos, Europe and other parts of the world, however, is dependent on personal networks of a very different kind. They are not structured and permanent but are activated when they are needed by individuals trading on their own behalf, and not as part of ethnic trading communities. Such networks have been labelled 'instrumentally-activated personal networks' (Mitchell, 1969: 39).

Clyde Mitchell defines personal networks as a set of linkages which exist simultaneously on the basis of specific interests and persist beyond the duration of a particular transaction. Such networks are used for all sorts of purposes and many different kinds of transactions in an individual's life.

> A network exists in the recognition by people of sets of obligations and rights in respect of certain other identified people. At times these recognized relations may be utilized for a specific purpose. (Ibid.: 26)

The underlying expectations which people have concerning other people persist over longer periods than those in which they are actually activated and may, as in the case of kinship, last for a person's lifetime.[2]

> The actors and observers in any social situation are able to understand the behavior of those involved because it is accorded a meaning in terms of the norms, beliefs and values which they associate with this behavior. (Ibid.: 20)

Economists also speak of networks and differentiate exchanges along them from other forms of exchange. When items exchanged between buyers and sellers have qualities which are not easily measured and are transferred in the context of long-term and recurrent relations, these exchanges constitute a network rather than a market transaction or a hierarchic governance structure. Such forms of exchange involve indefinite, sequential transactions within a general pattern of interaction, sanctioned by normative rather than legal means. Rather than driving the hardest bargain, as in market exchange, the aim of network exchange is to create indebtedness and reliance over a long period; it is not as obvious when a debt has been discharged as it is in market exchange. In a market transaction, participants are free of future commitments; in networks, transactions occur through actions of individuals engaged in 'reciprocal, preferential, mutually supportive actions' (Powell, 1990: 301–4). These are distinctive features of the arrangements made by the traders of our study, as they use family members to ship goods for them, and as they abide by the norms of reciprocity in their use of personal ties for other forms of assistance in their trading enterprises.

Efficiency and effectiveness are the basic reasons for the existence of networks for economic transactions. Entrepreneurs may use them as a strategy for several reasons: to obtain a competitive advantage, to lower transaction costs by generating trust through identity of values and motivations and emphasis on long-term relationships, and to get access to resources (Jarillo, 1988: 32, 34–9). 'These relationships have all the characteristics of "investments," since there is always a certain "asset specificity" to the know-how of, say, dealing with a given supplier instead of a new one' (Ibid.: 34). Networks appear especially where there is need for efficient, reliable information which is not otherwise readily available; people put most trust in information that comes from someone they know well, and trust and mutual dependency result in rapid communication of information (Powell, 1990: 304–5). Reciprocity is a key element in network organization. Rather than involving a precise definition of equivalence in exchange, it tends to emphasize indebtedness and obligation. In trade outside the law, all these elements are needed for its successful operation.

---

[2]Boissevain notes that most people using the network concept have done so for action sets and have not been concerned with latent links (Boissevain, 1974: 36).

So far we have discussed views on networks of anthropologists, whose focus is on relations between people, of geographers and historians, whose concerns are with spatial migrations, and of economists, who emphasize forms of exchange. We add an emphasis on the goods that circulate in these trade networks, and their cultural meanings. We want to include all three of the following: the people involved, the relations and obligations between them and their forms of exchange and co-operation; the spatial trajectories of people and goods and the arenas in which they are displayed and sold, which cannot be done just anywhere; and the goods, for which we need to understand the reasons internal to the network as to why particular goods and not others are traded. All three constitute the components of a network. This approach draws on the work of Bruno Latour and John Law. Starting from a structuralist base, they look at relations, and location in sets of relations, and at how relations are mediated through objects. 'Structures do not simply reside in the actions of people, or in memory traces. 'They exist in a network of heterogeneous material arrangements' (Latour, 1991: 16).' The social is made up of not only the human but also the material' (Law, 1992: 381).

Studies of long-distance trade mostly concern West Africa. Our study, however, is focused on West Central Africa, and some interesting points of contrast with West African trading diasporas emerge. Many West African traders are Muslims, for whom religion serves as a sanction for business transactions; Central Africans are mostly Christian, but religion plays no part in their business transactions. West African networks are highly structured; Central African ones are individually constructed, each trader must activate his or her personal relations to a specific end. West African networks often involve individuals from a common ethnic background; Congolese from both countries may have networks that include different ethnic identities, so that the boundaries of the network in which the actor devises strategies are not at all clear. There are a number of detailed studies of trade in different regions of West Africa, which give a clear picture of how it is organized. A few details will sharpen our understanding of the contrast with Central African trade.

Long-distance Trade in West Africa
Abner Cohen's classic early study of Hausa communities in Yoruba towns and their control over long-distance trade between the savanna and the forest belt of Nigeria showed the importance of traditional culture and religion in the organization of this trade. For the Hausa, the good life consisted of success in trade and the attainment of Islamic learning (Cohen, 1969).

Recent studies show that traders between Mali, Burkina Faso and northern Côte d'Ivoire make strategic use of ties of kinship, locality, religion, politics and finance, using networks reaching across frontiers and over several generations to circulate information, credit and goods. These traders invest in local politics; in marriage ties with important families; in financing religious ceremonies, Koranic schools and mosques; and in pilgrimage to Mecca. All such investments constitute the means whereby economic capital is converted into authority and position in the hierarchy of the religious community. Profits in the trade are in direct proportion to this social relations capital of the trader. These relations reduce the risks, which are particularly high in clandestine forms of trade across frontiers, in which agreements can be guaranteed only by the interdependence and recognition of reciprocal obligations between the parties concerned (Labazée, 1993: 144–70).

Islam also imposes and sanctions strict rules of conduct and ethics in the networks of big Hausa traders in their trade across the borders of northern Nigeria. Rich traders are closely linked to marabouts, to whom they give money and substantial gifts for reciting the Koran and for healing. Breaking one's word means exclusion from the business world and betrays one's religious faith, both of them fundamental for membership of Hausa society. Confidence between the big traders and their business partners, who are bound to them also by a religious tie, holds a religious guarantee more powerful than anything modern legislation can offer (Grégoire, 1993: 92–5).

From Senegal, diamond traders travel from country to country to Congo-Kinshasa and from there to other continents. They are supported by local residents who themselves migrated earlier from the Senegal river valley, in a chain of links based on kinship, marriage and friendship, cemented by the bond of a common religion (Bredeloup, 1993). Senegalese trade widely in other commodities besides diamonds. The Mouride Islamic brotherhood links large wholesalers in Dakar to networks of traders in New York, Paris, Brussels and Dubai. These Mouride emigrants form close religious and economic communities, which are hierarchically structured. The migrants who came first formed critical points of support for later arrivals; different networks specialized in organizing trade in different commodities. Betrayal of trust inevitably brings grave consequences for an individual's whole existence, and such stringent controls promote commercial success (Ebin, 1992).[3]

'Capitalizing solidarity'[4] is fundamental to the economic success of these networks. Three types of such social capital can be distinguished among these West African traders: the social capital of people that can be mobilized for a particular need by an individual; the religious capital of the approval of the religious community, gained by financial support and adherence to approved practices; and the political capital that comes from access to, and cultivation of, the essential connections within the state

---

[3]The scale of this trade boosts the wholesale business in New York, one Pakistani going so far as to claim that African customers account for the survival of many of his fellow New York wholesalers (Ebin, 1992: 95).

[4]Thanks to Simon Yana for suggesting this term.

needed to run successful business (Grégoire, 1993: 98–9). For an example of the last in Chad, families who have been in commerce for generations give their sons both a Koranic and a university or commercial education, thus insuring for their businesses the connections in the bureaucracy necessary for commercial success (Arditi, 1993: 216).

West Central African Trade
In contrast to West Africa, the West Central African trade of our study does not involve a continuing structured network of links between traders in particular commodities and over particular routes. Instead, it involves mobilizing networks on an individual basis according to circumstances, as the trade changes direction to respond to new market opportunities. Individuals activate linkages based on ties of kinship, ethnicity, friendship and nationality as they need assistance and advice in establishing themselves in a new country. The most important of these linkages, and the ones most often called upon, are those based on kinship. Such kin networks may not be organized for a specific purpose but the relationships on which they are founded can be activated by individuals as necessary.[5] They are maintained by means of considerable material investment over time. They are networks in the sense defined above: 'a set of linkages which exist simultaneously on the basis of specific interests and persist beyond the duration of a particular transaction', and are an essential feature of the functioning and success of this trade in all commodities.

Within and across the borders of Congo-Kinshasa, however, there have also been more structured trade diasporas of Asians and Greeks, and in Kivu, on the eastern border of the country, the Nande have formed such a diaspora, trading with East Africa and down to Kinshasa.[6] These ethnic diasporas are more like the structured West African trade networks and are inherently different from the instrumental networks of the long-distance international traders of our study.

Studying mobile traders: Multi-sited ethnography

Networks based on kinship and ethnicity have organized long-distance African trade for centuries (Cohen, 1969; Meillassoux, 1971; Curtin, 1984). State policies and social and historical contexts have all accounted for the rise of such forms of organization. As we shall show, they still do. But how have the changes associated with globalization affected trade networks?

Globalization is 'a coalescence of varied transnational processes and domestic structures, allowing the economy, politics, culture, and ideology

---

[5]The personal network exists situationally in that the observer perceives only those links, of all the potential ones which are activated and in use for a particular time, which he considers significant for the problem he is interested in (Powell, 1990: 26).
[6]These diasporas are documented in MacGaffey, 1987: 64–6, 74–8, and chap 6.

of one country to penetrate another' (Mittelman, 1996: 2). This process has accelerated in the last thirty years as the age of jet travel and rapid communications has extended social relations worldwide and caused local happenings to be shaped more and more by distant events. As the increasing mobility of human populations has stretched existing social relations and established new ones in extended networks, it has become increasingly difficult for social scientists to conceive of human diversity as comprised by bounded, independent cultures or nation states (Giddens, 1990; Hannerz, 1990; Cheater, 1995). But scholars also stress that, in this process, modernizing social forces and their material accompaniments have by no means eroded local cultural differences, as might have seemed inevitable (Comaroff and Comaroff, 1993: xi).

With our study of the ramifying and sometimes global networks of these highly mobile traders operating on the margins of, or outside, the law, we are following new developments in anthropology which call for research across and within multiple sites of activity. We have moved out from the single site of classical ethnographic research in order to 'examine the circulation of cultural meanings, objects, and identities in diffuse time-space' (Marcus, 1995: 96). In this multi-sited ethnography:

> The object of study is ultimately mobile and multiply situated, so any ethnography of such an object will have a comparative dimension that is integral to it, in the form of juxtapositions of phenomena that conventionally have appeared to be (or conceptually have been kept) 'worlds apart.' Comparison reenters the very act of ethnographic specification by a research design of juxtapositions in which the global is collapsed into and made an integral part of parallel, related local situations rather than something monolithic or external to them. (Ibid.: 102)

Multi-sited ethnographies trace within different settings complex cultural phenomena and follow the movements of a particular group of subjects. We attempt as much to understand something broadly about the system as to understand our local subjects (Ibid.: 110–11).

As ethnographers, we have each carried out research separately in multiple sites, but with this research on traders in Paris our work entered a collaborative phase for the longitudinal research in which each of us is engaged. In the course of this collaboration, we made short visits to other cities, but we primarily studied mobility by following the lives of the traders through their autobiographical accounts.

Research Location

The urban researcher must select 'certain actors, activities, or locations as the anchor points for fieldwork' (Sanjek, 1978: 257). George Marcus poses some critical questions for us here:

What is holism once the line between the local worlds of subjects and the global world of systems becomes radically blurred? How, then, is the representational space of the realist ethnography to be textually bounded and contained in the compelling recognition of the larger systems' contexts of any ethnographic subjects? (Marcus, 1986: 171)

One approach, he suggests, is to explore two or more locales and show their interconnections, both over time and simultaneously. The other is to construct the text around a strategically situated locale, treating the larger system as background and as a critical constituent of cultural life within the bounded system (Ibid.: 172). Our research essentially combines the two approaches.

In the longitudinal research in which we have both engaged and which we have developed in this joint study, we have focused on different locations and explored their interconnections. Bazenguissa has worked on the history of Congolese politics, focusing particularly on the relationship of the governed to the power structure. Through research on popular practices, such as *la Sape*, football, and frequenting *nganda*, he has investigated how the governed have invented a political culture of their own. He is also researching urban violence in Congo-Brazzaville during the process of democratization (Bazenguissa-Ganga, 1992a and b; 1996a and b; 1997). MacGaffey has studied the second economy of the former Zaïre, focusing initially in 1979 on trade and commerce in Kisangani, one of the country's three principal cities, looking at the activities of traders between city and hinterland, and with other cities, and then, since 1987, at second-economy trade across national and international borders (MacGaffey, 1987; MacGaffey et al., 1991; MacGaffey, 1992, 1994a and b, 1998).

Our joint research explores the organization of trade between Africa, Europe and other continents, in the strategically situated locale of Paris, where we carried out our collaborative fieldwork from January to June 1994. Bazenguissa, who lives in Paris, has followed up and continued it up to the present. His residence in that city, and his connections with the Congolese community there, determined it as the primary location for our study. Such contacts were an essential prerequisite for our research. For the study of second-economy trade with Europe, we might otherwise just as well have chosen Brussels; opportunity governed our choice.

How should the researcher construct the multi-sited space to be traversed? Marcus spells it out precisely:

Multi-sited research is designed around chains, paths, threads, conjunctions, juxtapositions of locations in which the ethnographer establishes some form of literal, physical presence, with an explicitly posited logic of association or connection among sites that in fact defines the argument of the ethnography. (Marcus, 1995: 105)

We visited Brussels, Leiden and Lille, following up contacts that we had in those cities, in a trip of several weeks during the research period. We relied primarily, however, on the personal narratives of the traders' lives to follow paths and juxtapositions, to move between locations and to construct multi-sited spaces. This is a method so far little used for this purpose (Ibid.: 109).

In Paris, the Château Rouge area was our primary location. This is an area several blocks square, adjacent to the metro station of that name. It could be appropriately called 'Little Africa': as you walk the streets, you hear African languages more than you hear French, and there are more Africans than Europeans in the streets. Most of the shops sell African foods, beauty products, cloth and music (they are owned by Africans and Asians). Many women wear African dress and carry babies on their backs. Dressmakers offer to make up the lengths of wax-prints sold in the stores into African-style dresses for women; hair salons style their hair. Street traders also sell African foods and beauty products – when the police are not around. Africans predominate in the cafés and bars. There is one African-owned bar frequented entirely by Africans. The atmosphere in this neighbourhood is friendly and full of gaiety; people are having fun and feel uninhibited. They call greetings noisily across the street and stop to talk and joke with those they know. Africans of all nationalities live all over Paris but many of them congregate here, not only to shop, transact business and meet friends and acquaintances, but also to spend time in a public space which provides surroundings and atmosphere that resemble home much more closely than do the Parisian neighbourhoods in which they live.

The traders we studied do much of their business in the Château Rouge area. Here they own or rent warehouses to store the goods they import, own or rent retail shops or sell on the pavements, and circulate through the bars, cafés, shops and streets to find customers and make trading deals.

Methods

Fieldwork is the active practice of anthropology. It is a form of social engagement, not a withdrawal into secluded academe, and is the way in which anthropologists connect directly with social reality and social change.[7] Quantitative methods and surveys are impossible for research on activities that are outside, or marginal to, the law. The qualitative methods and reliance on establishing trust and confidence that are a classic part of anthropological fieldwork are particularly suited to investigating activities that may be clandestine. They have been successfully used, for example, for studying the underground economy of drug dealing in Harlem

---

[7]We owe thanks to Keith Hart for this point.

(Bourgois, 1995). The nature of our research meant that we relied heavily on case material and the collection of life histories as our primary research tool. This method has previously been used successfully in Africa to investigate unrecorded trade (Schoepf and Engundu, 1991; Labazée, 1993; Lambert, 1993; Ebin, 1993). In addition to its usefulness as a methodological tool, a particular advantage of life-history material is that it has the potential to reveal dissonant voices, changing views, or the varying perspectives of persons of different classes or religions (John M. Janzen. Book review, *Journal of the Royal Anthropological Institute*, 1 (2), 1995: 436).

Collaborative Research

This study was carried out as a collaborative research project by a Congolese and an English researcher, the former trained in anthropology in France, the latter in England and the United States. It follows on the work of Stephen Gudeman and Alberto Rivera in Colombia (1989, 1990).[8]

Gudeman and Rivera propose the model of 'conversation' for the practice of anthropology (Gudeman and Rivera, 1989: 268). Following this model, we conducted 'continuous review' of our fieldwork, either when driving in the car around Paris, in cafés while waiting for informants who might, or might not, show up, and subsequently at intervals when we have been able to get together since our period of collaborative fieldwork. Our conversations have been in French. During the research, we reviewed the notes and transcripts of interviews, discussing the implications of what we had been told, and checking for accuracy and interpretation. Our analysis has unfolded as a joint endeavour in the course of these conversations, part of a process of 'actively negotiating a shared vision of reality' (Clifford, 1983: 134), one that was extraordinarily interesting and rewarding. In this process of collaborative research, we found, like Gudeman and Rivera, that:

> This dialectical drawing out and use of personal knowledge led us to question whether anthropology might be nearly impossible for the single foreign researcher, who, lacking a lifetime of personal knowledge, could never fill out, make the cultural connections, or turn into longhand what we increasingly understood to be elliptical field encounters; but it might also be impossible for the 'native,' for whom every verb and noun, every phrase and explanation, was too familiar to require conscious explication – or was an atavism, unconnected to anything else. (Gudeman and Rivera, 1989: 269)

---

[8]Collaboration with local scholars and experts has been utilized in several existing studies of unrecorded trade, for example, MacGaffey et al., 1991; Herrera, 1992a; Igue and Soule, 1992. See also, on the problems of research on Africa's unrecorded international trade, Ellis and MacGaffey, 1996.

Bazenguissa's intimate knowledge of African culture was invaluable for the setting up of this complex research project. He left his country for Paris in adolescence, so the diaspora community is very well known to him. His insider knowledge conferred on him an intimate knowledge of the field situation, which was crucial for detecting problems, seeking out research sites, setting up contacts and interpreting the information we obtained. His language skills were an essential asset for the project: as well as French, he speaks both Lari and Lingala, the languages of the traders. As Marcus notes, knowing the language is an important guarantee of the integrity of fieldwork just as much in multi-sited as in traditional fieldwork (Marcus, 1995: 101). One solution to the almost insoluble problem of the extensive language skills likely to be needed for multi-sited research is collaboration such as ours.

However, Bazenguissa's background caused him some problems as well as advantages: in particular, how to resolve the important epistemological question of maintaining distance and independent judgement in relation to experiences he had had himself. This was a challenge. The problem of maintaining distance was to some degree mitigated by the fact that he did not come from the commercial milieu, where he felt himself to be a stranger. Otherwise, he dealt with the problem by minimizing his interventions and leaving the traders to speak for themselves, and by making persistent efforts to take account of the complexity of the Congolese social system. MacGaffey, the foreign researcher, lacking a lifetime of knowledge of the culture, was able to probe for the extra explanation needed to convey the depth of understanding that the insider takes for granted.

Life Histories

We collected twenty histories from among the traders: these constitute the core of our data. The extraordinary richness and interest of the information they yield make up in quality for their small number, a consequence of the difficulties of the research. These life stories are not just important as a methodological tool; they are central to our account and critically important for our purpose. We need biography 'which is social not simply because it documents social contexts and social processes ... but, above all, because it places at the very center of the description, interpretation and analysis, the personal narratives of the people whose lives are actually interdependent and mutually significant' (Werbner, 1991: 4).

A primary methodological concern here was that the category 'traders' was made up of individuals belonging to different social spheres, so that their lifestyles and culture did not conform to a single model. We therefore divided our subjects into the three categories given at the beginning of this chapter. We collected histories from all three; each history related diverse trajectories. Immigrants living clandestinely without papers included the *sapeurs* and others out to make money in any way they could without regard for the law; the students who had failed academically included trainees and scholarship holders; and the government employees who had left their jobs because they were underpaid, or who had overstayed their training in France and been dismissed, included both recent arrivals and others who had been in Paris a long time.

We do not, however, primarily consider these histories to be exact accounts of the past: some of them constitute a particular construction the individual has put upon it. The life history as a discourse, while being a testimony on social facts, is above all a social fact itself, a particular kind of discourse. Its analysis must be founded on the selection of events the individual chooses to mention. For us, the potential of these life histories to give an exact account of the past was less important than the tactical and strategic significance the actors attributed to the particular events selected for them in the context of our inquiry.[9] We consider that the histories related to us are significant as mythical constructs as much as they are sources of verifiable information.

Some of the traders' reported memories seem to have particular importance for them. These memories are often invoked a number of times in the course of the history, and relate to events particularly notable for the narrator. They constitute the kernels of the story. They are the chronological markers that structure the biography. Personal occurrences (migration to Paris, divorce, family betrayals, arrest, etc.) are particularly stressed, and two kinds of memories seem to be given particular emphasis. The first concerns an inherited ability which facilitates entry to commerce; the second recalls occasions of ostentatious expenditure.

These individuals' lives were interrupted because of immigration, after which they had to start all over again economically. Some of them emphasized that success in trade was a 'gift', inherited down the family through an experience felt to be magical, known as *lokumu* or *lusolo,* and referring to business talent that ought to be developed to support the family (meaning the extended family). The miraculous nature of this gift makes the exact trajectory of its inheritance difficult to establish. Each history appeared to be a means of justifying the individual's present situation, his or her starting up in business, and the success that, in some cases, followed.

Ostentatious expenditure, on the other hand, affirms status acquired in trade outside the law. For the traders who live the ostentatious lifestyle of the *sapeur*, spending a large amount of money at least once in one's lifetime brings a certain prestige in the eyes of others and establishes a reputation. To pull off a coup in this fashion is, as the Congolese put it, 'to live'. Furthermore, this coup, at one blow, brings fame to oneself and simultaneously attracts attention to one's achievement. Thus, such moments, so intensely lived, remain vividly in the memory of these

---

[9]Elizabeth Francis comments that a life history is an intellectual construct 'whose structure and content reflect the priorities of the researcher and the images the informant projects back into the past, as much as tangible realities' (Francis, 1993: 93).

traders. When they recount what happened, they speak with great emotion. In contrast, those not living ostentatiously recall events with much less intensity.

Paying attention to such memories, and to the emphasis given to them, allows us to access the ways of thinking of these individuals and the rules of economic rationality they follow. These rules are not those of the official economy, and the usual model of business management has little relevance for them. The realities these traders confront require continual innovation and negotiation, because they have solved the difficulties of their existence by operating in the second economy outside the official system and its regulations. In reconstructing the meaning individuals give to their past history, we hope to provide a means of understanding some of the stakes they play for in their lives and some of the strategies they employ to achieve them.

> Life history here is no longer simply a narrative frame for stringing together life-cycle rituals, socialization patterns, and a generational history as experienced by one individual; nor is it left to unique individuals. Indeed, life history deconstructs in the fullest sense: not making the subject disappear, but rather illuminating the social and constructive elements of an individual that make him or her potent in social context. Insofar as a life is the locus of experience, it is important to specify the cultural meanings that figure in and compose it. (Marcus and Fischer, 1986: 183)

This approach to the interpretation of life histories has so far been little developed. We utilize it in our study as we attempt to explore the cultural meanings and the social structural elements that condition the lives of these Congolese traders. Van Velsen long ago commented that ethnographers with a structural frame of reference may indeed give accounts of actual situations, but that they do not present a series of connected events showing how individuals operating within particular structures handle the choices that confront them (Van Velsen, 1967: 140). We feel that life histories give this perspective. Our intention is to use them to illuminate social process, not to highlight personal idiosyncrasy (Ibid.: 145). Elizabeth Francis, in her use of life histories for research on the Luo, adopts this approach, observing that a focus on individual life histories is one way of studying economic change as social process (Francis, 1993: 92).

We asked the traders to give us an account of their lives in one or more sessions, which in some cases lasted for several hours. These sessions took place in a variety of settings, ranging from their place of business or a back room in their premises, to cafés, to a luxury hotel or to individuals' homes. Whenever the occasion was appropriate, we paid for drinks or meals for our informants. We were only once asked for payment for an interview, for which we negotiated a sum. When collecting life histories, to get started we asked for specific details of family background; then we invited people to tell their stories in their own way. Afterwards we asked them to fill in on details to complete a systematic set of questions we had developed. In this way, we were able initially to see what they chose to select as significant according to their own perspective, which was thus unstructured by us.

The life histories were tape-recorded in French and sometimes partly or wholly in Lari or Lingala, then transcribed in French by Bazenguissa, translated into English by MacGaffey, and checked again for accuracy by Bazenguissa.

Contacts, Snowball Sampling and Participant Observation
As already noted, these anthropological methods are particularly suited to research on activities that may be clandestine, because of their reliance on establishing trust and rapport. In addition to Bazenguissa's contacts in, and knowledge of, the immigrant community from Congo-Brazzaville, we needed a connection to get us into the milieu of the traders. Here we entered into and participated in a chain of reciprocity of the kind through which the trade operates. In Brazzaville, Bazenguissa had had a research assistant for previous research. This assistant wanted to come to Paris and Bazenguissa agreed to sponsor him. A return favour was thus in order and this young man agreed to work with us, introducing us around and vouching for our trustworthiness. He belonged in the milieu of the traders: he knew many of them well, he had no residence papers and no job, yet, as a *sapeur*, he was always very well dressed. His expertise was obvious, and his help was indispensable. When he was with us in the car or in cafés, he participated actively in our discussions, clarifying things informants had said, or checking on the accuracy of our translations.

Once contacts were made and trust and rapport established, we snow-balled out through introductions from one informant to another. Such a snowball survey, in which trust is established by interviewing friends of initial contacts, then their friends, and so on (Tripp, 1997: 27, 207–8), is the best method for research on activity outside the law. John Irwin describes the steps of this 'snowball sampling'. The researcher first establishes his neutrality, then keeps up regular contact in informal settings and builds up bonds of trust and friendship to make it possible to move from one contact to another. In this way, it is possible to get access to a wide range and number of informants and to engage in repeated, extended, informal interviews (Irwin, 1972: 121–3). The networks along which the researcher moves are based on personal ties of different kinds. Interview schedules employ open-ended questions to minimize intervention from the researchers and to allow respondents the opportunity to tell their own stories. This kind of sampling also allows the researcher to cross-check information when interviewing other members of an individual's network (Cornelius, 1982: 393–5).

Several factors helped us in this process. Bazenguissa's insider knowledge of Congo culture and his personal connections, commented on above, were of crucial importance. Prior fieldwork in the country of origin of informants can help in reducing their fears in activities outside the law (Ibid.: 391), and this was the case with MacGaffey's previous research experience in Congo-Kinshasa, which was helpful for establishing friendly relations with those from that country.[10]

We spent long hours in the Château Rouge area, in its shops, cafés and bars, participating in discussions, observing what was going on, and engaging in informal interviewing and conversation. We made an inventory of the different commercial activities of the traders and service providers to the immigrant African population and interviewed or collected life histories and case studies for each kind of activity, details of which are given in Chapter 3. We also visited 18 of the 60 *nganda* (unlicensed bars) of the two Congolese communities that are scattered around the city. We would spend a few hours in one of these bars, usually from 11 p.m. into the early hours of the morning, which was when they filled up. We would order drinks and the African dishes that are the speciality of these establish-ments. The music was generally too loud to engage in much conversation, so these occasions were used for observation and for making contacts that we could subsequently follow up to schedule interviews. We went to the nightclubs frequented by some of the traders, and we attended social events in the two communities, together and separately. We found ourselves drawn into conflicts: jealous interactions between compatriots, scary racial confrontations between Arabs and Congolese that sometimes verged on violence, and the running conflict between the police and the undocu-mented immigrants they were looking for. The police often got in the way of our research: they always seemed to appear at inopportune moments. We got a feeling of what it is like to be always evading the law, as we became apprehensive of finding ourselves in a drug raid, or were on occasion caught up in evasive action when the arrival of the police was imminent.

The Difficulties of Researching Activities Outside the Law

The investigator's primary problem in such research is to find ways to win informants' trust: people are, naturally, very wary of discussing activities that can land them in trouble with the police. Our research was arduous and often frustrating because, despite our excellent contacts, it was often very difficult to get people to talk to us. Reluctance to talk seemed to vary in direct relation to the intensity of the reaction of the authorities to an individual's activities.[11]

---

[10]In one instance, MacGaffey's earlier residence in a village in the Kongo region of Lower Zaïre and her visit to Nkamba, the holy site of the Kimbanguist Church, were critical for getting a Kimbanguist store-owner and her husband to trust us enough to give us their life stories, allow us to spend long hours in the store, and invite us to the wedding of the great-grandson of Simon Kimbangu, the founder of the church.

[11]Researchers working for De Herdt and Marysse in their study of parallel-market money changers in Kinshasa started with individuals known to the researchers because, as one said, 'it is too dangerous to interview just anyone' (De Herdt and Marysse, 1996c: 22).

The pervasiveness of drug dealing was a major reason for the difficulty in getting people to trust us. Also our fear of endangering through their association with us informants who might, or might not, be engaged in this activity was initially very inhibiting. We deliberately stayed away from any direct investigation of the drug trade, making it clear to our assistant that we were not going to question him about it, and never asking anyone for information about it. Our prime concern was the protection of our informants. Gradually we realized that our worries were excessive, and we acquired some data by happenstance. However, it was obvious that their involvement on occasion in such dealing was the reason why some people refused to talk to us, why others failed repeatedly to keep appointments we made with them, and why some would only give us such minimal information about themselves that it was essentially useless.

We spent many long and frustrating hours trying to make contact with particular individuals or waiting for people who failed to turn up after they had agreed to talk to us. One informant, owner of a very small *nganda*, who did talk to us at length and recorded her life history, had an array of material goods suspiciously large for her small source of income. It turned out that she was, as we suspected, involved in drug dealing: in 1997, we learned she was in prison for this activity. An exporter of second-hand cars in Europe, telephoned for us by a good contact, refused an interview on the grounds that it was too dangerous, because, we subsequently learned, of the connection of this trade with drug smuggling.

Trust, once established, however, was very strong: we were able to get people to record hours of life history that included detailed accounts of activities outside the law. A striking instance of trust was when the owner of a *nganda* lent us her daily account book and receipts, so that we should understand the financial aspects of her enterprise. Our concern not to betray trust did, however, close off completely some other potential means of obtaining information. Colleagues suggested that we should obtain access to police records to extend the range of our investigation, but it was far too risky for us to do this. We feared endangering our informants and any indication of contact with the police would have instantly destroyed people's trust in us. We were careful not to identify people by their full names in our notebooks in case they should ever fall into the hands of the authorities, and we use pseudonyms for our case histories throughout the text. Such concerns are especially necessary and preoccupying in research on clandestine activities.[12]

Many of our informants did not have residence papers and were thus living outside the law. There were continual alarms and breaking off of conversations because of the frequent police swoops into the Château Rouge neighbourhood looking for undocumented migrants. In some cases,

---

[12]For a full discussion of ethical concerns and precautions to be taken in fieldwork, see Wilson, 1993.

the problem of overcoming the reluctance to talk of people who, in addition to their undocumented status, were operating enterprises outside the law proved to be insurmountable. For instance, despite excellent introductions, we were unsuccessful in having more than the briefest conversations with the street traders, who were particularly vulnerable to the sudden arrival of the police. This activity is against the law, and, in addition, few of these traders had residence papers. Often a warning call down the street would result in a whole line of women variously selling food, clothing or beauty products, closing up the large bags containing their wares in a trice, blending instantaneously with the crowds of shoppers carrying shopping bags, and disappearing completely before the police got to them. Our most detailed information on this activity came primarily from those who had engaged in it in the past, but who had subsequently moved into more secure lines of business.

Apart from the problem of getting people to talk, we had to reach an understanding on the nature of the clandestinity in which some of the traders lived. We found that, although labelled '*les clandestins*', they are quite open about their lifestyle. They stroll publicly around the 18th *arrondissement* of Paris, often carrying out activities which are against the law despite the presence of the police. For example, they contrive to peddle foodstuffs and sometimes stolen goods on the street, as described above, and they frequent *nganda*, the unofficial bars situated in squats which are often found in disused buildings or houses, although these bars are known to the police. The authorities tolerate such activities for long periods of time, because, as far as they are concerned, if immigrants have no papers they do not exist. In such cases it is legal non-existence which defines clandestinity and not living a hidden existence. As for the attitudes of the traders themselves towards our research, they had a compulsion to reveal themselves and not to insist on clandestinity because, in fact, some of them lived to practise ostentation: being visible was an important element in their lifestyle. The *nganda* owner who allowed us to borrow her account books was bringing her activity out into the open and asserting its success by such an act. This need to be visible, not hidden, was one factor that made our ethnography of the traders' lives possible. Thus, although the authorities refer to undocumented migrants *as 'les clandestins*', the term does not, in fact, reflect the reality of the way they live.

2

Resisting Exclusion & Reacting to Disorder

The widespread decline of African states receives frequent comment. But little is said, or known, about the impact on individuals, families and communities of the disorganization, violence and disruption of social life and morality that results when the state ceases effectively to exist in terms of the performance of its normal functions (Desjarlais and Kleinman, 1994). Both Congo-Kinshasa and Congo-Brazzaville have suffered from political repression, chronic economic crisis, widespread brutality and violence, and a persistent deterioration of the institutional structure of state and society. The details of the lives of the traders in this study document one of the responses to this situation: taking up second-economy trade, first within the country, and then across borders and between continents. Since the mid-1980s, exclusion from the opportunity to make a good living or to fulfil ambition has been the dominant reason for such international trade for Congolese from both countries. The forms of exclusion they also experience as they move to Europe have been a reason for their continued second-economy activity there.

Our perspective differs from that of other analysts of informal trade in that we do not take the depressed view which sees commerce outside the law as a mere coping mechanism or survival strategy. It can indeed be such a strategy, but we view it, in addition, as a means employed by individuals to evade and resist exclusion from opportunity to better their lives in circumstances of state decay, economic crisis and civil violence.

The earlier waves of migrants to France came primarily to work, or for education and training programmes under state auspices. They formed a crucial support system and community for those who came later, who were motivated primarily by the search for opportunity. As French policies towards immigration changed and visas became difficult to obtain, the number of Africans living in France clandestinely, without residence and work papers, increased. The only possibility of earning money for these undocumented immigrants lies in business outside the law. For those who do have residence permits, resort to some kind of second-economy activity is also a frequent strategy since enterprise in the official economy is otherwise barely viable.

This chapter briefly recounts the deteriorating political and economic conditions in the two countries, to which second-economy trade and migration have been a defiant response. It proceeds with a short history of the changing patterns of migration of West Central Africans to France, and then looks at the characteristics of second-economy trade and its changing flows. Case histories of traders show the ingenuity with which they have surmounted the difficulties of getting to France, and also their fluctuating fortunes in trade.

Historical Background

I. Congo-Kinshasa

Immense natural resources make the Democratic Republic of Congo potentially one of Africa's wealthiest countries; yet, in the 1990s, it is one of the poorest, with a per capita income that, according to official statistics, is among the lowest in the world.[1] The economy went into a spiralling decline in the mid-1970s and, by 1992, was in ruins: the manufacturing sector was one of the weakest in Africa, agriculture was long neglected in government policies, and food imports had quadrupled since 1970.

President Mobutu Sese Seko came to power in a coup in 1965, following the turbulent events that threw the country into chaos after its independence from Belgium. In the years that followed, the administrative capacity of the state declined rapidly, for reasons which included the colonial legacy of the low level of education and lack of experience of the new civil service, the unbounded greed and corruption that characterized the regime, economic problems that deprived the state of resources, and the politics of the Cold War.[2]

The decline in government revenues from the long economic crisis and the pervasive corruption and clientelism among government personnel led to the collapse of the state's administrative capacity, a devastating deterioration of the economic and transportation infrastructure, with accompanying widespread food shortages, and the virtual disappearance of public health and education. From 1982, the World Bank and the IMF imposed draconian austerity measures as a condition for continuing their aid, the IMF undertaking one of its most comprehensive stabilization programmes in Africa (Leslie, 1987: 66). But the expected increased aid

---

[1]Given the size of Congo-Kinshasa's second economy, which is unrecorded, one must remain sceptical about such claims.
[2]For details see Young and Turner, 1985; Schatzberg, 1988; Willame, 1991, 1992; Braeckman, 1992; De Villers, 1992; Leslie, 1993; Young, 1994.

investment from donor countries did not materialize. By 1994, GECAMINES, the copper mining company that had been Zaïre's principal exporter, was barely producing;[3] business owners found themselves in dire straits and many firms closed; some of the big multinationals moved their operations elsewhere. For the general population, rampant unemployment and impossibly low wages meant that town-dwellers had to find means for survival and also essential supplementary income outside the formal wage system to make any improvement in their lives. Along with these problems, however, artisanal mining of gold and diamonds enormously increased after the liberalization of 1983. People flocked to dig these precious minerals and smuggle them across borders to buy and import the goods that were in such short supply. By the 1990s, the second economy appeared to be virtually replacing the official recorded economy.

Production of diamonds expanded again in the early 1990s with the discovery of new diamond beds in the north-east. By 1994, diamonds were the chief source of foreign exchange, primarily through informal markets. These unofficial exports of diamonds and also of gold replaced the official exports of mineral and agricultural commodities, which were in such drastic decline, as sources of foreign exchange.[4] These diamond earnings in informal markets were the principal economic support for the regime.[5]

In Congo-Kinshasa, we see the rise of a 'shadow state' like that described by William Reno for Sierra Leone. The shadow state develops from the emergence of rulers drawing authority from their ability to control informal markets. These markets provide them with alternative material and political support as the administrative capacity of the state collapses, with its exploitation for the private benefit of its personnel (Reno, 1995). Zaïre is a classic example of a country in which clandestine networks for the private and illicit control of informal markets have sustained a repressive regime. This has been a major factor in its long crisis and decline. The informal market in diamonds was the primary basis for the exercise of political and economic power by President Mobutu, by the politicians and businessmen in the clique surrounding him, and by

---

[3]In 1985 copper exports were valued at 711.80 $mill., 319 $mill. in 1982, and only 189.60 $mill. in 1994 (Maton 1993: Table A-2).

[4]Zaïre's formal exports have so dwindled that the World Bank no longer includes them in its statistics. Diamonds cannot replace copper as the primary source of government revenue. The critical difference, as Jef Maton has pointed out, is that diamond mining is much more difficult to tax than copper. This is especially the case under the present forms of diamond production and trade in which it is very difficult to combat fraud. Zaïre's shortage of foreign exchange exacerbates the problem (Maton, 1993: 7).

[5]An informal market is defined as 'legally proscribed production and exchange that contributes no revenues to government' (Reno, 1995: 1), corresponding closely to our definition of the second economy.

foreigners, especially Lebanese but also Greeks and Asians (Pakistanis).[6] Other informal markets besides diamonds, for gold, cobalt, coffee and other export crops, malachite and ivory, were also the basis for the long retention of political power by the Mobutu regime. As the shadow state grew, the formal institutions of government deteriorated further and lost their capacity to regulate economy and society, because state revenues disappeared into the pockets of state personnel, who used the administrative apparatus to further their own interests and to enable them to extract rents. The traders of our study who participate in these informal markets do not find themselves in competition with the politically powerful because their activities are too small-scale or otherwise uninteresting to these large-scale operators.

In the 1990s, these political and economic problems and their social consequences were intensified by stormy and violent efforts to establish multiparty democracy. In 1990, President Mobutu dissolved the single party (the MPR). Many new parties formed immediately, but the transitional government he appointed contained many of the old guard and was not the government of national unity the people wanted. Demonstrations in favour of the opposition leader, Etienne Tshisekedi, were violently repressed by the authorities. After much violence, a wave of looting, and the destruction of stores and businesses in December 1990, a Sovereign National Conference of 3,500 representatives of the people was finally opened in August 1991 to determine the form of the Third Republic; it called for radical reforms. But confusion, politicking and manipulation prevented any effective action, and in September polity and economy almost totally collapsed in another explosion of pillage and rioting. Underpaid soldiers and much of the general population looted and destroyed shops, businesses and homes throughout the country. Particular targets were foreigners, the more arrogant members of the ruling class, and the headquarters of the MPR. At least 200 people died in the violence; major urban centres were devastated and infrastructure was destroyed; 20,000 foreigners were evacuated, businesses were abandoned, and Chevron oil and other big foreign companies pulled out (Willame, 1991; de Villers, 1992: 128–55).

The long-time opposition leader, Etienne Tshisekedi, was elected Prime Minister by the National Conference in 1992 but Mobutu refused to accept his government and appointed another. In this political impasse, the elected government was powerless, as Mobutu retained control of the

---

[6]The Lebanese have strong connections to the political authorities, for whom they exchange millions of zaïres for foreign currency; in return they are offered means of evading customs duties, taxes and other controls (*Le Soft de Finance* (Kinshasa), 3 October 1992). The strategic importance of diamonds was clearly perceived by Laurent Kabila, who, early in his drive to take over the country in 1998, negotiated with De Beers (the diamond cartel) for control of the country's diamond revenues.

Central Bank and the money supply, of the only effective means of force, the *Division Spécial Présidentielle* (SPD),[7] and of the security forces, one of the most sophisticated in Africa (Braeckman, 1992: 72). Once more, Mobutu re-established his 'illusory peace, founded on institutionalized violence, systematic repression and fear' (Ibid.: 101).

The years 1991–5 saw drastic intensification of Zaïre's long economic decline, with dizzying levels of inflation and rampant unemployment.[8] Desperate to curb the inflation and find banknotes to pay the regular army, the government introduced a new currency in October 1993. More outbreaks of looting and violence resulted from this measure and in the region of Kasai and in other areas people refused to use the new zaïre (NZ) in order to show their opposition to the regime.[9]

In May 1997, the Mobutu regime finally came to an end and Zaïre was renamed the Democratic Republic of the Congo under a new President, Laurent Kabila. His Alliance of Democratic Forces for the Liberation of Congo-Zaïre (AFDL) had begun a swift advance from the east in October 1996 and by May 1997 Kinshasa was in their hands. Mobutu fled the country and died shortly thereafter. The army, unpaid and undisciplined, disintegrated rapidly, fleeing from battle and looting and raping as they fled, driving a population long disillusioned with Mobutu to the rebel side, and helping Kabila turn his rising in the east into a national one; people flocked to join him. The AFDL's war effort was boosted by their capture of mines and by Kabila's deals with foreign business interests to obtain financing from gold and diamonds (Solomon, 1997: 93–5).

The replacement of Mobutu by Kabila has not changed the despotic, authoritarian nature of the state. Elements of Kabila's supporters had turned against him by 1998, civil war broke out, and neighbouring countries actively intervened. By early 1999, efforts at peace-keeping resulted in stalemate in the fighting, but civil violence continued to be widespread. The situation that has confronted the traders all along thus continues and seems to have changed little with the removal of Mobutu.

With the demise of normal state functions and use of the remaining state apparatus merely to enrich its personnel and to further the interests of the politically powerful, the second economy appeared virtually to replace the official recorded economy. Whereas in 1955 39 per cent of the active population was employed in the formal sector, by the early 1990s the figure was only 5 per cent (De Herdt and Marysse, 1996b: 15). People have survived

---

[7]Recruited from the Ngbandi, the ethnic group of the President, they are a special division of the army, and the only one that is well paid (see Braeckman, 1992: 73–6).

[8]According to the IMF, inflation rose to 77.1% between 1986 and 1989, and to 2,805.8% between 1990 and 1994 (Luiz, 1997: 248). After the pillaging of 1991, one-third of the jobs in Kinshasa were lost (Devisch, 1995: 598–99).

[9]1 NZ equalled 3 million old.Z. Kasai has officially retained the old zaïre as currency and its economy has not suffered the inflation that has beset the rest of the country.

the long crisis of civil violence and economic collapse by 'fending for themselves'. They have set up small-scale enterprises, most of which are unlicensed and evade taxes and regulations, in petty trade, in retail, transport and manufacturing concerns, or in repairs or other service enterprises, or in some other way have earned money on the margins of the law. The looting that destroyed a large number of modern businesses created new opportunities for their informal competitors (De Herdt and Marysse, 1996a).

The most lucrative activities of the flourishing second economy, however, have been in smuggling or fraudulent import and export. The privileged access of the rich and powerful to foreign exchange and to the country's most valuable resources has allowed them to carry out the largest-scale operations of this trade. Through it, they have acquired the material support to maintain themselves in power. They have not, however, been able to monopolize it. Small traders and farmers have smuggled gold, diamonds and coffee across the frontiers, and imported manufactured goods, vehicles and spares, fuel, construction materials and food in return.[10] Traders with sufficient determination and ambition, or with wealth and the necessary contacts, have engaged in commerce with West and South Africa and with Europe and other continents. It is these traders in international and intercontinental trade, who are the subject of our study.

II. Congo-Brazzaville

Congo-Brazzaville is not nearly so well endowed with natural resources as Congo-Kinshasa and its economy relies heavily on its oil. Conversely, it differs in having one of the highest education levels in Africa. Another significant contrast between the two countries is that Congo-Kinshasa's unending crisis has meant that people have been accustomed to fending for themselves for longer than have the Congolese of Congo-Brazzaville.

The Republic of Congo was a French colony, notable for its strong education system and its urban growth (Eliou, 1977; Achikbache and Anglade, 1988; Makonda, 1988; Dorier-Apprill and Ziavoula, 1996). From 1963 to 1991, the period during which the present generation of clandestine traders grew up, two features in particular contributed to the construction of the Congolese political world: on the one hand, the ideology, proclaimed by the political class, of scientific socialism and Marxism-Leninism, which reinforced the military style of the regime; on the other, the strong popular fixation on collective identities (regional and ethnic) in politics, which structured the major lines in the field of competition for power and determined its alternatives.

In this society, education was critical. The youth of the country, whether they were children or adolescents, had a specific political status according

---

[10]For details, see MacGaffey, 1987, 1992; MacGaffey, et al. 1991; Omasombo, 1993.

to age. When only schoolchildren, they were pioneers of the revolution, then later they were obligatory members of UJSC, the youth party. Education served to bring access to the economy through public office, because other types of activity were devalued (see Bazenguissa-Ganga and MacGaffey, 1995). For this reason, at the height of the economic crisis, a high-school diploma was, officially, the minimum qualification which conferred the status of unemployed. Because such a close connection existed between education, economics and politics, young people have had to confront the political crisis directly.

Since the 1950s, the Congo Republic has suffered a chronic economic crisis (see Althabe, 1963; Devauges, 1963; Amin and Coquery-Vidrovitch, 1969; Bertrand, 1975). It has known only two periods of respite: the first from 1973 to 1974, the second from 1979 to 1983; both corresponded to oil booms. The second was the more important and increased the borrowing capacity of the country. In 1984, a fall in oil prices and revenues provoked a crisis in public finance because of the increase of the national debt. The setting up of a structural adjustment programme in 1987 was an attempt to remedy the situation (Diata, 1989). The reform measures were doubly contested, however: in 1985 and 1986, students and school pupils protested against the intensifying rigour of the selection process; in 1989 employees opposed measures to lower the retirement age. The latter in particular created conflict between the trade unions and the state, and resulted in a series of strikes in 1989 which paralysed political institutions. These various protests, originating from the people themselves, were taken up by former political leaders who had been dismissed from their positions. They demanded the establishment of multipartyism and democracy in the country.

The ethnic and regional basis of Congolese politics is rooted in its French colonial history, but it is important to emphasize that the ethnic identities of today do not just reproduce those of the precolonial era,: they are related to factors in the present political context. The Kongo ethnic group dominated national politics from 1958 to 1968, until they were evicted from power in a period of military rule (Ossebi, 1982, 1988b; Tsamouna Kitongo, 1990). At this time, the political scene was popularly seen as one of opposition between the Kongo and the Mbochi. When the Mbochi dominated the north, taking power with the socialist revolutionary party, the political division was described in spatial terms: the northerners, equated with the Mbochi, against the southerners, identified as Kongo.

A National Conference was held from February to June 1991 to resolve the political crisis over the demands for multipartyism. It put an end to military rule and gave victory again to the Kongo of the Pool region, who were to manage the transition period. However, any victory for them beyond the installation of new institutions was sabotaged by other Kongo from the regions of Niari, Bouenza and Lekoumou (collectively known as NiBoLek). The resulting resentments and anger culminated in civil war in

Brazzaville, lasting from September 1993 to February 1994 (Ossebi, 1992; Yengo, 1994; Gruenais et al., 1995; Bazenguissa-Ganga, 1997).

The political system in place following the National Conference reflected a form of factionalism, based on three powerful parties associated with youthful militias. The period of transition, from June 1991 to July 1992, ended in a succession of elections (municipal, legislative and presidential) intended to re-establish multipartyism. Three parties dominated: Pascal Lissouba's UPADS, Bernard Kolelas' MCDDI, and the former single party headed by Denis Sassou-Nguesso, the PCT. These parties were sustained by militias: the *Réserve Ministérielle*, the Zulus, the Ninjas and the Cobras. The first two supported UPADS, the Ninjas MCDDI, and the Cobras the PCT.

The militias are made up of young people 18 to 35 years old, primarily born in Brazzaville (see Bazenguissa-Ganga, 1996a and b). Unemployed school drop-outs, who have mostly had criminal, delinquent or other experiences of marginality, they are already practised in violence before joining the militias, although not in any political context. The crisis situation results in the politicization of these forms of social violence. These militias have fought on two occasions: in 1993–4, against the dissolution of the National Assembly, and in 1997, during the change-over of political power.

In July 1992, Pascal Lissouba took office, thanks to an alliance constructed between his party, UPADS, and the PCT (Weissman, 1993). But, in October that year, the PCT, dissatisfied with the allocation of ministerial portfolios, rejoined the opposition. This change of allegiance toppled the parliamentary majority which was constitutionally necessary for the Prime Minister to continue as head of the government. UPADS, through the President, decided to dissolve the National Assembly to keep control of the government. The opposition organized a peaceful march on 30 November, which came up against the Presidential Guard. This confrontation resulted in three deaths and some 100 injured. People mobilized in the streets and erected barricades. After a period to restore calm, the first round of legislative elections were held on 2 May 1993. The results were contested by the opposition with charges of fraud, but the President went ahead and set up a government. In turn, on 27 June, the opposition set up its own government 'of national safety'.

Political competition between presidential supporters and the opposition intensified and culminated in urban guerrilla warfare between 1993 and 1994, conducted sporadically by the now renowned militias. The most violent clashes took place between the militias supporting the President and the Ninja of the MCDDI. The battle for the control of the districts to the south (Bacongo and Makelekele) and east (Mfilou) of the capital officially caused 2,000 deaths, and resulted in the displacement of nearly 100,000 people and the destruction of nearly 13,000 dwellings.

Urban guerrilla warfare thus produced a new political order founded on the power acquired by the two factions. It consisted essentially of the sharing of power between UPADS and MCDDI. The setting up of a new government in January 1995, in which members of the two parties figured prominently, marked the end of hostilities and entrenched the positions gained during the clashes.

Further conflicts occurred in the process of political succession which has always involved violence in Congo-Brazzaville (see Bazenguissa-Ganga, 1997). The return of the former president Denis Sassou-Nguesso to Brazzaville disrupted the equilibrium reached after the clashes of 1993–4. Sassou had chosen, in mid-1995, to leave the country and retire to France. At the same time, he removed his militia from Brazzaville to his native town of Oyo. In January 1997, he was received in triumph in Brazzaville by a crowd of sympathizers and curious onlookers.

The presence of Sassou intensified competition for the presidential elections, and he renewed contact with his militia, the Cobras. In May 1997, in the course of the presidential campaign, his presence in a northern town, Owando, provoked clashes between counter-demonstrators and the Cobras. One counter-demonstrator, accused by Sassou's supporters of taking part in a plot hatched by the government to assassinate their leader, was killed. Other confrontations took place in the same month between the soldiers sent to the area to restore calm and the Cobras. About 20 people were killed.

Further such clashes in 1997 plunged Brazzaville into its second civil war, which in 1998 was still in progress. This situation of latent civil war makes people's situations ever more precarious. Those who can seek to emigrate from the country.

These brief historical sketches reveal the political upheaval and economic crises that have beset the home countries of the traders we studied, and which form the context of their lives. We turn now to the varying policies of different French governments over time, to see how they have affected migration from these two West Central African countries and the opportunities available to West Central Africans who come to France.

Trade and Changing Patterns of Migration to France

From 1946 to 1960 French colonial subjects had French nationality, but after independence in 1960 most automatically lost it. In the 1960s, the French needed cheap labour and encouraged African migration, giving Africans relatively easy access to the labour market in France. The Algerian conflict made Algerian immigration uncertain and sub-Saharan Africans provided a cheap substitute. Their numbers increased from 20,000 in 1960 to 120,000 in 1987 (Barou, 1987: 79). But, from 1974, France, like most of its European neighbours, stopped encouraging migration for wage labour, and made residence and work permits compulsory. As a result, from this time circular labour migration ceased.

Some workers still came but they stayed in France, bringing their families over and taking up permanent residence. Many companies were still eager to employ African labour, however, and hired young men who would come over clandestinely. But they were paid low wages and had no social security benefits. From 1976 the government tried to stop these practices, and a law was passed mandating financial penalties for such employers. In the 1980s, the situation changed again: the French Socialist government eased immigration policies and, in 1982, 150,000 illegal immigrants were legalized. Many Zaïreans came to France from Brussels at this time.

Details on four brothers from Congo-Brazzaville show how they took advantage of this clemency, following a common pattern among undocumented migrants, which is to start off in activities outside the law, and then eventually to obtain papers and find regular jobs.

The first of four brothers arrived in 1970 and lived without papers working in business outside the law ('les circuits'). In 1982, with the amnesty for clandestine immigrants proclaimed by Mitterrand, he obtained residence papers and got a job as a watchman in a store, which he still held in 1994, and gave up his irregular activities. He had been able to obtain two sets of papers under different names and so was able to help the third brother come to France. This one found work as a cook in a restaurant. The second had found a job in a bookshop, and the fourth worked in 'les circuits'. He found a job as a delivery driver, but continued his activities outside the law and has several times been in prison.

However, in the spring of 1993, after the political Right returned to power, the objective of the Minister of the Interior, Charles Pasqua, was to achieve zero immigration. The new emphasis, aiming to dissuade would-be immigrants and arouse public opinion against them, was on controlling frontiers, on verification of identity and on restricting families trying to reassemble their members (this could be done only once and entailed very strict income and lodging requirements). Parliament adopted these new rules on 13 July, 1993. The '*Loi Pasqua*' sought to prevent illegal immigration, restrict access to French nationality and reinforce identity controls. It has succeeded in decreasing the legal settlement of newcomers in France, in cutting down the number of clandestine immigrants, and in reducing the number of grantees of political asylum. Residence cards are given out very selectively and illegal immigrants cannot obtain social security benefits or the family allowances given to French citizens or permanent residents' families, to help care for children. Jean-Louis Debré, Pasqua's successor in 1995, continued his policies. In the first six months of 1996, 7,352 people were forcibly deported, compared with 5,868 in the same period of 1995. This tough stance on illegal immigrants aims to appease the National Front party of Jean-Marie le Pen, who won 15 per cent of the vote in the national elections on a platform of France for the French, claiming that if the 3.5 million foreigners legally in France returned home, France's 3 million unemployed French workers would find jobs (*New York Times*, 11 August 1966).

After independence from colonial rule, a new pattern of migration had developed as African governments sent their nationals overseas for education or training in the 1960s and 1970s. Young Zaïreans and Congolese were supported by scholarships and arrived in Europe with the intention of returning home. Some, however, got jobs and stayed on. These early migrants, arriving under state auspices, contrast with those who came later with no such protected status. The early ones constituted a crucial support system for others who came later on their own account.[11] Some of the early migrants also came because they had jobs, especially those working for the airlines.

In the mid-1970s the movement of *la Sape* (*Société des Ambianceurs et des Personnes Elégantes*) introduced a new motive for migration. The young BaKongo of this movement in Brazzaville wore Parisian designer clothing and flaunted it in an ostentatious lifestyle. Soon they got the idea of going to Paris themselves to obtain the clothes they wanted, which they called 'going adventuring' (*partir à l'aventure*). To finance this enterprise, they began to trade in clothes and appliances. It was thus the *sapeurs* who made France accessible in this period to those who were uneducated and of small means, rather than only to members of the upper class going for educational purposes (see Gandoulou, 1989a and b; Bazenguissa-Ganga, 1992a and b). The relations between early and late arrivals, however, were not always harmonious. After the *sapeurs* arrived at the hostel for Congolese students (*Maison des Etudiants Congolais*, MEC), they eventually drove the students away under the pretext that it was Abbé Youlou, the first president of Congo and a Lari (one of the major Kongo groups), who had purchased the building, giving them, as Kongo, a claim to it. Thereafter a large number of clandestine immigrants stayed there. This hostel was sold in the 1980s, thus ending the opportunity of free housing in Paris.

Zaïreans soon joined this movement of *la Sape* and it transformed many of the younger generation into traders. By 1979 other Zaïrean traders, not only *sapeurs*, were importing goods from Europe and an extensive commerce had developed.[12] In addition, some of those coming for education with state support also turned to trade because their scholarships were not paid regularly and they had to find money to live on. Zaïreans were earlier than the Congolese in diversifying their trade; the Congolese traded only in clothes, which they carried in their suitcases and not as freight. Trade increased as women began to expand their economic role in the household back home and to take up commerce, trading with neighbouring countries, with West Africa and with Europe. The 1980s

---

[11]A pattern found elsewhere (see, for example, Lomnitz, 1977: 189).
[12]For an example of a woman trader from this earlier period, see MacGaffey, 1987: 176.

were the peak period for the development of this commerce, as men and women went back and forth involved in a large-scale trade in commodities.

People in Kinshasa giving accounts of this trade in 1987 emphasized the large amounts of money made by some women traders.[13] These women smuggled gold and diamonds to finance their trade, and exported manioc leaves and palm oil to sell in Brussels to the large Zaïrean community there. They imported into Zaïre in return wax-print cloth, shoes, children's clothes, headscarves, table mats and blouses from Italy, France and Belgium, and jewellery from Antwerp. Commonly, a woman's husband would provide her venture capital. Many of them were second wives (*deuxième bureau*): the first wife would take care of the children and the household, and the husband would set up his second wife in trade. Middle-class women often relied upon their husband's position for protection, because women were accorded more respect if they were married. Some women, as they became very wealthy, would divorce their husbands and become the first wife of another man; others remained independent and much sought after, and took young men as their lovers.[14]

The following case history is of a middle-class woman who had the wealth and contacts that enabled these women to dominate this very profitable trade.

Louise, the wife of an army officer, lived in Kinshasa. When visited for an interview in 1987, she and her husband and some friends were drinking whisky and watching an Israeli/Russian basketball game being played in France on their large colour TV. Their living-room was air-conditioned, luxuriously carpeted and furnished with deep upholstered armchairs, and chrome and glass side-tables. Louise, who had secondary education, started to trade in 1984 with a suitcase of wax-print cloth provided by her husband. Prior to this venture she had been a housewife. This provision of venture capital by her husband entitled him to a share of her profits and a controlling share in her business. By 1987, she was trading in children's clothes, blouses, shoes from Brussels and Paris (which she brought back by air) and velour upholstery cloth. She had tried jewellery a couple of times but found that it was so costly that people could only pay for it in instalments and it took her too long to recover the money. She sold to wholesalers, except for shoes, which she sold direct from her house. She financed her trade by buying CFA francs on the black market in Kinshasa, taking them to Brussels and buying Belgian francs at a parallel money market bureau de change she knew of in the Grande Place. She would stay two weeks to collect and ship her goods. She would often take orders from her customers and had a Zaïrean woman partner, who lived in Brussels,

[13]Interviews in Kinshasa, MacGaffey, January 1987.
[14]Recalling the *vedettes* described by La Fontaine (1974)

who helped her. She would get the address of European wholesalers from shopkeepers in Kinshasa when she saw things that she liked. Her best trips cleared 180,000 Z, her least successful 50,000 Z. She made about three trips a year, so she was making the equivalent of around $6,750 a year at the rate of exchange at that time. On her return to Kinshasa, she paid customs duties on her goods at the port of Matadi; sometimes, she said, she would come to an arrangement with the customs official.[15] *She found it cheapest to ship by boat, and would take their car to Matadi to supervise the trans-shipment of her goods to a rented truck, or to rented space in a truck, to get them to Kinshasa.*

During this period, people were going to France and Belgium '*pour chercher l'argent par tous les moyens possibles*' (to make money any way they could). The political and economic events of the late 1980s, however, caused the trade to diminish, with Congo-Kinshasa's plunge into acute political and economic crisis from the troubles associated with the move to multiparty democracy and with Congo-Brazzaville's civil war. In 1994, global recession and the devaluation of the CFA franc compounded these problems. In addition, after 1988–9 other European governments tightened their visa regulations and became unreceptive to migrants. Thereafter, it became extremely difficult for Africans to get visas for both Belgium and France and the direction of trade shifted to South Africa.

Undocumented Migrants in France

For the reasons just given, a large number of migrants from Central Africa are in France without residence or work papers. Precise figures on the number of these migrants do not, of course, exist, but some other figures are available and enable us to form some idea of the numbers involved.

Census figures give the number of Zaïreans and Congolese officially resident in France as follows:

1982	8,940 Congolese	6,712 Zaïreans
1990	12,235 Congolese	22,568 Zaïreans
1994	13,000 Congolese	23,000 Zaïreans

(Source: Institut National des Statistiques et des Etudes Economiques, Paris, 1992)[16]

The increase by 224 per cent in the number of Zaïreans during the period 1982–90 reflects the influx from Brussels when the French Socialists eased

---

[15]She gave no details, but other reports of such arrangements gave figures of one-quarter of the money paid going to the customs, one-quarter to the official, and half being retained by the trader.
[16]Figures for an earlier period exist for Congo (numbers of Zaïreans were judged to be insignificant). The census of 1975 showed 3,435, in 1982 there were 7,620 (2,200 under 14 years old), and in 1984 the figure was 13,223 (3,908 under 16 years) (INSEE,1992).

immigration regulations, the increasingly severe economic crisis in Zaïre during this period, and the expanding phenomenon of *la Sape* in Kinshasa. The figure is the second highest for immigration to France in this period, after Guinea (228 per cent), and is followed by East Asians (166 per cent), Haitians (150 per cent) and Pakistanis (135 per cent).[17] These figures refer only to those migrants admitted officially. It is possible, however, to get some approximation of those clandestinely in the country from the number of applications for political asylum, since Zaïreans and Congolese who are in France clandestinely generally ask for asylum, sometimes living there without residence papers while they wait for an event at home to justify such an application. The right to residence while seeking political asylum lasts for six months and is granted with an allowance of 2,000 francs a month. During this period, the French authorities make enquiries about the individual concerned. In 1982, Zaïreans took full advantage of the clemency measures: many of the 150,000 legalized at that time had been seeking political asylum.

Census figures for 1992 show that, in this year, with 9,400 requests for asylum, Africans came second after East Asians (13,000);[18] 1,300 requests were from Zaïreans (622 of which were granted). Political refugee status was granted to a total of 1,800 Africans, 17 per cent of the total given out[19] (in 1991, the number had been greater: 2,300). It is difficult to distinguish between a real political exile and one who is merely seeking a way to obtain residence papers, but, for this very reason, a large percentage of the 1,300 Zaïreans applying for asylum in 1992 can be assumed to have been clandestine immigrants, giving us some idea of their number. For earlier years, the annual report on immigration of the Minister of Social Affairs and Immigration notes that requests for asylum decreased by 10.8 per cent

---

[17]Zaïreans were sixth among numbers of African migrants in France in 1990, as follows:

Algeria	613,000	Côte d'Ivoire	17,000
Morocco	573,000	Mauritius	13,000
Tunisia	206,000	Congo	13,000
Senegal	44,000	Madagascar	9,000
Mali	28,000	Togo	6,000
Zaïre	23,000	Guinea	6,000
Cameroon	18,000		

(Source: Lebon, 1993)

[18]In 1992, the principal countries of origin in Africa for seekers of political asylum were as follows:

Zaïre	3,100	Angola	300
Mali	1,000	Tunisia	200
Guinea	800	Mauritius	65
Mauritania	600	Morocco	50
Algeria	600		

(Source: Lebon, 1993)

[19]In France, the right to political asylum is only granted for three years; it must then be re-applied for.

in 1990 from 1989 but were still double the average for the years 1985–8. This increase appears to reflect the expansion in clandestine immigration from 1989.

What are people's motives for undertaking this difficult move? Histories from the different categories of traders show how individual motivations in the migration process and in the movement into trade are responses to restrictive political and economic situations. Such trade is perceived as the opportunity of greatest potential by those who have the initiative, the ambition and the contacts, and who can get together the necessary venture capital to take it up. They are the people to whom we shall now turn.

Motives for Migration and for Entering Trade

We shall look first at the educated traders and their reasons for leaving home. In both Congo-Brazzaville and Congo-Kinshasa, education has always been the minimum qualification to enter the salaried workforce, especially for state employment. The majority of the migrants we talked to in 1994 in Paris were aged between 30 and 40 years and had arrived in France in the 1980s. The educated ones came for the following reasons, in order of importance: first, scholastic failure, either from lack of ability or because the structural adjustment programme made the selection system more rigorous; second, the difficulty for university graduates in getting state employment; third, unemployment; and fourth, leaving state employment because it did not pay enough to live on.

The unstable political and economic system in their home countries ruins the prospects of many individuals and motivates them to move to Europe. An additional economic reason for taking up trading appears in the increase in numbers of those trading between Kinshasa and Brazzaville after 1964.

> The connection of the zaire to the DTS [Special Drawing Rights] and its devaluations of 22% and 25% in 1976 and 1979, respectively, which lowered purchasing power, have given rise to an absolute passion for trading. This situation intensified from 1980 to 1983. During this period, 67% of traders were registered. Their increasing number was undoubtedly a consequence of the successive devaluations given above (Kongo, 1987: 414).

The following case histories show how ethnic clientelism and political troubles disrupted the careers of two men. In both Congo-Brazzaville and Congo-Kinshasa those without the necessary connections or ethnic background find themselves excluded from promotions and jobs. The history of Paul, from Congo-Kinshasa, shows how ability and ambition fail to override this pervasive reality.

Paul studied in the Institute of Commerce in Kinshasa and became a computer programmer. He then passed the test for a job in the presidential service brilliantly and worked for five months. At the end of this time, he found himself passed over for promotion because he was not of the right ethnic group. Frustrated by finding his progress in his career thus blocked, he decided to come to Europe for study. He got a scholarship from his church, paid for by the state. In Paris, while getting a doctorate in business law, he has also worked. He had a job as a warehouseman in a railway company, but decided he could do better on his own. He took out a commercial licence to work as a service contractor doing deliveries, for which he has his own van. He and his wife import African foodstuffs from Congo-Kinshasa. She sells them and other goods bought from local wholesalers in their rented store.

Jerome is from Brazzaville. In his case, the problem was the political troubles of the time.

Jerome studied accounting in Pointe Noire for three years, specializing in customs work, then got a job with a freight company, who sent him for further study in France. While he was there, the directors of the company fled from Congo for political reasons. When Jerome finished his studies and was told to return home, he asked to be sent his ticket but the branch company had closed and he received no reply. He went to Paris and lived with his nephew for a year, finally finding a job with a freight company. He worked for this company for seven years, then, urged on by his wife, went into business for himself as an importer and wholesaler of African foodstuffs. He engages in various second-economy activities in the course of his business dealings.

When they arrive in France, migrants often encounter another form of exclusion in the form of discrimination against Africans in the job market: those who are well qualified cannot always obtain jobs suited to their level of expertise, so some university graduates find themselves working as unskilled labourers, at boring or low-paid work, or unemployed (Bolya et al., 1994: 331–3). Two Congolese from Congo-Kinshasa who had this experience were François and Chantal. Both resorted to second-economy activities.

François, the eldest of his family, was sent to Brussels to study. He qualified as an electrical engineer but has only been able to get temporary work as manager of a warehouse. He cannot find a permanent job that fits his qualifications. Aged 30 and married, he now lives in Lille. For a year and a half he exported spare parts for cars whenever someone he knew was going home and could take them. He also tried exporting a second-hand car for a taxi, but was swindled by family members managing the business for him.

Chantal obtained a degree in France in the Science of Education but despite this qualification could only find a boring job as a secretary at the then Zaïrean embassy. The job had no future and she hated the monotony of her work, so she gave it up and set up a dressmaking business. She considers herself to be an artist as much as a business-woman and she wanted an occupation that would allow her to be creative, have ideas and put them into practice, 'rather than doing the same thing all the time like a robot'. She had learned dressmaking from her mother, who was a teacher at a social centre and sewed a lot at home. Chantal used to sew for herself and for her friends, and has expert knowledge of materials and how best to use them. To run a profitable business, however, she finds she needs to run part of it without a licence: she employs seamstresses to work in a back room producing garments for her.

It is not only difficult to find jobs and avoid underemployment, but other options are limited: the venture capital needed to set up in business, as well as the rate of taxation, is so high as to be prohibitive for most people, without resort to illicit means of wealth accumulation of some sort, or without access to the personal wealth of the dominant political class. Chantal refused to tell us where she obtained the venture capital for her shop, making it clear she had something to hide. In another case, one of the street traders we talked to had trained as a midwife in Kinshasa, but in Paris found she could only get a job as a nurse's aide. For this reason, she had taken up street trading.

So far we have discussed the reasons for migration and entry into trade of the educated. The less educated are primarily motivated by two different ideas. For those from Congo-Kinshasa, it is the predatory outlook originating with the diamond and gold diggers which provides a model:[20] they leave to go into exile (*ngunda*), to 'break stones' and earn money. This includes an element of banditry: anything is permitted and justified by the idea that one must fend for oneself where and how one can. The imagination of those from Congo-Brazzaville is fired by the political opposition that is manifested in *la Sape* (see Gandoulou, 1989a and b; Bazenguissa-Ganga, 1992a and b).

The following case history of a Congolese from Brazzaville shows the difficulty of earning a livelihood in the deteriorating political and economic situation at home in Congo, and also his ingenious use of the opportunities that come his way to make a living in Paris.

In 1994, André operated an unlicensed business in Paris as a photographer at social events and in bars and cafés. In Brazzaville, at the

---

[20]After the legalization of the artisanal mining of gold and diamonds in 1983 in Congo-Kinshasa, there was a rush of young people into this activity.

age of 30, he had decided to go 'adventuring' in France, hoping to find means to support his wife and child. He had been unable to achieve success in anything he tried at home. He failed to graduate from secondary school in 1987 and his various attempts thereafter to run a market stall for hardware and electrical goods, start a taxi service, and set up an ice-cream business had successively failed. He had learned photography in school, and also from a friendly Russian aid worker, who owned a camera and lived in the same building as André's cousin. In Paris, in order to pay his rent, he borrowed a camera and started taking pictures at social events, birthdays, weddings, baptisms and in nganda *(clandestine bars). He describes coming to France as 'a dream full of hope', but has found it very difficult to make enough money with his photography to send anything home to his family. 'It is a hard job', he says. It is often difficult to get people to pay and he finds himself in competition with about ten Congolese from Kinshasa and two from Brazzaville in the same line of business.*

Once in France, exclusion from opportunity, and the means for a decent life, is evident in many areas of life for African immigrants. One observer finds drastic mechanisms for excluding them from society (Nair, 1992: 49). 'The victimization, harassment, aggression and murders carried out against today's immigrants will leave many lasting marks that will only fade very slowly from their memory' (Ibid.: 12).

The difficulties that traders encounter in France mean that once again they are impelled into second-economy trade and other activities.

The Fluctuating Fortunes and Changing Flows of Trade

The histories of two traders, both *sapeurs*, will first show some of the ways people surmount the difficulties of getting to France. Eloise, from Kinshasa, exploited differentials in exchange rates as a means of accumulating the money she needed to get to France.

Eloise was in her twenties in 1994 and had had three years of secondary school in Kinshasa. She started in petty trade at the age of 15, first selling soap and powdered milk, then progressing to lingerie, which she bought from a Lebanese wholesaler in Kinshasa. She would buy goods for zaïres for the equivalent of 600 CFAF, and then go to Brazzaville and sell them for 2,000 CFAF. On her return to Kinshasa, she would sell these CFA francs on the parallel money market for many more zaïres than she had paid for the original goods, thus making a handsome profit from the exchange rate. It took Eloise five years to get the 150,000 CFAF that she needed for a ticket.

For Charles, getting to France was much more complex. His story shows extraordinary determination, creativity and persistence in the lengths he goes to to find means to live his life in ways he finds fulfilling:

> *Charles, from Brazzaville and aged 29, is a playboy and an adventurer. He dropped out of school before finishing primary education, then frequented pop band concerts, became a* sapeur, *and had fathered five children by different women by the time he was 25. His motive for coming to France was to get the fashionable clothes he wanted for* la Sape. *He needed to make money to buy them and to buy his ticket to come to Paris. At the age of 17, he had tried to stow away on a boat without success, then from 1983, he engaged in 'Bizness', selling forged passports and other documents provided by a patron for whom he worked. Passports sold for 50,000 CFAF, and visas for 75,000 to 100,000 CFAF, of which he got 50 per cent. Customers were plentiful because the socialist government in Congo made it difficult to obtain passports at this time. After four years, he was caught and arrested. During the four years, he had also been trading, buying goods in Kinshasa and selling them first in a kiosk in Brazzaville, then in itinerant trade to the villages along the railway line, a well-known way of making money quickly: he said he made 50,000 CFAF in 10 days.*
>
> *He next decided to try and get to France through Angola via Belgium or Portugal, where visa and passport regulations were less stringent. He made money in Angola by selling goods for a diplomat (for whom such activity was forbidden). The diplomat bought jeans and T-shirts in Brazzaville and brought them through customs without paying duty without any trouble because he had diplomatic immunity from customs searches. They divided the profits between them. In four months Charles had the money he needed, the diplomat helped him get a visa, and he went to Brussels and then to Paris, where he asked for political asylum.*

Over time, the two visions, of the 'breaker of stones' and the 'adventurer', have mingled: the digger has become a *sapeur* and the movement of *la Sape* has turned more and more towards contraband trade.

Undocumented clandestine migrants are only in a position to earn money on the margins of or outside the law and must turn to second-economy activities, and those who do have residence papers and who have moved into licensed retail or wholesale business, or the import and export trade, generally find they need to combine second-economy activity with their official activities to make profits or, in some cases, to stay in business at all. The difficulties of finding employment commensurate with qualifications and the expenses of setting up in business have left trade as the best option for many of these migrants.

Traders specialize in particular commodities in their trading, but these keep changing as the traders take advantage of the market of the moment:

success depends on being able to adjust one's activities swiftly to new opportunities as old ones disappear. For example, during a period in the early 1990s before the political crisis escalated, luxury foods were a profitable item. Traders would take back smoked chickens or sausages to Brazzaville, sell them in the market during the day, then in the evening sell beer from their houses along with sandwiches of thin slices of sausage. These foods could be sold for three times as much as they cost in Paris.

A striking feature of the trade is the extreme fluctuation in the fortunes of the traders, as is shown in the following case history of a woman making a living off the trade between Brussels and Congo-Kinshasa.

> *Annette keeps a store in the Galerie d'Ixelles of the Matonge neighbourhood of Brussels. It is a hairdressing business and she also sells pagnes (cloth sold in six-metre lengths to make a woman's costume of wrap-around skirt, blouse and a wrapper to be tied around the hips or used to carry a baby on a woman's back), blouses and dresses, hair lengths, shoes, wooden bracelets and cold drinks. 'The trade was at its peak between 1982 and 1990 and was primarily carried on by women. There was a lot of to-ing and fro-ing by people coming from Kinshasa to buy things to take home to sell, primarily Dutch waxprints, blouses and other clothes, toiletries such as perfumes and lotions, shoes and jewellery; business prospered. Aeroplanes arrived every Tuesday, Thursday and Friday, and my salon was crowded as women came to beautify themselves and buy things to take home. After 1989, the situation began to deteriorate: the value of the zaïre dropped sharply and it became much more difficult to get a visa for Belgium. People no longer came and trade dropped off drastically.' By 1994, the CFA devaluation of that year had made the situation worse, and customers were mostly political refugees and students: neither had much money to spend.*

Annette was trying to figure out how to move to another country where the situation might be better. She asked about prospects in the United States, where she had heard it was possible to make good money.

Hong Kong and Dubai, in the United Arab Emirates on the Persian Gulf, are major centres for the trade. Many traders from Congo-Kinshasa go to Dubai. They call it the supermarket of the Middle East: it imports and re-exports huge quantities of goods and is a Mecca for second-economy traders from Africa and Central Asia. Its particular advantages are: the ease of getting an entry visa; the frequent flights in and out by many airlines and the services of freight companies that go by sea or air; its feeble frontier controls and low rates of customs duty; and its status as an entrepôt city (Marchal, 1997: 16–18).

When trade opportunities decline in one direction, information on new and lucrative possibilities in other places passes rapidly by word of mouth. The direction of trade flow, in instantaneous response, may change with extraordinary rapidity. As trade between Central Africa and Europe was diminishing, new opportunities developed to the south: the major trade from Congo-Kinshasa in 1994 was to South Africa rather than to Europe. The fastest-growing Congo-Kinshasa overseas community in the mid-1990s was in Johannesburg.

The South African Option

The first Zaïreans who came to South Africa were those who diverted trucks of cobalt produced by the GECAMINES mines in Lubumbashi to sell on their own account. Subsequently, they began to bring with them people who wanted to cross the border clandestinely, concealing them in their trucks. Then, towards the end of the collapse of apartheid, around 1990, a number of educated professionals entered the country to take up positions that could not be filled locally because of the lack of educated and trained black South Africans. In 1997, there were about 500 Zaïrean doctors in the country. However, these professionals lived in the white quarters of the city, not in the same neighbourhoods as those who made a living outside the law.

South Africa, faced with anti-apartheid trade restrictions, increased its trade with African countries. In September 1988, Presidents Mobutu and Botha met at Mobutu's palace at Gbadolite; the next year, a visit to Pretoria by the Zaïrean Prime Minister, Nguz Karl I. Bond, cemented the new ties between the two countries. From 1990 three flights a week from Kinshasa to Johannesburg brought a flood of Zaïreans; others too poor to buy aeroplane tickets arrived, having travelled overland through Zambia, Zimbabwe or Botswana. Numbers increased after the crises of September 1991 and January 1993.

Until March 1992, under the terms of an agreement between the two countries, Zaïreans were issued a two-week visa and a three-month temporary residence permit at the South African border. If they found a job, they could become permanent residents. In 1992, Zaïreans were estimated to constitute about half the immigrants arriving in South Africa. Zaïrean immigrants for that year numbered between 4,500 (Fidani, 1993: 52–3) and 9,000 (De Herdt and Marysse, 1996b: 94). After 1993, when the South African authorities began to get worried by this influx, the residence permit was no longer issued, the two-week visa was not renewable, and Zaïreans travelling to South Africa had to give a security deposit of US$1,000 to the South African representative in Kinshasa. But, at the end of the fortnight, migrants simply went underground to avoid being sent home, and lived with the help of the networks of compatriots which had come into being over the previous five years (*Le Monde*, 15 April 1994). The scale of the problem of illegal immigration is becoming overwhelming for South Africa, however, and there is no saying how long this option will remain. In 1993, 96,600 illegal immigrants were deported to 39 countries, more than double the number in 1991. One estimate of the total number of illegal immigrants in 1995 was between 3 and 5 million (Carim, 1995: 221).

The flood of Zaïrean immigrants included businessmen, traders, sellers wandering round on foot, smugglers and students. They lived in the suburbs of Johannesburg. Ponte City, for example, a 51-floor luxury apartment tower, was two-thirds occupied by Zaïrean families in 1994. Many more professionals, academics and engineers as well as doctors, went to South Africa as the crisis intensified in Zaïre and its universities and hospitals closed and GECAMINES became defunct. Skilled people, left without employment by this crisis, found they were in demand in South Africa's hospitals and mines (*Le Monde,* 15 April 1994).

Informants in Brussels, where traders were finding they sometimes had to wait six months for a 30-day visa for Belgium, said that the attraction of South Africa, in addition to the ease of entry, was that the same goods were cheaper there than they were in Europe. Since 1989, South Africans living in Zaïre had imported frozen foods and other goods. With the new situation, Zaïreans themselves were going to South Africa to find the goods they wanted and were trading them in many African countries (Fidani, 1993: 54). For some years, planes have flown daily from Zaïre to South Africa carrying diamonds, coffee, gold and cobalt, and have brought back fresh meat to be sold at very high prices in Kinshasa (Braeckman, 1992: 208). In response to the expansion of this trade, small airline services from Shaba to South Africa have greatly proliferated in recent years.

Our account of the violence and dislocation of the political, economic and social life of the two Congos has shown why people turn to the second economy and its trade within their national boundaries, with other African countries and with other continents. The discrimination and harassment they suffer in Europe provide new reasons for them to continue in these activities. The description of some of the characteristics of the trade leads us to the next chapter, to our investigation of traders in Paris and to the details of the goods and services they provide and of how their trade operates.

3
Commodities, Commercialization & the Structuring of Identity

The meaning in consumer goods is one of the ways in which we give our lives a consistency in the face of the overwhelming change to which it is subjected. (McCracken, 1988: xv)

Goods are constituents of self-hood: the practice of identity encompasses a practice of consumption. (Friedman, 1990: 327)

The new ease of communication and the rapid movement of people and commodities have intensified the mingling of cultures worldwide in the last thirty years. Meanings, people and goods flow between different regions, and the world becomes one network of social relationships. But it is one that is marked by diversity, not by uniformity (Hannerz, 1990: 237). The mingling of cultures is not merely a result of the breaking down of traditional culture and the disjointed adoption of half-understood elements of Western culture. It is 'the emergence of creative and fully viable new syntheses' (Fabian, 1978: 317–18). Nor is it a product of the mass consumer culture of Western political and economic domination, but rather a diversity of popular and local discourses, codes and practices (Featherstone, 1990: 2). In this chapter, we examine the use of material goods in the construction of an African urban identity among immigrants from West Central Africa in Europe, which exemplifies just such a creative synthesis of African and Western cultural elements. Second-economy traders, such as those whose life histories we have collected, provide many of the goods and services used in this process.

We have primarily documented traders who cater to the consumption patterns of Africans from Congo-Kinshasa and Congo-Brazzaville living in Paris. These immigrants do not constitute a separate residential community since they live scattered all over the city. But they do form a 'market population',[1] unified by their West Central African origin, the

---

[1] Our thanks to Sandra Barnes for suggesting this term.

commonality of their culture, and their demands for particular commodities to satisfy their culturally determined needs. The process of constructing and marking identity requires material goods; it is restricted by the negotiation between self-definition and the range of possibilities permitted by the commodities available in a particular market (Friedman, 1990: 314).

This European variety of African urban culture is different from the urban culture in Brazzaville or Kinshasa, a difference that is commonly found between diaspora populations and those who remain at home. Its blend of cultural elements includes African foods, Western clothing, African dress, the mixture of musical traditions that make up African popular music and the Western technology that reproduces it, and beauty products invented in the West and adapted for African usage. We find relevant here Paul Willis's comment on the importance of African and Caribbean cultural traditions to young black people in Britain: 'they use their cultural backgrounds as frameworks for living and as repertoires of symbolic resources for interpreting all aspects of their lives' (Willis, 1990: 8). He finds that the background of such traditions is necessary for the development not only of the identities of these young people but also for helping them to affirm and assert themselves against a pervasive racism that excludes them from full participation in British culture because they are not white. West Central Africans in Continental Europe confront the same problem. Michel de Certeau is illuminating here:

> Like law (one of its models), culture articulates conflicts and alter-nately legitimizes, displaces, or controls the superior force. It develops in an atmosphere of tensions, and often of violence, for which it provides symbolic balances, contracts of compatibility and compro-mises, all more or less temporary. The tactics of consumption, the ingenious ways in which the weak make use of the strong, thus lend a political dimension to everyday practices. (de Certeau, 1984: xvii)

The Two Worlds of Congolese Immigrants in Paris

Central African immigrants in Paris are divided into those who are docu-mented and employed in professional, skilled and semi-skilled employment, and those who are undocumented and excluded from oppor-tunity by the political and economic situation in their own countries and by the recent anti-immigration policies of France. The way the latter actively engage with, rather than submitting to, such constraints is to resort to international second-economy trade and to live as clandestine immigrants in Paris.

Those who are employed and have residence papers have little knowledge of the world of the unemployed and undocumented that is the primary focus of our study. They live within the law but they are connected with those who live in this other world outside the law, sometimes through ties of kinship but primarily through their demand for the goods and services provided by these second-economy traders.

These West Central African migrants are divided by nationality, which is primarily manifested in language difference. They all speak French: not only is it the language of the country they are now living in, it is the official national language of both their own countries. But, among themselves, they speak the lingua franca of their own country. Lingala is spoken by those from Congo-Kinshasa, while Lari is the language of residents of Congo-Brazzaville. These linguistic differences are important identifying features for the two nationalities, defining each in opposition to the other. The elements of their cultures other than language exhibit only minor differences.

Cultural identity is subjective and situational. Groups are not defined by innate permanent cultural characteristics: 'we' is defined by 'they'. 'The identities to members and categorizations by others are more or less fluid, more or less multiple, forming nesting hierarchies of we/they dichotomizations' (Cohen, 1978: 395). Congolese from Congo-Brazzaville and from Congo-Kinshasa do not, in fact, intermingle very much in their daily lives, but they do identify with each other as Central Africans in opposition to Africans from other regions of the continent. Nationally, there are clear signs of a developing consciousness for Congo-Kinshasa, produced by the experience of general popular discontent with the Mobutu regime, the widespread popularity of Congo music, a distinctive national dress (now in disrepute) invented by Mobutu, and the many diaspora communities 'whose common experience is of national origin and exile'. Ethnic identity within the country is constantly in flux in response to changing political relations internally and externally (W. MacGaffey, 1997: 54–5).

Engaging the Problems of Social Exclusion

To engage with life's problems involves action. Nicholas Dodier observes that:

> When a way of engaging is sustained by a person through all situations so that his interior motivation orientates relations with the world, when this way of engaging induces the individual to seek and select the necessary supports for his intended action, or, when the constraints of the situation are unfavourable, to resist or oppose what confronts him, we can speak … of a true ethos.[2] (Dodier, 1995: 191)

---

[2]'Lorsqu'une forme d'engagement est portée par une personne au travers des situations, tel un guide intérieur qui oriente le rapport au monde, lorsque cet engagement incline cette personne à rechercher et à sélectionner les appuis pertinents de son action voire, lorsque les contraintes de la situation sont défavorables, à résister ou à s'opposer à ce qui lui est offert, on pourra parler … d'un véritable ethos.'

But Dodier wants to expand the concept of ethos, which he finds too static, too tied to the idea of a stable culture, into the action of engaging or, to put it another way, of 'taking on' life's problems. The action of engaging implies flux. We find his perspective illuminating for our data: commerce is not a cultural phenomenon that is fixed. The reality we observe is of individuals carrying out clandestine commercial activity, who mobilize not only an adaptive competence to deal with their environment, but equally an ability to work towards an objective that, should it be achieved, could block or disrupt the functioning of the whole system. We see people taking part in second-economy activities and engaging in actions which involve choice and alternatives and which, in the aggregate, bring about shifts in the power structure of society.[3]

We wish to stress the heterogeneous nature of our data. We consider it more relevant to consider how groups and categories form and how they are in flux and in process of change, than to present them as if they were fixed and homogeneous. There is no single model of the migration experience and the strategies involved. It is an open and dynamic process, expressed by these migrants in many different and vividly evocative terms. It is to these language usages and their meanings that we now turn. They encapsulate the attitudes of resisting constraints and engaging with problems that are so evident in the life histories we collected.

The Terms the Traders Use
In her study in Japan, particular narratives and performances of selfhood led Dorinne Kondo to investigate how selves are variously constructed in specific situations, how these constructions can be multiplex and contradictory, and how they shape and are shaped by relations of power. She observes that it is necessary to attend carefully to meaningful, experiential aspects of work and the implications of these meanings in the wider system of power relations (Kondo, 1990: 230).

In the 1980s and 1990s, the most notable reason for migration for Congolese from both countries has been the search for opportunity by those who find themselves excluded in various ways at home. This new reason for migration is indicative of a defiant response to the closing down of chances for people to better themselves at home, as more repressive political conditions have developed and the economic situation has worsened. It is more and more the case that fewer people have jobs and the pay of those who do have them is ever more derisory: it is widely recognized that to 'fend for oneself' (*se débrouiller*) is the only way to survive.

This situation is reflected in the changing definition of 'work'. People devise their own uses of language to express their perceptions of official society, as well as of the ways they defy it. An early study showed that, in

---

[3]This point is developed in MacGaffey, 1992.

Kinshasa in 1945, 'work' implied salaried employment: a comment on a market vendor was that '*elle ne travaille pas, elle se débrouille*' (she doesn't work, she's just fending for herself) (Comhaire-Sylvain, 1968: 29). In Paris in 1994, when we asked an informant from the milieu of the traders whether a particular Congolese worked or not, the response that 'yes, he (or she) works' meant any way of earning money, including activities outside the law, such as unlicensed trade and services, and drug dealing, trading in stolen goods and other activities known as '*bizness*' or '*les circuits*'; all are means of fending for oneself. '*Le travail*' in 1994 encompassed '*se débrouiller*', whereas in 1945 it had not. This new definition is part of the challenge these young people mount to the hierarchy of meaning attached to work and employment in the larger system of power relations.

We find that the language these young people use expresses this challenge, and that 'talk is not just a reflection of social organization; talk is a practice that is one of social organization's central parts ... In maintaining or changing local power relations, talk unites structure and agency over time' (Gal, 1989: 347). The principal terms used to refer to the migration experience and the activities it involves are '*l'aventure*' and '*la débrouillardise*'. The first originated in Congo-Brazzaville, the second in Congo-Kinshasa. '*Partir à l'aventure*' means going to France to acquire high-fashion clothes and change one's status, the movement known as *la Sape*.[4] Upon return to the home country, the status of '*Parisien*' is bestowed on a young person. The meaning of the expression '*la débrouillardise*' comes from the legitimization of the illegal practice of artisanal diamond digging after the secession of the state of South Kasai in the 1960s. Because this secessionist state lacked a budget, its leader, Albert Kalonji, decreed '*débrouillez-vous*' to be Article 15 of the constitution of the ancient territory of the Luba-Kasai, including MIBA territory. He said 'This land and its subsoils belong to the Muluba people. Fend for yourselves (*débrouillez-vous*), though not in the MIBA concessions'. He thus liberalized the diamond industry (Biaya, 1985: 86, n. 36). This simple order, '*débrouillez-vous*', was subsequently given to the whole nation by President Mobutu, and has since become associated with all illegal activities: corruption, theft, diamond smuggling and so on.

The collective idea of '*l'aventure*' or '*la débrouillardise*' is summed up in comments by traders: 'One must manage on one's own by whatever means one can to make money and live', and 'If you have the spirit of adventure, you go for it. If they tell you there's a land-mine there, you have to go on regardless. You only consider the danger after the action has been taken'. These ideas make clandestine immigration an experience of self-fulfilment in which the actor is constantly evaluating himself. '*L'aventure*' entails the

---

[4]In what follows, details of the movement are taken from Gandoulou (1984).

use of physical and mental skills, and even sometimes putting one's life in danger. In '*l'aventure*', migrants do not stake assets which are exterior to them (such as a title or a property). Rather, they put their own potential and power – their very selves – on the line. It is clearly because these actors have nothing but themselves to rely on that the events of the migration experience are felt so intensely. The emphasis on the dimension of risk shows that the clandestine migration and activities of Congolese can be seen as a way of life geared towards self-realization: by this mode of operation, the immigrants reveal and fulfil themselves, and construct their personal identities.

Another term, '*mikiliste*', is used by young people in Kinshasa. It is derived from *mikili*, which means country in Lingala; thus a *mikiliste* is someone who has travelled abroad and 'been around'. The term refers to the disadvantaged, not to young people coming from privileged backgrounds. In this context, *mikili* corresponds mainly to France or Belgium, but also, by extension, to the Western world. The *mikiliste* is considered to be so changed by his experience that he is a stranger in his own country: he has left it to accumulate wealth in the *mikili*. On his return home from Europe, he distinguishes himself by his style of dressing, his lighter skin tone, and a circle of acquaintances giving him access to the political and artistic worlds. It should be noted here that Congolese migrants in Belgium socialize across socio-economic lines. For example, in the immigrant community of Matonge district in Brussels, underprivileged young people mix easily with the children of political leaders, often forming friendships with them. When these young people return to their home country, these friendships become political assets and facilitate the starting up of businesses, or the undertaking of any activity requiring official authorization. The wealthy and powerful from Congo-Kinshasa were to be found in greater numbers in Brussels than in Paris, but *mikilistes* often came to Paris after a stay in Brussels.

The term *kobeta libanga* (stone-breaking) is an expression used by Congo-Kinshasa artisanal gold and diamond diggers to justify certain activities that they see as part of the fight against unemployment, hunger and uncertainty. It signifies the will to succeed by one's own efforts no matter what the cost, even through morally and socially reprehensible actions. This lack of respect for rules is reinforced by *Article 15*.

All these terms (*mikiliste, aventurier, kobeta libanga* and *Article 15*) are metaphors for improving one's life by whatever means available. This goal is the reason for migration to a European country, to a society which offers possible escape from poverty and other negative social, economic, political or psychological experiences. Traders say explicitly that they are in France to 'become someone' and to change their status. Thus the most common words they use to describe their experiences are French words and are thought of in French, but they are given a different sense.[5]

---

[5] Gandoulou gives many more in a long list of them (Gandoulou, 1984: 209–10)

Music is an important domain for elevating or reinforcing status during migration. Success becomes public when a famous singer launches the name of the immigrant by including it in the refrain of a song. The individual's status is fully established, however, if this song including their name is then recorded on disc. He or she is then consecrated as a '*mwana Paris*' (child of Paris), '*mwana Bruxelles*' (child of Brussels) or '*mwana Bundes*' (child of Germany).

The terms '*l'aventure*' and '*l'aventurier*' are used in both Brazzaville and Kinshasa, but have different meanings. In Brazzaville, they are positive. Having lived in France and been celebrated in songs, the '*aventurier*' is the equivalent of a '*mikiliste*', except for the fact that he or she has not made political contacts, because in France the spheres of politics, student life and '*aventure*' do not mix. In Kinshasa, '*aventurier*' can signify someone who 'picks up' girls, but also someone who has failed to make their way elsewhere in their attempt to leave their area of origin (the village, neighbourhood or city). Following this failure, the '*aventurier*' hides and does not return to his home area. '*Mikiliste*', on the other hand, means someone who has succeeded in this effort.

These young traders manifest '*la débrouillardise*' in their commercial practices. Their enterprises represent specific forms of resistance to the oppression suffered in the countries of origin, as well as to the constraints of clandestine life in France. Trade is a way of confronting the problems these people face; it is not a given activity. They could conceivably resort to other types of activities, such as mugging or participation in organized crime. Our investigations of clandestine milieux in France show a parallel world with its own rules of exclusion, determined by its own form of commercial logic. It is to the details of the commercial operations of this world that we now turn.

Trading in the Second Economy
Commerce outside the law is called by several names, among them '*bizness*' and '*co-op*'. '*Bizness*' is a distortion of the English word 'business', and is used indiscriminately to describe all clandestine commercial activities. '*Co-op*' is an abbreviation of 'co-operate' or 'co-operation' and refers to the entire system of relationships involved in a clandestine business deal and the making of the necessary contacts for commercial purposes.

The goods sold are often procured by theft, which entails taking risks. Several euphemisms are used to refer to this activity, such as '*bouger les choses*' (shifting things). The traders have a tendency to justify their fraudulent practices in France as recovery of goods or riches stolen from their country during colonization. Thus they perceive their migration experience as a sort of reverse colonization. Imprisonment for actions taken in the quest for money is not taken seriously. In fact, it enhances reputation in their milieu, because, once you come out, you are still in France and can continue your activities as before. Expulsion from French territory, however, is the most damaging possible punishment, because it signals failure in the process of 'becoming somebody'.

Traders in the second economy have their own system of rules. One must not kill anyone but only take material possessions, and both break-ins and muggings are forbidden. *La débrouillardise*, they say, should avoid 'violent' money. The general agreement is that nothing good can be done with wealth acquired by violent means.[6] Those who do earn money in this way are ostracized. They are also believed to 'go crazy', and end up poorer than they were when they started. In the view of the *aventurier*, earnings should be amassed little by little; patience is a principal virtue. In reinforcing their aversion to 'violent' money, these young people differentiate their style from that of the Arabs, as shown in the following statement by a *sapeur*:

> *We have our principles. The Arab style of theft must be distinguished from ours: 'we don't do it their way, we do it our own way'. For example, we say that that way is for the Arabs. They do it like that, and we do it like this, so we won't mix everything up. We're different from them because they're more advanced. We're amateurs and they're professionals. They can show up for a robbery with weapons. If they want to break into a store, risking who knows what unknown elements are there (alarms, guards, etc.), they'll pull out a weapon. But the Congolese tries to go about the same thing intelligently; he says to himself, 'I have to leave quietly, so nobody calls the cops and there's no trouble'. Their style involves violence, ours does not.*

One has to note, however, that a feeling of helplessness does seem to be evident in this statement. It is certainly also the case that some Congolese deal in drugs and quickly earn large amounts of money, rather than accumulating it patiently little by little.

Traders say that their aim is to save enough to start a business in the home country later on. They also tend to justify their activities outside the law by the fact that they are only living temporarily in France, which makes it easier for them to do what is forbidden back home. The frequency of theft in Paris reflects this idea. In their own country this activity is sometimes punishable by death. In France, theft is considered to be a measure of self-accomplishment for Congolese young people, hence the emotional recollection of such activity. This situation has led to the perception that to undocumented migrants France represents a lawless world. In fact, this is not the case because, firstly, *la débrouillardise* starts in the home country

---

[6]These ideas are comparable to those of the Luo in Kenya, as described in Parker Shipton's *Bitter Money*. Luo classify money into two kinds, one good, one evil or 'bitter'. Money from forbidden transactions, most commonly sales of land, gold, tobacco or cannabis, is ill-gotten. It is conceived of as barren and of no use to its owner (Shipton, 1989).

before they ever get to France and, secondly, the clandestine practices of Congolese in France are subject to their own rules, for example, the prohibition on violence and killing. They do have respect for social rules, but they are not necessarily those of the state.

A large proportion of merchandise acquired outside the law is sold within the milieu. Any individual may alternately occupy the roles of customer and vendor. The customer is often either a relative or a compatriot of the vendor. It is highly likely that a Congolese living in the Paris area will buy from a compatriot, but the relationship may also be defined by customer loyalty, with the regular purchase of items from the same vendor. In such a case, a buyer–seller bond may be formed between two people of different nationalities. Details of these relations are given in Chapter 5. The customer makes every effort to maintain such links because he or she is usually also a vendor. Buying is therefore a potential occasion for doing business. Thus the 'wheeler-dealer' attitude is shared by both customer and vendor.

There are no means to transmit *la débrouillardise*, since it is an individual and not a standardized mode of operating. The following statement from the *sapeur* quoted above makes this clear:

> *Most compatriots have this spirit before leaving the country. If in France you're often broke while everyone else is getting by, your ideas change. You adapt and get by as well. If you remain a* sapeur, *you know that to buy those pants or those shoes, you have to do this scam. Automatically, you have to join in. Nobody tells you you have to join in, but you know it. To get something. If you don't join in, how are you going to live? Nobody takes care of you. Everybody's in the same boat. Someone can put you up but they won't give you any money, so it's up to you to get by every day, to figure out how to make money.*

Unification begins, however, when people share experiences. In this case, a culture and a cultural identity are formed around the experience of social exclusion, though this culture is the result of different activities and not the basis for them. Clothing, music, and the terms used to refer to migration and its motives and experiences, *kobeta libanga*, *l'aventure*, *la débrouillardise*, *mikilisme*, etc. and the value systems they embody create a cultural unity for these traders. This unity is further reinforced by the interpenetration of the ideas of *la Sape* and *mikiliste*, which now apply to all the young who show by their clothes that they have been to Europe. Furthermore, all the terms are current now among those from both Congo-Brazzaville and Congo-Kinshasa. *La Sape* has lost the original connotation of political opposition that it had in Brazzaville. In Paris, it has become a sign of success. The statuses acquired by the young during migration – *Parisien* and *mwana Bruxelles* – encapsulate this complex cultural reality and the identity that goes with it.

Many documented Congolese immigrants are as resourceful, as full of initiative and persistence, as are the clandestine immigrants. Whether or not a person's occupation corresponds to his or her career and level of education is not so important as earning an income which ensures an acceptable standard of daily life in France and, for those from Congo-Kinshasa especially, allows one to send a significant amount of help (in money or goods) on a regular basis to family who have remained back home. Despite their being a heavy burden, migrants make considerable and regular contributions to kin back home, as we shall see later in Chapter 5.

We now describe the goods and services these traders supply.

Culture and Consumption

Consumers buy goods within a specific cultural framework and use them:

> To create cultural categories and principles, cultivate ideals, create and sustain lifestyles, construct notions of the self, and create (and survive) social change. Consumption is thoroughly cultural in character. (McCracken, 1988: xi)

All these usages are evident for the goods and services provided by the traders in our study. These are not just any goods but those specific to the lifestyle of the immigrants. As Igor Kopytoff points out, 'commodities must be not only produced materially as things, but also culturally marked as being a certain kind of thing';[7] they are culturally constructed and in the process given culturally specific meaning (Kopytoff, 1986: 64, 68).

Commodities in demand by all West Central African immigrants in Paris are African foods, wax-print cloth (*pagnes*) to be made up into women's outfits (as well as the accessories to go with these outfits, such as shoes, head scarves and jewellery), beauty products, and discs and video cassettes of popular African music. Clandestine immigrants, in addition, specifically desire designer-label clothes for the lifestyle of a *sapeur*, and the beer and other forms of alcohol of particular kinds consumed in *nganda*, some of which are smuggled. Services used by all immigrants include photographers to commemorate social events, hairdressers, seamstresses to make up dresses and other clothes, financial transfer services, taxis and repair garages. Clandestine immigrants also use the services of those who establish squatter housing, manufacture false papers, provide transport services and provide depots for storing goods.

---

[7]'A commodity is a thing that has use value and that can be exchanged in a discrete transaction for a counterpart, the very fact of exchange indicating that the counterpart has, in the immediate context, an equivalent value' (Kopytoff, 1986: 68).

We shall begin with an account of how different goods entered the trading circuits in chronological order.

The History of Commodities in the Trade
One of the earliest commodities was drugs. Musicians were the great drug sellers at the beginning. In the former Zaïre, popular singers who made a coup selling drugs advertised the fact in their songs. This had the effect of spreading the practice among the young. A singer with Papa Wemba, Strervos Niarchos (who changed his name to a misspelling of the name of the Greek shipowner, Stavros Niarchos, a wealthy and powerful man), was among the first in this trade. Papa Wemba had created a song which praised the young man's qualities as a *sapeur*. Thanks to this success, he was able to enter several drug-dealing networks. Initially the principal drug was marijuana, which first appeared in the Congolese diaspora in France after 1975. Drug dealing was widely disseminated in 1977 and 1978 with the increasingly large influx of young BaKongo *sapeurs*. It was an easy way to earn money quickly, so selling marijuana attracted many people. At the end of the 1980s, a hard-drug network, specifically for heroin, developed. The smugglers supplied themselves in Holland and England, or made connections with Arab networks. The two Congolese communities got to know each other through the medium of this drug smuggling. Before they engaged in this trade, very few Zaïreans went to the MEC (*Maison des Etudiants Congolais*), where these drug-trading trips were organized.

Several studies show the importance of luxury clothing imported into the urban culture of the two Congos (Gandoulou, 1984, 1989a; Friedman, 1990, 1992; Bazenguissa-Ganga, 1992a and b; Biaya, 1994; Gondola, 1997a). There were two distinct periods in this activity. Luxury at first meant ready-to-wear instead of the hand-sewn clothes produced locally. Only later did it consist of the French designer clothing of *la Sape*.

The first period lasted until the end of the 1970s: Congolese bought clothes in France and took them home to sell in their own countries. There were three means of doing this: immigrants returning home on vacation brought clothes in their suitcases and sold them; some people came to France to buy for themselves; and others sent clothes home to be collected and sold by their contacts. The discount stores of Tati in Barbès in the 18th *arrondissement* were the principal sources of supply because of their low prices. Traders bought men's, women's and children's clothing to order. After a while, other stores became important, including some around Tati and others in the suburbs, such as Auchan in La Défense and Rosny 2 in Rosny-sous-Bois.

The second period began with the increase in migration to France of the young *sapeurs*. Their commerce was organized out of MEC. Initially it was capitalized by stealing clothes to be sold to students or Congolese tourists returning to their country. In 1984–95, the *sapeurs* tended to acquire these clothes outside France, primarily in Italy, and they sold them not only in the MEC but also in cafés around the metro stations of Château-d'Eau and Strasbourg Saint Denis. Since the early 1990s, the streets of the Château Rouge neighbourhood in the 18th *arrondissement* have become the place for these sales. This activity is becoming increasingly more open: in cafés, the seller sits at a table and discreetly displays his goods to a customer; on the streets they are displayed without any attempt at concealment unless the police come into view.

The networks of clothing sellers are distinct from those of drug dealers, but symbolically a relationship exists between the two commodities. Drugs are referred to as *putulu*, a word which is also used as an exclamation of admiration to refer to someone who is well dressed. From the beginning, the MEC has been the meeting place for different groups of young people, primarily distinguished by whether they are drug dealers or not. They indicate which they are by the kind of clothing fabric they prefer: the dealers wear leather, the others linen. The dealers have not succeeded in imposing their lifestyle because among the young people of the two Congos the use of marijuana is not widespread.

African foods were finally added to the trade. Congolese eating habits used to be characterized by substitutions. Prior to the 1980s, speciality African foods were almost unavailable except for some brought over by individuals. Semolina replaced manioc as the basic starch. Mixed with potato flour, it became an acceptable substitute for *fou-fou* (manioc flour). Similarly, salted dried eels were eaten instead of other salted dried fish (Gandoulou, 1984: 110). A very few speciality food shops could be found in the 14th and 12th *arrondissements* and in the 'African village' in the Mouffetard market. But these foodstuffs were very expensive and the vendors lacked sufficient Central African customers. In consequence, the most frequently used means of making these products available was to bring them back after a visit home. The traveller used the airlines' 20 kg baggage allowance for this transport. The export of food and the necessity of preserving it, since it could not all be eaten at once, introduced some innovations in eating habits. Foods usually eaten fresh, such as leafy vegetables like *saka-saka* (manioc greens), *mfumbwa* (leaves gathered in the wild and finely shredded) and *dongo-dongo* (greens) began to be dried. The nature of the food eaten, with this change from fresh to dried items, thus reflected the shift in geographical space.

Goods and Services Supplied by the Traders Today
Food and Drink. 'Eating is an act of self-identification' (Friedman, 1990: 314) and, for Congolese in Paris, eating the foods they used to eat at home is an important token of cultural and self identification. By the second half of the 1980s, African foods such as manioc, peanuts, salt and smoked fish, a variety of vegetables and mangoes were widely available.

Manioc holds a special place among these foods. For members of the diaspora from both banks of the Zaïre river, it marks both national and family identity. It is considered to be the basic food; eating it implies a way of looking at the world and at society. Until the end of the 1970s, attitudes towards it seemed to express the cultural dissonance associated with the journey to Europe. When a migrant returned home, he or she would usually eat manioc last. When they finally did so, it was taken as a sign that they had regained their national identity.

But, in addition, there is an ambiguous attitude towards manioc. This food was generally perceived as the incarnation of savagery. Thus, in certain places in the home country considered as civilized and smart, manioc was not permissible and was looked upon as dirty. For example, when Congo-Brazzaville put a luxury train known as the Blue Train into service, it was formally forbidden that manioc be consumed in it. Again, after the inauguration of the Hospital Centre of the University of Brazzaville, it was forbidden to bring manioc to the patients.[8] The consumption of manioc in France, which represents, for Congolese, the centre of civilization, therefore involves an ambiguity: how can something thought of as 'savage' be associated with civilized living? Symbolically, France is simultaneously the home of these migrants and yet not their home. In the minds of these young people, France and Congo are two aspects of the same world, of which France represents the centre. From this point of view, going to France is not only to traverse geographical space but also to go to the centre of the world. Moreover, this journey is a way of putting oneself to the test, of trying out one's competence, and of expanding one's identity. Thus the departure for France, besides the fact of actually making a journey, also signifies a journey into the interior of the self. One moves and the experience of life intensifies.

Besides manioc, plantain bananas, maize flour and rice are the staple starches. They are accompanied by smoked or salt fish and vegetables. Green vegetables include *saka-saka*, *fumbwa* (or *mfumbu*) and other leaves. They may be cooked in peanut or palm oil sauce, sometimes with canned pilchards or other fish as an ingredient. Other vegetables are bitter eggplant, okra, *safu* (a sour fruit with a purple skin, soft flesh and a large pip), hot peppers and several kinds of dried beans. These foods are imported from different countries of West and Central Africa or from the Caribbean, and sold in African or Asian-owned speciality food shops, or by street vendors.

From these foods, eaten every day, Congolese women cook the splendid repasts, consisting of many different dishes, that characterize all festive occasions: weddings, anniversaries, the end of mourning celebrations, parties, social evenings, children's birthdays. Favoured dishes are *saka-saka* with pilchards or other fish and peanut sauce; big platters of grilled salt fish or chicken wings; fried plantains, boiled manioc, rice or maize pudding; mutton or beef stew, or chicken cooked in a peppery palm oil

---

[8]In both Congos and in other African countries, food has to be brought to patients in hospitals by their families.

and peanut sauce; and always freshly prepared hot pepper sauce on the side.

Drinks consist of beer, whisky, sparkling wine, champagne and still wine. Most of these drinks are bought in shops and large Parisian establishments. Beer is the most culturally valued drink, as is manioc among foods. Young men drink to get drunk, a mark of masculinity, and also of delinquency and a whole way of life. Drinking is also an important element in picking up women: paying for a drink is a way for a man to declare his interest. For men, expenditure consisting of the purchase of several beers is a way of showing off status. One exhibits capability ('*capacité*') and power ('*puissance*') or the success of a coup. Women do not drink beer; some studies have shown that they think it makes their sexuality deteriorate (Enquête Collective, 1986; Codou, 1987). They prefer to drink whisky or sparkling wine instead. Drinking thus has significance over and above the act of drinking.

The most expensive beers are the brands Beck and Skol imported from Belgium. They are brought across the frontier by smugglers and sold to *nganda* owners. This trade is a speciality of Congolese from Congo-Kinshasa. The smugglers have vans and often go to Belgium in the evening, returning in the early hours to Paris. Cases of twelve bottles are sold at 250 FF on credit.[9] The vendor gets his money back with the empties a week later. A smuggler always has beer in his van so as to be able to supply the needs of his customers.

Clothes. Many African women in Paris continue to dress as they did at home. They wear a *pagne*, or length of wax-print cloth, as a wrap-around long skirt. It is sold in a six-metre length, part of which is used to make a blouse. The highest-quality wax-print is made in Holland, a poorer quality is produced in the UK and West Africa, and an inferior variety in Congo-Kinshasa. Trade in this cloth is principally in the hands of women, some of whom have become very wealthy on the proceeds. These big traders name the patterns and set rapidly changing fashions in them (see MacGaffey, 1987: 169). But other fabrics are also in demand: a couturier displays lengths of cloth in colourful patterns and a great variety of Lurex and voiles to suit the urban African woman's dress style that is particular to Paris.

The variety making up this dress style was much in evidence at the wedding of the granddaughter of the head of the Kimbanguist church which we were able to attend. There must have been well over a thousand people present and a repast of many of the dishes described above was served to everyone at the end of the event. About half the women wore Western-style dresses, and half some variant of African dress, some made of wax-print, some of luxurious silk or brocade fabrics. Several groups representing different organizations were dressed in identical long wrap-

---

[9] In April 1994, 5.68 FF (French francs) = US$ 1.00.

around skirts, blouses and head scarves. Some wore brilliantly patterned wax-prints, some flowered or other bright-coloured cloth; one group was in black skirts, white scoop-neck bodices and short black and silver Lurex-knit jackets. The bride was dressed in Western style, in a white embroidered bridal gown with a long train and veil, and with a silk and satin flower bouquet. Her mother was strikingly elegant in a dress patterned in small gold medallions bordered with black, with black trim, a black velvet turban and gold jewellery.

These are the clothes of the well-dressed middle class. The *sapeurs*' ideal, however, is designer-name clothing.[10] Those among them who cannot aspire so high are still carefully turned out in stylish clothes. The outfits of one *sapeur*, a *nganda* owner, included a short, black patterned dress, pale grey sling-back shoes cut high in front, a silver ankle chain, a necklace and an ivory bracelet. She wore her hair short and tightly braided. The next time we saw her, she was wearing a wig of artfully tousled neck-length brown-black hair falling forward over her face, a baggy white sweater over tights with a pattern of Chinese characters down the sides, and black suede lace-up boots with patterned cloth tops. Other *sapeurs'* outfits included a short tight skirt and short jacket in black leather, with elaborate make-up and lots of gilt jewellery; a black leather, metal-studded jacket and trousers, gold earrings and gold-ornamented sunglasses; and, in more sober mode, another wore an expensive looking navy V-neck pullover, pleated skirt, blue striped blouse, black pumps and gold earrings, with hair straightened and bleached gold on top. When this young woman left us, she spent a considerable time arranging her wrap to her satisfaction in the mirror: self-presentation is very important. One young man was very suave in a long wool overcoat; another, on one day, wore blue jeans, black turtle-neck sweater and a heavy light blue cotton shirt with the sleeves rolled up, and, on the next, poplin trousers, jacket and shirt in shades of beige, a plain black belt, gold ring with green stone, cross pendant and sunglasses.

Beauty Products. Beauty products include: skin lighteners, soaps and lotions, hair straighteners, wigs, and the hair extensions for braiding into elaborate hairstyles. These are essential elements for the presentation of self as a new identity is constructed. They must be used before the return to Brazzaville. Until the 1980s, make-up products such as l'Ambi Vert, Mounganga and Venus came directly from the home country. Some people brought them from Brazzaville to sell to Congolese in France; otherwise, they could be obtained by asking a friend to send a packet by an intermediary who was travelling to Paris. Since that time, close on twenty varieties of skin lighteners, among them Dehar (which comes from Nigeria) and Deprosone, have

---

[10]In 1984, Gandoulou observed labels from the following fashion designers in the *sapeurs*' outfits: Gianni-Versace, Kansai-Yamamote, Balenciaga, Ventilo, Valentino, Ventilo-Valentuomo, Mario-Valentino, Marsoto-Uomo, Veri-Uomo, Ongane, Paco Rabanne, Renoma, Giorgio Armani, Capo Bianco, Marcel Lassance, J.-M. Weston, Yves Saint Laurent, Chimbamoto, Daniel Hechter.

been introduced. These products are normally only sold on prescription in a pharmacy. They are illegally acquired by theft or by obtaining them from home. Some traders have contacts with pharmacists who sell these items to them. Since there is a demand for these products in France, the speciality stores circulate them around, selling them semi-wholesale for 6 FF to women retailers, who then sell them in the street for 10 FF.

Music: Compact Discs and Videos. Modern African popular music is heard all the time in shops, in African cafés and *nganda*, and in people's homes and in their cars: it is a vital component of urban immigrant culture. Videos of concert performances, compact discs and tapes of the music of Papa Wemba, OK Jazz, Rochereau, Kofi Olomide, Mbilia Bel, Mpongo Love, Viva la Musica, Victoria Eleison, Wengue Musica and others are sold everywhere, in shops and by street vendors, to satisfy the huge demand.

Some video cassettes are produced by Télé-Zaïre and imported into France; they are transmissions of concerts, of theatrical performances in Lingala, and of comic shows that are in vogue. Otherwise videos and compact discs are produced in France. Most producers have neither an office nor a professional address. When they receive a verbal contract, they set up two or three recording sessions in a studio. The artists, knowing that the producers will not pay copyright fees, prefer to do the production themselves if they can. They then propose a sale to Sonodis or Sonima, companies which produce compact discs of popular African music. Discs may also be stolen from stores and then sold in the street and at parties. All are of interest to Congolese from both countries.

This element of African popular culture in Europe has long been part of the urban culture of Central Africa. It was tied to Western technological innovations such as gramophones, records and certain instruments. Playing and dancing to mostly Western music was part of urban life in Stanleyville (now Kisangani) before independence. The popularity of African recorded songs started with the marketing of recorded music soon after the Second World War (Fabian, 1978: 317–18, 331, n. 14).[11] Congo jazz became famous and widely known in Africa in the 1950s when it was distributed by Congo-based record companies and Radio Brazzaville. The great musicians were mostly singer guitarists (Bender, 1991: 42).[12]

---

[11]In Kisangani, in 1977, an enterprising entrepreneur of the emerging indigenous bourgeoisie found the opportunity for his first profitable enterprise by buying records in Kinshasa and selling them for a high mark-up in Kisangani (see MacGaffey, 1987: 100).

[12]In the early years of the century, the ethnic mixture of the inhabitants of the cities of Kinshasa and Brazzaville resulted in the mingling of musical traditions from both Central and West Africa; this was to be the basis for the popular music of today. Later influences included Ghanaian Highlife and Caribbean and Latin American rhythms. Music using the drum and the thumb piano, played at mourning ceremonies, marriages and births, was replaced in the rapid urbanization of the early 1930s by the electric guitar and the tambourine, flute, clarinet and accordion of the modern band. Radio-Brazzaville and Radio-Congolia, started during the Second World War, were instrumental in disseminating this new popular music (Gondola, 1997a: 234–48)

Popular music has been a vehicle of political discourse (Gondola, 1997b: 65). At first, it was one of the responses against the colonial system; today it is one of a series of practices and attitudes reacting to exclusion from the urban world (Gondola, 1993: 156). In the 1950s, while the leaders of the African elite were merely seeking reform of the colonial system, popular music was demanding its total abolition. The first ethnic political organizations used the bars where this music was played as meeting places, though not until 1932, in Congo-Kinshasa, was the sale of liquor allowed to Africans in public places, and only in 1946 were Africans in Congo-Brazzaville allowed to patronize bars frequented by Europeans. Thereafter, the bar, in which the playing of popular music was an essential feature, became the inviolable domain of African initiative, both cultural and political, a refuge that rapidly became the place for having a good time (Ibid.: 156–63, 165).

These material goods supplied by the traders make up assemblages for the individuals who buy them that reflect ideas about identity and values, ideas which are specific to time and place and which creatively synthesize African and Western elements. We can see exemplified here the statement of Mary Douglas and Baron Isherwood that: 'Goods assembled together in ownership make physical, visible statements about the hierarchy of values to which their chooser subscribes' (Douglas and Isherwood, 1979: 5). The services these traders provide are also a part of this process.

Photography: Constructing Images of the Self. We learned of at least a dozen photographers, ten from Congo-Kinshasa and two from Congo-Brazzaville, who take photographs of people at social events. They began this activity in their own countries, either as professionals or as amateurs. They do not always own a camera, so they may have to borrow one. André, one of these photographers, related how he was helped by a compatriot:

> The guy who welcomed me to France was a photographer in Congo-Brazzaville. He lent me the equipment to do business. I had not known him in Congo. I had no family connection with him, nor was he even a friend; I did not know him until I got here.

Photography is one way in which a public image is constructed. A photo is simultaneously private and public: it is both a presentation of the self and a construction of social identity in the migration experience. Gandoulou shows how the image of a Parisian used to be constructed through a series of photographs taken in places that symbolize Paris, such as the Eiffel Tower, the Arc de Triomphe, the Champs Elysées, les Halles or luxury stores (Gandoulou, 1984: 98–9). Evoking such places was part of the process of constructing the new identity of *la Sape*. These photos were destined for friends at home to involve them in this undertaking. Today, however, there is less emphasis on the context. Formerly, when the community in Paris was small, photos were important to close the distance with the home country. Now, with jet travel, this distance has been, in effect, cancelled out and the community has been consolidated. The photographic image is no longer important in itself; what is important is the fact of being photographed and of being seen publicly in the process. Thus it was that in 1994 photographers would complain about people who asked to be photographed but then would never come to claim the photographs.

In 1994, the accounting for a photographer was as follows:

Price to customer for a 13x17 print: 35–40 FF
Cost to photographer:
    Film of 36 frames: 32–38 FF
    Development per print: 15 FF
    Additional costs (flash bulbs, battery): 5 FF

Thus the photographer cleared between 19 and 24 FF a print, if he could collect the money. He would demand the price in advance but often could only get an agreement for payment on delivery. Covering an event lasting the whole evening (from 10 p.m. until dawn) requires four to five films. Film is primarily purchased and developed at FNAC (a big Paris discount store).

The subjects are mostly posed. Spontaneity is not sought after since the photograph is done to order and the subject chooses the decor, the place and the people in it. People arrange to be photographed with friends, so that these photographs make the social visible by capturing part of a personal network at a particular moment. Such images preserve the memory of an event and are proof of one's participation in it. The photograph captures a fugitive moment, in which the most important thing is to show off one's physical image and elegant clothes; this is what has been achieved by means of all sorts of risks and sacrifices. Photographs are often full face, since recognition is essential and self-fulfilment through adventuring should show in the face.

In the process of constructing appearances, individuals take advantage of the proliferation of public and private occasions at which they can exhibit successes achieved in the migration process. Photographs are most often taken in nightclubs, concert halls, party rooms, at the stadiums, and at private celebrations that take place for the end of mourning, for marriages, anniversaries, baptisms, reunions, etc. All such festive occasions take place on Saturdays and Sundays

Taxi Services. To provide a taxi service, one must own a car. A sign is not necessary, but some cars do carry them. Taxi drivers primarily find their passengers at the airports on days when flights arrive from Congo-Brazzaville or Congo-Kinshasa. They approach potential customers and propose a fare at about one-third of the usual rate. A driver may negotiate with three different customers, in which case, if they want to accept, they should not have too much luggage. The taxi deposits each customer in turn. These taxis are also used for a range of other services: a trader sometimes rents a taxi to pick up his freight imported from home; someone without a car may need to meet a compatriot or kinsman at the airport; a taxi driver may also stop in front of Africans waiting at a taxi rank and negotiate to take them where they need to go. We can also include here the service provided by those who rent trucks to people wanting to move house.

Financial Transfers. Organizers of unofficial financial transfers arrange payments of money (or goods or food) to those back in the home country. Formerly, flight attendants or friends performed this service, but there was a high risk that the money would be embezzled and never arrive. To try and keep the courier honest, people generally invented some tragedy to gain sympathy as a reason for the transfer, such as the death of a parent. The slowness of bank operations and the likelihood of theft of postal orders by mail personnel today also motivate recourse to unofficial means for the transfer of large sums of money.

Unofficial transfers involve at least two people who know each other and who each invest quite a large sum of money. It is necessary to have two people involved so as to be able to come up with a large enough sum, of the order, say, of 300,000 FF. These partners then need an agent, to act as an intermediary in Kinshasa or Brazzaville, who personally takes the money out there and then works with this capital. From time to time, a close member of the family of one of those concerned, or a trusted friend going to the country, is given money to take out to replenish this capital. The partners are thus confident that it will not be stolen. When a transaction is required by a Congolese living in France, the partners contact their agent in Brazzaville or Kinshasa by telephone and give him all the information for identifying the recipient. The Congolese sender in France then asks that his consignment arrive in the form of either money or a package of goods or food. In the latter case, one of the partners then asks the agent to buy the goods on the spot with some of the capital he has or, otherwise, to pay out the money himself. Afterwards, the recipient comes to the office to confirm by telephone to the sender that the transaction has taken place. All this happens in the space of a few hours. It is a reliable but very expensive service: a quarter of the amount transferred is required as commission. The precautions involved show how it is possible, in certain activities, to set up a system that effectively avoids risk, however para-doxical this may seem for an organization outside the law. The banks are not involved in this transaction in any way.

Squatter Housing. Until the middle of the 1980s, Congolese could live free at the MEC or pay rent for a studio or hotel room. After the MEC was sold in 1985, the massive number of Zaïreans who came to Paris at this time found themselves confronted with a housing problem.[13] They responded by setting up squatter housing. Squats were to be found in 1994

---

[13]From Gandoulou's account of MEC, one can calculate that about 248 people could live there at a time, but there was a rapid turnover.

all over the Paris region, but particularly in the communes of Saint-Denis, Grigny and Mantes-La-Jolie.

Squats are often set up in abandoned houses in areas destined for construction projects. The owners find it very hard to sell, so they abandon the house and wait for the compensation the state will pay. Squats are also often located in blocks of HLM (*Habitat à Loyer Moderat*), low-income housing now scheduled to be pulled down.[14]

Men establish squats. To do so, they watch out for buildings or apartments in which the lights never go on. When they find one, they wait a while and watch it. Then they knock on the door daily for about a week. They will also write a letter to a false name at the address and insert it in the letter box. If it is still there after a week, they break in, take possession and put a new lock on the door. Many locksmiths work in the milieu of the traders and will do the job for 200 FF.

The person who establishes the squat gets it for nothing but he is the one who takes the risk by breaking in. Once the squat is established, he can sell the right to the premises. He advertises it by word of mouth. The purchase price varies with the squat, generally from 1,500 to 2,000 FF. The lower price is for friends. The resale price varies with the length of occupation: if you buy one for 2,000 FF you can expect to sell it for 4,000 FF in one year, 6,000 FF in two years. So buyers can quickly recoup the original cost if they want to, and of course they pay no rent. The longer the squat has been in existence, the less risk is attached to living in it, hence a progressively higher price. Once the money is paid, all business relations between seller and buyer are finished; it is considered to be a sale, not a rental.

There are well-established procedures for connecting utilities. Telephones are easy to get for squats. All you need is a '*quittance de loyer*' (proof that you have paid rent), and such forms are as easy to come by as they are simple to forge. PTT (the telephone company) will then open a line. They subcontract to another company for this. It will be one which is paid according to the number of new lines it opens, so it is not eager to enquire too closely about those who want the new line. Electricity is connected in a similar manner.

Provision of False Papers. There are two kinds of suppliers of false papers. The first produce consular documents and visas – an activity which started a long time ago. In 1984, Gandoulou showed how, in order to facilitate the acquisition of a residence permit saying 'employed', the friends of a new arrival would take him to the MEC (or nearby) to contact 'specialists' who could get him the necessary papers to obtain such a permit. This service cost about 500 FF (Gandoulou, 1984: 94). At the end of

---

[14]This scheme originated as a way of helping families in difficulties. Applicants were given various sorts of means and needs tests for eligibility. The suburban ones are called *les Cités Dortoirs*. They were built in the 1960s but have not been a success and are associated with delinquency. When this housing is rebuilt, it will be redesigned in more holistic communities.

the 1980s, with the tightening up of the immigration laws, it was still possible to acquire residence permits and visas in this way, but it required the complicity of the authorities. It has now become very difficult.

The second providers of false papers consist of specialists who write credible accounts for those assembling dossiers to request political asylum, for which, in 1994, they asked the sum of 2,000 FF. Sometimes, it is necessary to wait for an opportune moment when a political crisis arises in the home country, so that these events can be used to make the application more credible. The necessary skill for writing these documents requires a certain amount of education.

The Arenas of Commercialization

The commercial skills of the traders are primarily practised in five places: the customer's home, the street, *nganda* bars, football stadiums and shops. We choose to call them arenas because they are the sites in which people strive to prove themselves and be successful. They are sites in which bargains are negotiated according to cultural ideas rather than in terms of economic logic based on price. We discuss these arenas in the chronological order in which they were used in the traders' activities in Paris. The traders first participated in second-economy activities in their own countries. The experience and expertise they gained were useful to them when they resumed such activities in France.

The Customer's Home

Here the vendor goes to the customer. The customer's house can be considered an arena because the trader's 'flair' for trading, his powers of persuasion and his ability to stabilize customers are tested. Traders need to work continually on their social relationships, which presuppose skill in negotiating with customers, in listening and in the conversion of orders into appropriate products.

This way of selling works best for those who already have an established clientele. Transactions are primarily in drugs, clothes and food, but caterers and hairdressers provide their services in the home as well.

There are practical reasons for this mobility. For the hairdresser it is obviously the lack of a salon. The supplier of goods, on the other hand, is fulfilling orders but can also solicit other business if he has goods that are interesting, since this method of selling may open up opportunities for finding new customers. The vender goes to the house and customarily will drink with the customer. They may also eat together, and the transaction includes time for conversation on political and other topics. Sometimes, these occasions enable the venders to meet friends of their customers and offer the potential for new business.

The personal relations between vender and customer are evident, first, in the crucial importance of the address-book where the telephone numbers of customers will predominate, and secondly in the regularity of the orders placed by customers. Repeated orders maintain the tie with the supplier, who makes sure to keep the customer up to date on good deals.

Selling to customers in their homes was the first method employed by Congolese traders in France. It has several advantages. Going to the customer's home is more secure and less risky than selling door-to-door, since the police do not suspect any clandestine activity, but think that people are just visiting. Commercially it is effective, since the traders of drugs, for example, may find at the same time a potential clientele for clothes and speciality food products. Initially, the transaction takes place between friends, but by the end the trader has earned a reputation as a supplier of a particular product among his or her compatriots. It is a way of marking status, of being recognized and assuming a role among a group of friends and acquaintances. Reputation and the power to attract customers are essential elements for success in second-economy trade. As we show in Chapter 5, fear of losing reputation acts as a sanction to back up transactions in this trade in the absence of formal legal contracts.

This way of operating tests the existence of a clientele and, over time, stabilizes it. The first transaction ends with promises from those present to see one another again, or for the vendor to telephone to take an order or pass the word that he or she has some interesting goods. At the end of the first meeting, the customer pays cash or negotiates credit. Seeing that he has entered into a relationship with the customer leads the trader to hope that he can minimize his risks. However, the fact remains that customers do not always pay. By selling on credit, the trader is gambling on his credibility, because this mode of operating is very risky. Details are given in Chapter 5. Being able to recover debts indicates that an individual has powerful influence among his network of friends. When someone is paid, it means that they are feared or that their friends want to make sure they will remain an ally.

In a way, the goods are only a pretext for consolidating the relationship. Even after giving an order or paying a deposit, one can retract, so no problems are evident. Only the vender assumes the risk: he can be reproached for not having sufficient know-how to seek out the desired goods. He also serves as an intermediary for making deals which serve the customer's needs.

The Street

Street traders are found particularly in the 18th *arrondissement* near the Château Rouge metro and the Dejean market. A large majority of the shops selling African speciality foods in Paris are in this area. Many are owned by Asians but Africans are beginning to compete by owning a few shops and by street trading. This trade was started by women, and it is still primarily a female enterprise. They sell African speciality foods, beauty products and clothes for women and children. The few male venders specialize in selling stolen goods and men's clothing imported from other European countries.

Food, clothes and beauty products were introduced successively into street vending. Four food products were the first: manioc, *fumbwa*, *saka-saka* and smoked fish. The earliest sellers sold only manioc. Their customers relied on the shops for their other needs. *Fumbwa* was the second product sold, its advantage being its light weight. The vender could have a large quantity on hand for this risky trade, in which it was better not to be too encumbered if the police approached. Once *saka-saka* and smoked fish were added, the ingredients for the two national dishes of Congo-Brazzaville, '*trois pièces*'[15] and *saka-saka*, were available.

Some streets of the Château Rouge neighbourhood are lined with as many as fifteen women venders. In 1994 they sold beauty products as well as food (especially the skin lighteners normally only sold on prescription), and sometimes clothing. Each seller has her own place, which is respected. Newcomers set up beside a friend selling the same product. These women have large bags full of their goods open beside them on the pavement to display what they have. They hold up items and show them to passers-by to encourage them to buy. These goods are not cheaper than in the stores, but purchasing them is quicker and more convenient. One means of restocking a bag of goods is to park a car full of reserves on another street. On one occasion, a woman had a suitcase in her car containing about 100 manioc puddings to restock a bag in which she had 37. She bought these puddings at 7 FF each and was selling them for 12 or 15 FF. Some women pay for space in a depot where a trader will store the foodstuffs she or he imports and will also sell to these venders.

Men station themselves towards the interior of the neighbourhood, since they are mostly sellers of stolen goods and need to be more concealed. As well as men's clothing, they sell metro passes, watches, perfumes, compact discs and audio and video cassettes. They will gather outside a café at the end of the day and exchange news. Selling stolen goods is a risky activity because of the constant presence of the police. To return home each day signifies success, because one has avoided arrest. Women are in the less risky circuits, for which the penalties incurred are only fines and not imprisonment. The majority of women street traders are now from Congo-Kinshasa, and the men venders are mostly from Congo-Brazzaville.

Nganda
Nganda are Congolese and Zaïrean clandestine bars. They serve food as well as drinks and are run, and generally owned, by women. In Paris, they

---

[15]This dish combines smoked fish and *fumbwa* with a peanut sauce.

operate outside the law in a number of ways: most are located in squats, and the owners have no licence to sell liquor or anything else and they are often immigrants who have no residence papers. Their function and importance as arenas for commerce and for ostentatious, competitive consumption and display are highly significant in the world of the traders. They will be discussed at length in Chapter 6, so we shall not dwell on them here.

Soccer Stadiums

In summer, the sport associations of the two countries organize soccer matches against the associations of other African countries. They rent a stadium for the summer in *départements* north of Paris, principally Saint-Denis and La Courneuve. Matches are played every Sunday. They are announced on flyers distributed in the 18th *arrondissement*. These are always the same, showing the same time each week of 14–22 hours and promising the attendance of some well-known popular singer. But most of the time the events do not begin until the end of the afternoon and the artist does not show up at all. But, even if the artist does not come, it does not matter because the stadium becomes, during the summer, an important place for meetings and for people to get together.

Besides meeting people and having a good time, the stadiums are an arena for business. Traders promote discs and video cassettes; photographers deliver negatives to their customers; suppliers announce the stocks of goods they have obtained through their contacts; *nganda* owners and street traders have stands for food and drinks and generally enliven the proceedings.

Women *nganda* owners and traders, varying in number from twenty to fifty, pay the association for the right to have a stand. Each of them, as they arrive on a particular Sunday, takes a place and sets up chairs, parasols, a barbecue, and food previously prepared at home. They all sell the same items: beer, fruit drinks, doughnuts, meat on skewers, manioc, salt fish, etc. Each trader pays a fee, and each tries to attract customers by all possible means. How they present themselves, their conversation and seductive ways are the most important means of gaining customers. In this competition, a little help from any visiting celebrity who stops by is always welcome.

Shops

Shops are all located in the Château Rouge area. Here we note the paradox that most of the shops selling African speciality foods are run by Asians. There are only about a dozen Congolese owners, and the first of them did not open until 1992. This kind of business seems, at first, to be conforming to the law, but the shopkeepers are also participating in the second economy in various ways, as we shall show in the next two chapters. These owners are immigrants with protected status (those who originally came for education or training, or who were former civil servants). They not only sell food in their shops, but also clothes, beauty products and compact discs, and some have beauty salons, hair salons or photographic shops.

Congolese shopkeepers generally have a clientele of their compatriots. The name of the shop often reflects this by trying to appeal to a specific nationality. Two are called '*Marché Total*' and '*Les Quatres Marchés*', which recall Brazzaville, while two others, '*La Kinoise*' and '*La Ndjiloise*', refer to Kinshasa. These names attempt to invoke the experience of being in one of the two Congo capitals. They are set up to reproduce the image of the market-place; the goods are in cases in bulk and can be handled by the customer. The shopkeepers sell practically everything that can be bought in the markets back home. The only other thing needed would be to be able to bargain over the price that is posted up. Some traders say that, were it not for health regulations, they would put their merchandise on the floor the better to reproduce the atmosphere of the market at home. The owners, to stay competitive, seek to have products which are unavailable in the Asian shops, hoping that their customers, while buying these items from them, will notice other products they need and buy from them rather than from the Asians.

The skills involved in running these shops have been learned through participation in the second economy. They are particularly relevant in the accumulation of capital, in keeping down costs and for stabilizing a clientele.

The Organization of Sales Circuits

We divide the principal sales circuits into two kinds, one simple, the other complex. These circuits mobilize three separate roles: the person who introduces goods or services into the clandestine milieu, the middleman, and the customer. We end the sequence with the customer, even though sometimes his or her buying may initiate contacts with other circuits. We shall see here how the spirit of *l'aventure* and *la débrouillardise* is manifested in the trading of goods.

The Structure of Simple Circuits
Simple circuits involve only two or three roles. Those with only two mainly comprise services and directly link a vender and a customer. The latter is often ignored in analyses of African commercial circuits. Here it is noteworthy that the customer and the vender belong to the same milieu and their roles may be interchangeable in other situations. Customer loyalty must be built up and constantly maintained. Two roles only are involved in the activities of mobile hairdressers, photographers and taxi drivers. These are based essentially on the competence of the clandestine provider, who operates according to the wishes of the customer. The circuits are autonomous and have no boss; each person fends for themselves, according to initiative and the opportunity of the moment.

The sale of squats, financial transfers, street trading and the sale of goods that are stolen or otherwise obtained outside the law combine three roles. For the sale of squats, we have described above the roles of the person who establishes the squat and of the customer. The locksmith who is called in has no permanent relationship with the vender, since there are many locksmiths from whom to choose. In financial transfers, the customer is the one who wants to transfer the money. He or she works through a hierarchy of roles of the two partners and their agent. The former have invested their capital in the business and are responsible to the customer. This circuit is constructed to resolve the problem of trust by offering guarantees to the customer, who in this undertaking thus maintains his autonomy.

Street trading links an airline flight attendant or a wholesaler or retailer, the vender and the customer. The first venders were Senegalese selling maize; then the Congolese joined them. At first, the venders ordered their manioc directly from Congo-Brazzaville, asking a family member to ship it to them and sending money to pay for it through someone with whom they had a friendly relationship. No commission was charged, it was a service that was part of the relationship. But it was hazardous because one could never quite be sure that the money had arrived and supplies frequently broke down. Women from Congo-Kinshasa and Cameroon soon joined in, and then the market was discovered by airline personnel from Central Africa. They eliminated the flaw in the old supply system, removing its risks and uncertainty by importing manioc in their baggage allowance. Having previously established relations with the venders and exchanged addresses, as soon as they arrive at their hotel they telephone to say how much manioc they have brought. Supplies have become much more dependable and the venders no longer have to pay customs and transportation costs. Flight attendants are now the primary source of supply for street venders, though they also buy from wholesalers and from retailers.

For the sale of goods that are stolen or imported without licence or without paying the full customs duties, three roles are involved; the first two are known as the *sachiste* and the *douanier*,[16] the third is the customer. The *sachiste* is so named because he supposedly carries goods in little bags ('*sachets*'). The *sachiste* often obtains his goods through theft, a fact which obliges him to hide them. In fact, the 'little bags' can be duffle bags, backpacks or any other receptacle used to conceal the goods. The *sachistes* are not always thieves; some purchase goods in other European countries to benefit from price differences, while others receive goods from the home country.

The procedure for their transaction is as follows. The *sachiste* hands over the goods to be sold by the *douanier* at a fixed price; the *douanier* accepts and then sells for a higher price so as to make a profit.

---

[16]These are French words but are not used in the French sense.

The *sachiste* does not want to engage in selling for three main reasons. First, as a thief or *bougeur*, as he is called, he considers it beneath him to do so. His status is with the *grands* ('patrons') and he does not want to get mixed up with the *petits* ('clients')[17] who engage in this sales activity. He therefore hands his goods over to his own *petit*. These transactions take place every evening at Château Rouge where the young meet in cafés. With the opposition of *grands/petits*, a hierarchy appears. This is an integral part of the functioning of this circuit, in the sense that it gives a minimal stability to these roles by giving one authority over the other. This hierarchy is not general, however; it only holds within this particular activity.

Secondly, the *sachiste* may lack confidence in his competence as a seller, having neither a clientele nor a reputation in the milieu. In addition, he may not have mastered the art of persuasive sales talk, or 'commercial politics' as it is called by the traders. Thirdly, the *sachiste* prefers to organize this structure for cheap products that move quickly, with the aim of concentrating himself on the trade of other, more valuable, goods. The *sachiste* may also resort to this method of selling when he is overstocked, as a large quantity of goods is difficult to explain in the case of a police check.

The *douanier*, the *sachiste*'s associate, is the seller. He will have many contacts and be well known in the milieu. He is considered a *douanier*, because he exacts the 'customs costs' (or 'tax') from the *sachiste*. The price fixed by the *sachiste* takes this 'customs cost' into account. An example will clarify this series of transactions:

A *sachiste* wants 500 FF for an item
The *douanier* sells it for 700 FF
The *douanier* returns 500 FF to the *sachiste*
The *sachiste* gives 100 FF to the *douanier* (the 'tax').

The voluntary payment by the *sachiste* towards the profit of the *douanier* cannot occur until the sale has taken place, which demonstrates that the latter has an established customer circuit. The *douanier* is free to sell the item at a much higher price than that fixed by the *sachiste* on condition that he return to him the amount agreed on, and he will always try to get this higher price. His profit corresponds to the additional value added because of the risks he takes, which come from his direct contact with the customer. Also, since he sells the goods publicly, there is the further risk that they may be seized by the police as he has no proof of

---

[17]These translations do not really fit. There are no English equivalents. A feature of the context of Kongo matrilineal traditional society was the ambivalent relationship between mother's brother and sister's son. In the past, it was carried over in the *grand/petit* authoritarian relationship in trade, where juniors were supposed to do the bidding of their seniors. The maternal uncle was the protector against witchcraft, but he might also practise it. The sanction for his authority was the threat to cease acting as protector and to no longer abstain from witchcraft. One performed services to avoid his anger or disapproval.

purchase. When this happens, it is difficult for the *sachiste* to get his money. If the *douanier* is afraid, he will pay the *sachiste* out of his own pocket, but, if not, he will say to him: 'Listen, if you have the receipts, you can go to the police and get back your merchandise; it's not my problem'.

Depending on his skill, a good *douanier* sometimes earns more than the *sachiste*, despite the fact that the latter, if he has stolen the goods, risks arrest. This is especially the case with cheap goods. As Charles stated:

> *What I buy in Italy for 10 francs, I ask the* douanier *to sell for me for 20 francs and I know that he's going to sell it for at least 30 or 40 francs, so it works out fine.*

The 'customs cost' must also be added in to this calculation.

The Structure of Complex Circuits

We label as complex those circuits which combine more than three roles, as well as those combining different circuits. In the former, we find the export of used cars and spare parts, the importing of African foods by owners of wholesale and retail businesses, and drug trafficking. All are extensive because they involve moving goods from one continent to another. Export of used cars and spares combines an owner, an associate, a driver and a negotiator of the resale in specialized stores. Food importing links the supplier, an associate overseas, a team of workers and the customer. Details are given in case histories in the next chapter.

Drug trafficking can be a means for young people to get to Paris from Kinshasa or Brazzaville, when they are recruited to act as one-time couriers. This trade combines five or six roles: the dealer, an associate, the courier, the wholesaler, the retailer and the customer. This set-up is the result of the increasing complexity of trafficking. At first, each actor took risks individually to smuggle the drugs and sell them in Paris. After a few years, the smuggler had to be in contact with an associate whose job it was to find wholesalers. For the protection of the smuggler, and so as to prevent him from being robbed, the associate did not put him in contact with the wholesaler. The associate has thus taken on some of the risks involved in this traffic.

Marijuana is transported in suitcases or travelling bags. When the smuggler is stopped, he makes out that he is carrying exotic foods. To reduce this smuggling, the French authorities demand from food traders a certificate issued by the Hygiene and Epidemic Disease authorities. Customs officials and the French police do not verify this systematically at Roissy airport, but it is asked for in any cases taken to court.

A drug courier requires some training in self-presentation to acquire the necessary confidence to carry off getting past the authorities. To gain such assurance, each courier uses his own method to avoid being arrested; some will go and see a specialist in magical charms before leaving. Those who decide to smuggle drugs make the calculation: 'I am young, I must try for a coup. If I am caught, I shall be put away for five to seven years. When I come out of prison, I shall still be young and can start my life all over again'.

Over time the circuit dealers establish themselves, and the majority of them, once they have amassed plenty of money, form complex circuits. The dealers return to Brazzaville or Kinshasa from Europe, find two or three young folk, and offer them a ticket and a visa in exchange for the transport of a suitcase. In some cases, the dealer has an associate in the country who makes this arrangement, takes care of all the details and accompanies the courier to the airport with the suitcase. The dealer without an associate sets up the whole arrangement himself, and gets to Europe a few days before the courier. In either case, the dealer meets the courier at the airport to pick up the suitcase. When the operation is successful, the dealer gives the courier a sum of up to 500 FF, then leaves him to his own devices. These couriers do not know France and, despite the risks they have taken, cannot count on the dealer for lodging. For them the main thing is to have arrived: they know they will have to figure out how to get by on their own.

Shops, *nganda* and the stadiums are all public places that bring different circuits into contact and provide opportunities for clandestine trade. Many of those present will be potentially both buyers and sellers and engage in constructing their own circuits by making contact with potential customers.

Having described the traders, their trade, the goods and services they provide for a particular market and how they operate in Paris, we now turn to the ways in which these traders contest various kinds of boundaries in order to make their enterprises profitable.

4

Contesting Boundaries

The Defiant Search for Success

> Boundaries themselves have a salience that surpasses the merely practical. They are both political problem and political solution. They are entailed by the exercise of power, but undermine power and make possible the escape from it. (Thornton, 1996: 150)

This chapter is about the ways in which the traders of this study contest different kinds of boundaries in their trading activities, as they struggle to resist the oppression of the state and their exclusion from the opportunity to improve their lives. These boundaries constitute specific points where power can be challenged and evaded and thus undermined, and they therefore provide potential means for escaping or resisting it. The traders transgress the boundaries of state laws, refuse to abide by the regulations governing the crossing of national frontiers, and push the norms of participation in institutions beyond their limits. They also compete with each other in their search for profits and, in so doing, transgress the boundaries of co-operative behaviour.

James Scott puts forward the idea that the discourse of speeches, gestures and a whole range of practices as well as speech, takes place 'offstage', beyond the observation of the powers that be. He calls this discourse a 'hidden transcript', and finds the frontier between public official transcripts and hidden transcripts to be a zone of constant struggle, not a solid wall, between those who dominate and those who are subordinate (Scott, 1990: 4, 14, 27).[1]

The capacity of the dominant to define this frontier – though never totally – is a significant measure of their power. Scott finds the continuing struggle over such boundaries to be perhaps the most vital arena for everyday forms of class struggle (Ibid.: 14). The struggles in question here

---

[1] Scott's public and hidden transcripts include activities as well as acts of speech.

are between the dominant classes in the two Central African countries, whose power is based on their official position and its use by individual members to further their own interests, and the subordinated classes who contest the limits set upon their lives by these oppressive actions.

The Central African traders in this study are individuals who have found themselves excluded from opportunity in various ways; they are excluded by the dominant class from the necessary contacts for obtaining education and the contacts needed for positions in the state or other good jobs, or to fulfil their ambitions in the jobs they do have. As we have shown, some who originally went to France or Belgium as students or to undertake training programmes found themselves thereafter unable to get the type of job for which they were qualified and ended up underemployed in unskilled low-paid work with no prospects. Others, in the lower echelons of government employment at home, found their ambitions frustrated because they had no hope of advancement or were passed over for promotion because they lacked the right patronage or contacts, or were not members of the ethnic group in power. In this situation of exclusion and marginalization, these people felt their best strategy was to take up second-economy trade.

In what sense does this form of trade constitute resistance, what exactly are the traders resisting, and are they aware that they are so doing? The voices of the traders themselves bring us the answers to these questions. Their terms for their activities and their comments on what they are doing show that they perceive their actions as constituting resistance to oppressive state authority at local and global levels, and to its constraints on their aspirations and ambitions. One African scholar from Congo-Kinshasa explicitly describes smuggling as 'an act of rebellion against the political and economic systems and the dominant groups' (Vwakyanakazi, 1982: 339–40).

The term used for second-economy traders in Manianga, in western Congo-Kinshasa, is *lutteurs* (Makwala, 1991: 98). Informants in 1994 said that originally this word referred to people who struggled with carrying heavy loads, but the meaning has now changed to mean people who struggle against 'the system', those who will not accept exclusion from opportunity, who fend for themselves (*se débrouiller*) with the will to succeed despite the constraints and oppression of the authorities.

In Congo-Brazzaville, the pillage following the coup in 1997 was directed particularly against the unfair distribution of oil revenues. The perception was that profits from the nation's oil wealth were going only to the directors of the oil companies, rather than being shared by everyone. There were two slogans among the pillagers: one was 'N'Kossa, chacun aura sa part', meaning that all should share in *N'Kossa* – the name of the biggest off-shore oil well, which was discovered at this time, and about which public statements had implied that it would improve the lives of all Congolese; the other was 'On tue le cochon', which referred to the traditional practice 'of killing the pig', a ceremony in which a pig was killed as a gift and a share was given to everyone. The pillage was thus explicitly seen as a forced means of redistributing wealth that should have belonged to everyone.

People who cheat the state or break its laws feel that, since their leaders steal the state's goods, they can do the same. They say: 'If the authorities want us to stop, they must first stop stealing the state's goods themselves.'[2] One trader in Paris in 1994 said that his reasons for leaving Congo-Brazzaville for Paris, and for living there without residence papers and engaging in trade outside the law, were that 'in Congo there was no electricity, no running water, no roads and no work because a handful of people "eat" the money given for improvement projects and road repairs'. Another trader from Brazzaville listed activities outside the law, such as owning *nganda*, living in squatter housing, importing cloth and jewellery from Brussels, street vending and running unlicensed airport taxi businesses, commenting that all of these originated with Central African immigrants. But, she said, expressing her defiance and justifying her participation in these activities: 'We are here to make money, one must not be afraid. It is necessary to use a hammer to break stones'. This phrase refers to the idea that other people took from the state resources that they felt belonged by right to them, specifically referring to the mines, where one found the *'casseurs des pierres'* (breakers of stones).[3] In Europe, traders and others explicitly state that operating outside the law, even in theft, drug dealing and other criminal activities, is justifiable because: 'In the past Europeans looted Africa, now it is the turn of Africans to help themselves to the riches of Europe'.

Thus traders do perceive their activities as resistance, but they do so in a broad sense. They do not undertake particular strategies to achieve it: the dimension of resistance is conscious and present but it is not organized or co-ordinated. Through case histories, we shall now show, in turn, how the traders contest legal, territorial, institutional and co-operative behaviour boundaries as they search for opportunity and profit.

We shall first consider the ways in which they transgress the boundaries of the law. The definition of what is legal or illegal shifts over time since it is subject to political pressure.[4] The power to define legality is a mechanism

---

[2]People say: *'Les hommes politiques volent les biens de l'état. Nous emprenons ce terrain. Nous faisons la même chose qu'eux. S'ils veulent que nous arrêtons, il faudrait qu'ils s'arrêtent de voler les biens de l'état.'*

[3]Awareness of second-economy trade as resistance to an oppressive state is also explicit in Congo-Kinshasa. In Kivu, the easternmost province, Nande second-economy traders say 'There's a great outcry against fraud but at least we bring back manufactured goods and medicines that are needed and sell them, instead of putting foreign currency into Swiss bank accounts and living in Europe, as the rich and powerful in Kinshasa do.' An ex-minister of the provincial government said bitterly that he had tried in vain to get import quotas but 'the only way to get goods or fuel was in exchange for coffee or gold in Uganda or Rwanda' (MacGaffey, interviews, 1980).

[4]Howard Becker, in his study of the sociology of deviance, urges us to remember that the rules created and maintained by labelling behaviour as deviant are not universally agreed upon and conflict and disagreement over them are part of the political process of society. 'The question of what rules are to be enforced, what behavior regarded as deviant, and which people labeled as outsiders must also be regarded as political' (Becker, 1963: 7).

for reinforcing the interests of the dominant class,[5] but this means that the boundaries of the law are not permanent and immutable and that they are susceptible to challenge and contest. Case studies show how the traders contest the control of the dominant class by transgressing the legal boundaries of the regulated economy as they engage in unlicensed trade and other enterprises outside the law, combine licensed and unlicensed enterprise, evade taxes and, in some cases, acquire venture capital in activities that could land them in jail.

Next we look at territorial boundaries. National frontiers, demarcating geographical space, are politically drawn lines that are laid down, fought over and change over time. We are familiar with how they are disputed at the level of national politics, but less aware of how they are contested by individuals. In order to engage in more lucrative forms of trade and, in some cases, even to make their trade profitable at all, traders evade visa requirements and refuse to abide by other regulations and the payment of excise taxes governing the crossing of national frontiers.

We continue with less obvious forms of contesting boundaries. Traders creatively stretch the limits of normal participation in institutions in order to expand their trading enterprises and take them in innovative new directions. And some of them abandon normal scruples and seize chances that come to them through breaking the norms and bounds of co-operative behaviour in their dealings with each other. Such betrayals occur because sanctions for breaking these norms are weak, as we shall show in the next chapter. There is a contrast in this respect with the strong sanctions based on a religious community, which exist for the Islamic traders from West Africa, described in Chapter 1.

Contesting the Boundaries of the Law

Unlicensed Itinerant Trade

Traders in Paris go to different European countries, buy goods and either return to Paris to sell them to the African community there, or take them to sell in Congo-Brazzaville or Congo-Kinshasa. In Italy, they buy clothes, purses, jewellery and shoes (especially women's sandals); in Germany, they buy clothes and leather goods; and in Holland, sports clothes. In some of these countries and in others, they also buy drugs. As we showed in the last chapter, customers are found in Paris by word of mouth, by telephone, in the streets and cafés of the Château Rouge neighbourhood, or at the football stadiums in summer. One man from Congo-Brazzaville has set up

---

[5]For examples of this in the administratively weak state of Zaïre, see MacGaffey, 1987: 200–3. In Sierra Leone's informal diamond markets, institutional boundaries of legality inherited from the colonial period became one more manipulable resource for the politically powerful (Reno, 1995: 126).

a shop out in the Paris suburbs where he sells goods bought in Château Rouge, including the stolen goods that may be sold there.

In their life histories, traders give detailed accounts of such trade. For some of them, this is a continuation of their unlicensed trading activities back in Africa. Charles, from Brazzaville (Chapter 2, p.46), recounts how he started out in the travelling trade in the villages along the railway line in Congo, using it as one of the ways to accumulate money to get to Europe.

I went to the villages to sell in the markets to people who could not come to shop in Brazzaville. We were unlicensed traders, though the big traders on this circuit had licences. We had to hide from the market police all the time; when they appeared, we disappeared. I bought goods in Brazzaville in the boutiques of the Senegalese in Poto-Poto market: T-shirts, shorts and trousers, new, not second-hand. A dozen T-shirts cost 3,000 CFAF[6] and I sold them for 6,000 CFAF. I sold only clothes; the other traders sold other goods, for example, make-up, perfume, shoes. These markets started towards the end of the month, after the 23rd and finished on the 30th. We then returned on the 1st of the month to Brazzaville. Every day we moved from one village to another where there was a market, leaving on the train in the evening after we finished selling, in order to sleep where we were going to work next day. In all the villages, there were empty houses one could rent. We paid 100 CFAF a night, put our mats on the floor to sleep, were given water by the landlord to wash in the morning and food to eat after the market was finished. We rented them as a group, ten of us for example might be able to sleep in one and we'd pay 100 CFAF each. Sometimes we'd rent rooms from friends.

I knew about this kind of commerce through a friend, who is still a big trader. He knew that I wanted to go to France but that I did not have enough money. He told me: 'Listen, if you want to make money quickly, trade along the railway. Every month you can have at least 50,000 CFAF profit for 10 days work'. There were about 15 itinerant traders who were young. We did not know each other beforehand. There were many more big traders.

The high mark-up on Charles's goods shows how these urban traders were able to exploit the rural villagers: subordinated themselves, they in turn exploited those below them in the hierarchy. Some of the villagers, however, managed to turn these traders' trips to their advantage by renting them accommodation.

The histories of two women traders, who have been active in different forms of unlicensed trade, show the persistence, the ingenuity, the

---

[6]In 1994, 500 CFA francs = US$1.00.

ambition and determination to succeed, and the bold moves outside the law to contest constraining bureaucratic regulations and requirements that characterize many of these traders. Both women are from Congo-Brazzaville, and both are middle-class.

Josephine is a young woman in her twenties who supports herself and her child by trading without a licence. She started in commerce when she was training to be a flight attendant in Paris in 1983. She needed money because she was a *sapeur* and wanted to buy expensive clothes. Her mother visited, bringing a lot of salt fish and manioc so that she would have plenty to eat, but, instead, Josephine sold it to her friends. Thereafter, her mother, who worked for an airline and therefore could send freight free as a perk from her job, sent her more. Soon Josephine was selling these foods to the Congolese embassy as well as to her friends, and had found more contacts, mostly friends of her mother's who were flight attendants and could bring goods in for her in their free baggage allowance, so she also did not have to pay freight charges. She changed to selling beauty products, particularly the skin lightener, Dehar, travelling to Kinshasa to buy it, and using the free tickets given to her mother for her immediate family by the airline. She decided that rather than selling to individuals, she wanted to become a supplier to the Chinese retailers (*les Chinois*) in Château Rouge.[7] Her account of how she broke into this market, hitherto closed to Africans, shows the tremendous boldness and tenacity these traders have to summon up to be successful as they refuse to abide by regulations and strive to beat the competition:

> At first, the Chinese refused to buy goods from me. They said I needed to have papers[8] and that they had their own suppliers, but I bluffed them. I saw the bookkeeper in one of their shops and went in. After greeting her, I told her that I wanted to see the manager. She asked why, and I replied that I had something to propose to him. I put on a very serious air and pretended to be in a hurry. She told me to wait. When I saw the manager, I lied to him. I gave my mother's name and said that I was Madame Keita and that I had come from Africa. Then I said there was a friend of his who wanted to buy some African products from me, and that I had some Dehar to offer him. He thought a bit and asked what kind it was. I told him MC3. He said that that was good and took me into a corner to ask the price. I told him, 15 FF a unit. He said that was too much, that he didn't want it and goodbye. I told him that was not how one does business: we are just in the middle of discussing the matter, so why leave? He asked me what was my

---

[7]All Asians are put into the category 'Chinese'. They own most of the stores in the Château Rouge neighbourhood. At the time Josephine started in trade, there were no African-owned shops there.

[8]She has no wholesale or import licences.

final price. I told him 12.50 FF. I said that at the moment there was a shortage of Dehar on the market and soon it would not be available. I had gone a long way to get it. 'If you don't get it from me, you won't have any' (indeed there was none available at that precise moment). He asked me how much I had and I told him 100 dozen. He said to bring it all. It was then Monday. He asked me to deliver it immediately. I said that that was not possible, and that I would bring it tomorrow. He said, no, he must have it at once. I told him I had no car; he said he'd pay for a taxi. I said no, because I lived in the provinces and that I would bring it tomorrow. He said, OK, tomorrow morning. I said no, in the evening. After I left the Chinese, I called my mother (in Brazzaville!) and asked her to send 100 dozen Dehar immediately, because it had to arrive by tomorrow. Well, I got it and delivered it to the Chinese. He sold it to the others who had none. After that he began to trust me. Just a week later he called me: 'Congolaise, OK, I want more Dehar'. From that moment, I started to ask if he wanted other things. Anything that he wanted, I said yes, because I knew that I could always get it. This Chinese gave my phone number to another Chinese and so on. So whenever they have needed anything and there is a break in their stocks, they have called me. There have always been flights and I have always been able to get the goods.

In this trade, she made 20,000–25,000 FF a month. She depends for her success on the co-operation of her mother, and on the use they make of the perk from her mother's job, to reduce the costs of air-freighting the product she sells. She can thus undercut the competition.

Marie is an older woman who in 1994 owned a shop selling African foodstuffs in Château Rouge, and who had previously accumulated considerable wealth in unlicensed transborder trade. The daughter of a tailor, she was raised in Brazzaville, completed Catholic secondary school, and then trained as a nurse in the prestigious A. Cissé Hospital, later renamed Loukabou by the politicians, in Pointe Noire. She married and had four children and was later divorced. Nurses were highly ranked professionals, and in her job she earned a salary of 25,000 CFAF. She was able to buy a *parcelle* on which she built a house. But she was ambitious, energetic and enterprising, and she wanted to earn more money than she could make from her salary. Since she was on and off duty for 48 hours at a time, she decided to use her time off to go to Kinshasa and trade. The details of her trading activities reveal how much she relies on personal connections for advice and assistance in getting started, for getting accommodation in foreign countries, and for finding customers when she sells her goods.

In 1973 on my first trip, I went to the market in Kinshasa with a co-worker, who was a cleaner at the hospital, and she showed me where to make purchases. I had between 1,000 and 2,000 CFAF and I bought little things like soap and baby clothes in small quantities and sold them to friends and acquaintances in Brazzaville, giving them credit if they needed it. They would pay me back a month later. I finally made a profit of about 2,000–3,000 CFAF, which helped to supplement my salary. Sometimes I would go with only 8,000 CFAF, sometimes with 12,000 CFAF. At this time I had no thought of going in for large-scale trade. I traded between Brazzaville and Kinshasa for three years.

Then a friend who had been to France on a training programme suggested I go and spend my vacation there with her: 'I've seen what it is like in France, and it would be good for you, you are so enterprising. Why don't you give it a try?' So I did as she suggested and took leave of absence from my job. At this time, no visa was necessary to enter France, so in 1976 I went there for a month and stayed with a friend whom I had known at work. She was single, with two children, and was in Paris on a training programme. She also worked during holidays and in the evenings as a café cleaner. Because I was a state employee, I had no difficulty in Brazzaville in taking out a loan at the bank for 300,000 CFAF (a considerable sum at that time), and I used this money to buy blouses, scarves, slips and shirts at Tati in Paris.[9] When I returned to Brazzaville, I sold them to friends and acquaintances in my neighbourhood. Goods from abroad were rare and people were eager to buy them. Everyone came to my house and wanted to know what it was like in Europe and I would sell them little things. I sold all of it for 400,000 CFAF: things I had bought for 10 CFAF I sold for 100 CFAF. Since the quantity was not large, I did not pay customs duties, the things were just mixed up with my own clothes. I was among the first women to go to France from Congo, bring back goods like this, and tell people about it. At that time, it was only men who went there, for training programmes, as students or as politicians.

The helpful advice and instruction of other women, friends, family or, as in Marie's case, co-workers, often appeared as a factor in the entry into trade of the women in our study. Marie, along with flight attendants on airlines, was a pioneer in this trade between Congo and Europe. Her account continues to show how she rapidly began to make money, relying on personal contacts for her customers.

I went back to France three months after I had used up my stock. I bought blouses again and filled orders on several other items. Back in Brazzaville, I quickly sold everything, earning 600,000 CFAF: this time I already had customers, who had told me what they wanted, some

---

[9]Tati is a huge department store with three branches in Paris, six in the provinces. It sells goods of all kinds in quantity at discount prices, made profitable by the high turnover.

had even ordered five to ten different items. They did not pay me in advance, it was all done on trust, and when I came back they all took their orders. I had no commercial licence. I made at least four trips and earned 1,000,000 CFAF. My great opportunity came when ten ministers' wives gave me orders for blouses. I bought 500,000 CFAF worth. Each cost 3,000 CFAF and I sold them for 15,000 CFAF. They paid cash. I was the only person selling this quality of blouse and they each bought several as they came in a variety of colours and styles. I paid customs duties on them because I had a huge trunk with 300 articles and couldn't get through without paying. I made 4,500,000 CFAF. There was no competition in this trade and I was very successful.

I decided to buy a new Renault car for 300,000 CFAF to export to Brazzaville and set up a taxi service. In 1976, I made a down payment of 50,000 CFAF to a French car company (CSCO) in Congo, which made all the shipping arrangements.[10] Three months later, I bought a second car.

This was the time of the first oil boom when people had money to spend. Luxury stores were selling goods at very high prices and traders such as Marie could undersell them. In setting up her taxi business, Marie made an investment that is common for successful traders.

Street Trading in Paris

Migrants without residence papers frequently use this form of unlicensed trade to make a living, relying on family back home to send them goods or buying from other traders who are licensed importers on a larger scale.

In the early years there was not much competition between venders because their customers were acquaintances or friends (Congolese, Zaïreans and Angolans), who came to buy smoked fish or green vegetables from the Asian shops that sold these foods. The venders selling manioc stationed themselves just outside the metro, so that, although the Asians also sold manioc, these customers had already bought it by the time they reached the Asian shops. The quality is said to have been better because, since this is Central Africa's staple food, African women are better at keeping it fresh. The market expanded because there was nothing to pay to set up and no formalities; all one had to do was to get the manioc and come to sell it. Venders have proliferated in the last four years and are seen as serious competition by Africans owning food shops.

Street vending is said to be quite a lucrative business, primarily because there are no overheads, but it is a hard way to make a living: informants spoke of the misery of standing outside for long hours in all weathers.

---

[10]The company later went bankrupt, put out of business by second-hand Japanese cars imported from Europe.

Nevertheless, women persist in it: Rachel did it for five years, saving her money to buy her own shop. The small scale of this enterprise means that profits cannot be very large, yet the vender mentioned in Chapter 2 found this means of earning money more worthwhile than being underemployed as a nurse's aide.

The police are very much in evidence in the Château Rouge area, arriving suddenly and demanding to see people's papers as they search for undocumented migrants. As already noted, when they come in sight, a warning is called down the street, or signalled by a whistle. The venders will quickly close the large bags containing their wares and blend instantly into the crowds of shoppers. If the police catch them, they confiscate their goods, a loss that we were told could amount to 300 FF. This figure gives at least some idea of the amount of capital that may be invested daily. One woman remarked bitterly:

> When they catch you, they take all your goods and your money, then let you go. It is like at home, they take your money. It is only when you have no money that they begin to enquire into the question of [residence] papers and take you to the police station.

Here again is a comment from an informant that vividly illustrates both the mechanisms and the consciousness of oppression. This arbitrary enforcement makes the boundary of the law in reality flexible and thus open to contest. Such incidents highlight the complexity of relations between the traders and the police, who are well aware of most of these extra-legal activities.

Setting Up Housing Outside the Law

Africans arriving in the city have difficulty finding a place to live. They do not have steady work, and have no wage slips to assure the landlord of a regular income. They also find themselves barred by racial prejudice from finding apartments to rent. One of the solutions to this problem is the well-organized line of business described in the last chapter, of setting up and selling squatter housing in abandoned buildings. Some 20 people were reported to carry on this form of enterprise in Paris in 1994. Some traders combine this form of earning money with unlicensed trade.

Living conditions in squats are dingy. In one HLM block we visited with letter-boxes scrawled with Muslim African and Arab names, one elevator was broken, and stairwells and corridors were dirty and covered in litter. In addition, finding schooling for children living in squats is a problem. Squatters resort to various subterfuges to obtain legal addresses from which their children can attend school. One *nganda* owner has a squat in a house where one legal tenant still remains, so the house is still a legal address and her daughters can go to the local school. In another case, the legal address used was so far away the child had to take a 45-minute metro ride to school.

Relations with the authorities with regard to squatting demonstrate how flexible the boundaries of the law are and how they can be contested. The following two cases show that the authorities may tolerate squatters but that this tolerance can change rapidly following a shift in the political climate, in this case the anti-immigration policy of Minister Pasqua. As James Scott has noted, 'many forms of authority can tolerate a remarkably high level of practical nonconformity so long as it does not actually tear the public fabric of hegemony' (Scott, 1990: 204). He considers the ability to choose to overlook infringements of the law or other acts of insubordination to be a key exercise of power (Ibid.: 89).

> *Nanette had a problem with the woman from whom she bought her squat. The man who sold the right of occupation to this woman was trying to get it back on the pretext that she had not paid him. The two of them tried to get Nanette to leave, but she refused. She had nowhere to go and anyway had the right to stay since she had, in fact, paid 6,400 FF for the squat (it had been in existence for over ten years). She demanded at least 3,000 FF but they refused and began to assault her. Her seven-year-old son went for the police. When the police arrived, they said it was not their affair because it was a squat, and were going to leave, but because it was a man beating a woman, and continuing to do so even while they were there, they decided after all to intervene and they arrested him. They then told Nanette she could stay in the squat!*

This case reinforces our earlier conclusion that those who live clandestinely do not live a hidden life: they simply do not exist as far as the authorities are concerned, because they have no legal status. This situation, however, is ambiguous and may change if it is expedient for those in power. This is what happened in our next case, a continuation of Charles's history.

We have recounted in Chapter 2 and above how Charles managed to get to France. When he arrived in Paris, he stayed with friends and applied for political asylum. He was given a refugee card and a monthly living allowance. With this status of temporary legality, he was able to look for a job and after persisting for three months found one, working as a painter of seats in the metro. Charles's friends, with whom he was staying at the time, were all living clandestinely and working in activities outside the law, selling drugs, stealing and forging checks. They resented his working on the right side of the law, and ended up forcing him to leave at the end of a month. Excluded from the official system, they were, in their turn, excluding those who worked within it. Charles slept at the Gare du Nord for two days, then heard of a squat and lived there for 14 months.

When his papers ran out and his request for asylum was not granted, he lost his job. It was then that he took up *bizness* and began setting up and selling squats. His life history shows how traders can use this activity to capitalize their international trade.

> *I would break into a house, then let someone have it for 1,500 FF. I would draw up a lease for them. After a few days the HLM people would come. If you had papers they rehoused you, if not, you could stay for a year, and a few months after that they would eject you. In this business, I was able to make two or three sales a month. Since I like to live well, buy good clothes and good food, this did not enable me to save anything, so I took up trade as well. When I sold a house, I would buy clothes and electrical appliances. Since I do not have papers, I preferred to buy clothes because I could keep them in a suitcase to use if I was expelled from France. I would go to Congo, sell them, and return quickly to France.[11] Selling squats lasted until the HLM agents decided they no longer wanted squatters. After that, they came and took possession whenever someone took over a house and ejected them.*

This story shows the effort of this young migrant to be part of the official system and his rejection: he is not accepted for residence and can only remain in the country by living without papers, so he has to find clandestine work.

An important form of trade that ranges from activities within the law to ones that incur criminal penalties is trading in second-hand cars.

The Second-Hand Car Trade

Wealth accumulated in extra-legal trade is often invested in second-hand cars, which are exported to the home country to be used as taxis or resold. Japanese cars are preferred. Until January 1994, exporting second-hand cars to Africa was a flourishing and very profitable trade.[12]

The large majority of second-hand cars exported are reportedly stolen, particularly those in the trade with Eastern Europe. There are various strategies for such theft. One is to steal a car with its documents. Police reports on stolen cars will not be available if the car is exported from another country.[13] Another strategy requires the complicity of car wreckers: a stolen car can be taken to the wrecking dump and can then emerge as if it is a repaired old car, which can be exported but which is out of circulation, no longer on the records and therefore without papers. Stolen cars can also be given the papers and plates of wrecked cars. Stolen

---

[11]Charles borrowed the residence permit of a friend and with it was able to get the visas he needed for travelling.

[12]An indication of the level of profit comes from an example given by an informant from Cameroon in Holland: a ten-year-old, four-wheel-drive Toyota Tercel, much sought after because it lasts so well, could be bought in Holland for 2,750 DF (Netherlands guilders) and exported to Cameroon for 1,400–1,500 DF. Customs duties cost 3,000 DF, so the total cost was 7,150 DF. The car could easily be sold in Africa for the equivalent of 12,000 DF, so the profit was 4,850 DF. (In March 1994, 1.97 DF = US$ 1.00.)

[13]This situation has probably changed with the new European Union policing system.

luxury cars and drugs are often part of the same *bizness*: these cars are used to transport drugs (hidden in inner tubes) across frontiers. The relaxing of frontier controls within the European Union has facilitated the expansion of such trade.

Many cars are legally imported into Nigeria or North Africa, then enter the smuggling circuits and go to other countries of West Africa and to Congo-Kinshasa. Cars bought in France, Spain and Holland may be shipped from Antwerp. Up until 1993, Antwerp only checked the papers, but, by 1994, numbers on engines were being checked as well. They can, however, be fixed and given new numbers by a garage that does this kind of business.

An employee of an African embassy in The Hague, whose salary was hardly ever paid, told us he managed to live by selling second-hand cars for this trade. From January 1993 to January 1994, he sold cars to fourteen people, ten of them women. One woman bought five (for taxis, for selling and for her personal use). In 1988, revenue from a taxi in Cameroon was 10,000 CFAF a day, but, by 1993, as the trade began to decline, it was difficult to earn as much as 5,000–6,000 CFAF a day.

As we noted in the case of Marie, women who are successful traders or *nganda* owners commonly invest their profits in cars and send them home to be used as taxis. The trade to Congo-Kinshasa in cars that were mostly used as taxis also included Dutch spare parts and Japanese used-car engines to sell in Kinshasa, and this easily covered the shipping costs and customs duties for the cars. Since the vehicle could be amortized in one year, it was possible to buy a new taxi each year.[14] Thomas from Congo-Brazzaville, a participant in this trade, originally came to Lille to study. He ended up underemployed in a job washing dishes at a restaurant. Realizing he had no future, he gave up his job and invested his savings of 20,000 FF in a second-hand car, which he shipped home and returned there himself to run it as a taxi. He comes back to France annually to buy two or three cars. In 1994 he owned at least six. He said that, if a taxi did well, it was easily possible to get back one's investment by making 60,000 FF in 10 months. Thomas preferred to run his taxi business himself, rather than, as he put it, 'wasting his time in France'. He has built a house in Lille, where he leaves his wife and son, sending them monthly payments of over 10,000 FF.

Holland is the centre for the second-hand car trade, for three reasons. First, it has rigorously enforced rules that cars on the road must be in good condition. Once the car is three years old, it must be inspected at designated garages to check its mechanical and physical condition. All defects must be repaired before it is allowed back on the road. Cars bought to export for use as taxis in Africa are about eight to ten years old. Secondly, there are many credit facilities for car purchasing, which makes it very

---

[14]Official figures on the export of second-hand vehicles from the European Union to Zaïre for 1992 were 1,030 (we are grateful to Prof. Stefan Marysse of UFSIA for these figures).

easy to obtain them. Thirdly, there are second-hand car auctions held weekly, on Tuesdays in Utrecht and on Saturdays in Amsterdam, for both cars and trucks.[15]

Spare parts are regularly exported to West Central Africa, generally as a package in the accompanied baggage of a friend, or as freight in trunks, containers, and even in the crates of the cars themselves. An associate, friend or relative must be there to pick them up when they arrive. They are often sent in the name of a customs official to avoid paying customs duties (he will be paid something for this, but less than the official dues). There is a high demand for these spares, since there are so many second-hand cars in the two capitals.[16]

The second-hand car trade has declined because of the devaluation of the CFA franc in 1994, the effect of European recession, which increased car prices and transport costs and made it hard to save money, and the economic crises in these Central African countries, which meant that the principal customers for taxis (bureaucrats, employees, students) were no longer using them.

Besides operating outside the law in unlicensed trade and other enterprises, traders contest legal boundaries in other ways.

Evading Taxes

Our findings conform to those of Hernando de Soto in his study of the informal economy of Peru, where he found that the high costs of legality drive people into illegality (De Soto, 1989). George Marcus comments on the telling criticism of capitalist society embedded in the discussion of ethnographic subjects (Marcus, 1986: 189). The trenchant comments of some of our traders on the system in which they live provide good examples. Jean, a Paris retailer from Congo-Brazzaville, who imports African foodstuffs to sell in his shop, remarked that there are lots of people who do not want to be legal because they have to pay so many taxes, and added: 'People get the feeling they are working for someone else'. Another retailer commented: 'The state doesn't want us to work; they make it so difficult'.

Jean pays several half-yearly taxes on his two shops in Château Rouge: Value Added Tax *(Taxe sur la Valeur Ajoutée)*, which is 5.5 per cent on food products, and as much as 18.6 per cent on some cosmetics products; social security; and URSAF (social benefits for the small-business owner). He evades other taxes in order to keep his business profitable: he employs two assistants to work in his shops who have no residence papers and whom he does not declare to the tax authorities; he has suppliers who are unlicensed and he does not declare his purchases from them. He explains how risk-free it is to avoid this tax:

---

[15]Interviews, MacGaffey, The Hague, May 1994.
[16]Interviews, Bazenguissa, Lille, May 1994.

> *It is easy to conceal illegal purchases. In grocery stores like ours the tax collector cannot exercise control, there is no means of doing it. Those who supply me don't always write bills. I don't tell the taxman that I buy from pedlars and, when I do, I don't leave any record. Only by writing out a bill does one declare what one has bought.*

Generally, however, he is very cautious:

> *You get caught out somehow. One can go to Roissy (the airport, to collect goods brought by flight attendants), but, one fine day, someone will ask for your commercial licence and, if you don't have it, they will confiscate your goods. There is always some point where the state catches up with the illegal.*

He consults his Togolese accountant on how far he can judiciously go.

Taxes are also evaded by non-declaration of some of the activities of a licensed business. Chantal, the seamstress (Chapter 2, p.44) has a back room for making women's clothes to order, with seamstresses hard at work on sewing machines, none of which is reported. Another way of avoiding tax is to run some other unlicensed business on the same premises. One shopkeeper runs a *nganda* (an unlicensed bar serving African food as well as drinks) in a small curtained-off room at the back of her licensed retail shop selling imported African foodstuffs. She also has a card-playing establishment upstairs. Another example from a different sort of enterprise is a licensed car body shop owned by two immigrants with residence papers. The wife of one of them runs a *nganda* on the premises, and four migrants from Congo-Brazzaville, without residence papers – a mechanic, a painter, an electrician and a bodywork expert – also run an unlicensed repair garage there. Each of them pays 100 FF per job as rent to the owners, and each buys his own tools and supplies and finds his own customers. Their repairs are much cheaper than those done by licensed official businesses (for example, 500 FF for a job that would cost 1,200 FF elsewhere).

These are all ways that people contest onerous taxes and resist or compensate for state levies that they find excessive and repressive.

Acquiring Venture Capital

It is exceedingly difficult for a trader to accumulate enough capital to set up a shop or other licensed business. Costs are very high and people combine savings from salaries, bank loans, and moneys earned outside the law. Jean (p. 92 above) gives an account of this process which shows the use of all these strategies. He arrived in France in 1981 on a state scholarship and has become a French citizen. His father was a gendarme, his mother a petty trader; his wife's father was an ambassador and her mother a housewife and then a big trader. Jean and his wife, aged 35 and 33, own two shops: a grocery shop and a hairdressing salon and video shop. They purchased the businesses and repurchase the leases for the shops annually which costs them the equivalent of three months' rent. This is risky because the owner may refuse to renew the arrangement. Buying the lease halves the rent (5,000 instead of 10,000 FF). They bought the business for 300,000 FF:

> *We had to do all kinds of things to accumulate this capital. I had a job for ten years; then in 1992, I negotiated my notice in a friendly way so that my boss gave me some money. This served as a start. For four years I had been operating an undeclared wholesale business importing manioc and other goods from Congo-Brazzaville and selling it to the Chinese and I had accumulated money from this. Then I went to the bank to ask for a loan. I had to wait several months and was very careful during this time to be sure there were no problems with any of my accounts at this bank. My wife had two boutiques for clothing, watches, shoes and accessories in Brazzaville. She traded back and forth and contributed to our savings. She subsequently lost her whole investment in these stores because of the civil war.*

They struggle against the high costs of moving into business in the official system, the reluctance of the banks to lend them money, and the political troubles that have wiped out their business investments in their home country.

Others take a different route and finance their enterprises by pulling off a coup in some activity outside the law. They steal expensive goods such as electronic equipment or clothing, and hawk it around the cafés and bars, keeping the goods meantime in their parked car nearby.[17] Some traders participate in the stolen luxury-car trade. Some resort to dealing in drugs or acting as drug couriers on visits to other European countries.[18] One couple told us they had paid 70,000 FF ($12,000) needed for a security deposit on the shop they rent for 9,500 FF a month, from savings from his job over six years and from her five years of trading between Paris and Kinshasa and street trading, but they were reticent about details. They had a family of seven children and savings on such a scale from these activities seemed to us unlikely. Our suspicions of what other sources for amassing their capital might be were aroused when we were told that drug dealers often frequent their shop and that a street vender associate of the wife made trips to London to buy drugs.[19] We got the impression that to these people drugs were simply another, and valuable, commodity.

---

[17]On one occasion, the police raided a bar owned by a North African and found a lot of stolen VCRs and suits. They closed down the bar, but the owner soon opened another nearby.

[18]Fottorino (1991: 86) mentions purchases of stolen goods as a way of laundering drug money.

[19]In 1994, the drug market was dominated by medium to small players. The quantity and value of drugs being shipped to the European Union was rising rapidly and the organizations bringing them in were reported as increasingly violent. Cocaine came from Colombia, heroin from South-East Asia. Europol, the new EU drug intelligence unit, had already intervened to help French, Belgian and Greek drugs officers in recent raids, using computer links (Richard Dowden, *The Independent*, 9 March 1994).

Women in particular said that they had started out in small-scale trade on gifts of money from fathers, husbands or lovers. Men were more likely to have had jobs and saved their salaries or to have made a coup or found some activity outside the law to finance their trade, like Charles above.

Territorial Boundaries: Crossing National Frontiers

'Frontiers are a game: people rarely pay dues.' (Congolese trader)[20]

For centuries frontiers have been contested by wars and invasions, and by smugglers, who, without the political barrier of the frontier, would simply be traders supplying commodities to a particular area that lacks them from another area that has them. Frontiers present potential opportunities for traders for several reasons. Price distortions from one side of a frontier to another may make it much more profitable to take goods across the border than to sell them locally; political interference with the market forces of supply and demand may make large profits possible by bringing goods made artificially scarce in one country across the frontier from another; and the populations of areas which have always been linked by trade may refuse to accept its prohibition or taxation by governments and simply cross the frontier clandestinely, continuing their trade and avoiding the tax.

That transborder trade offers profitable opportunities for those living on borders has been documented for Congo-Kinshasa by Vwakyanakazi (1991), Makwala (1991) and Rukarangira and Schoepf (1991). Comparative material from West Africa is given in Donna Flynn's study of trade across the Bénin–Nigeria border, which shows the economic and political power, and the strong sense of border solidarity, of the residents of the border region of Shabe because of their position in the interstices of the border-lands.[21] Economic opportunity fluctuates with the rise and fall in the flow of unofficial trade across this border, but border residents form a bi-national social grouping and manipulate their marginal situation to their economic advantage by inserting themselves as mediators or brokers between non-local traders and the state.

---

[20]This comment echoes De Herdt and Marysse's observation of the attitudes of the parallel market money-changers in Kinshasa, who treat this activity like a game, a way of passing the time, a dance (De Herdt and Marysse, 1996c: 21).

[21]The perceived threat posed by the states of Nigeria and Bénin, specifically through the customs guards, has led border residents to 'assert and emphasize their common border identity in a variety of ways'. This identity is defined in terms of their roles in transborder exchange and of their relations with the state and with non-border residents: they 'defiantly assert their independence from state structures'. In one instance they burned down shelters built to house customs guards (Flynn, 1997: 318, 320).

> Struggles between wanting to reject restraints placed on them by
> customs guards and wanting to maintain working relations with
> those same guards in order to extract more profit from their presence
> are constantly pulling locals in opposite directions. (Flynn, 1997:
> 323)

To make transborder trade profitable, traders must find ways of evading customs duties levied by officials at the border posts or of bypassing the frontier posts altogether. They also have to devise means of getting around visa requirements, which can prevent them from entering certain countries. Although the literature on unrecorded and unofficial transborder trade in Africa has recently expanded (Meagher, 1990; Grégoire, 1991; MacGaffey et al., 1991; Nugent, 1991; Herrera, 1992a and b; Igue and Soule, 1992; Ebin, 1993; DIAL, 1997; Fleisher, 1998; Flynn, 1997; Marchal, 1997), only a few studies include details on exactly how these problems are solved (for example, Rukarangira and Schoepf, 1991; Vwakyanakazi, 1991). The accounts of clandestine border crossings given by some of the Paris traders provide a wealth of such details and reveal the traders' striking resourcefulness, their daringly light-hearted attitude and their motives. The words of one trader put their problem in a nutshell: 'If you have to pay the full dues, you make a loss'.

Great crowds of people embark and disembark at the ferry quay in Brazzaville as they trade back and forth from Kinshasa. There are various methods for avoiding customs charges at this particular frontier post. One is to pay for the services of young men who make a living as smugglers ('*passeurs*'). These young Congolese are known as '*Romans*', because 'they are like gladiators and carry very heavy things'. As the goods start being unloaded from the ferry at the dock, the '*Romans*' rush on board to the traders and offer to get them past customs without paying duty. This they do by taking a load of goods on their heads, plunging into the river and swimming to land to get the goods on to the beach. The police and customs officials know all about this, of course, and wait for them. Those they catch have to pay; those they cannot catch get through free. This occupation requires considerable physical strength and is also dangerous, since the current of the Zaïre river is very fast. The risk for the trader is not only that the officers may catch the smuggler, but also that he may sell the goods to someone else and report that they have been confiscated.

Some traders simply stay on board the ferry and sell their goods to those who come on board. The latter then unload the goods and cope with the customs officers. A trader who takes this option makes several trips a day without disembarking.[22]

---

[22]We have no data on the comparative costs of paying the smugglers or lowering the prices of goods to allow for the customs duties paid by the buyer.

Another option is for the trader to bribe the customs official. One trader described the way she operated:

> *Rachel, who has a food shop with her husband, Paul, was a trader between Kinshasa and Brazzaville before they came to Paris. She said she sometimes paid customs and sometimes did not; it depended on luck. She did not use the 'passeurs': it was too risky because they would often steal your goods. She considered it better to take goods through herself and pay the customs duty. Sometimes she was able to negotiate a lower rate by buying off the customs official.*

A trader from Kinshasa smuggled *pagnes* from SOTEXKI (the Kinshasa factory), cloth for making men's trousers, and cooking pots across the river to sell in Congo-Brazzaville. She gave us the details of how she got her goods across the border upriver from Brazzaville and Kinshasa.[23]

> *Véronique and her grandmother crossed the river clandestinely in the Loukami region of the Pool (17 km from Brazzaville), and sold their goods in the villages of the region, travelling on foot or taking trucks. After a while, they banded together with other traders and rented houses so that they could stay in Congo for three months at a time. They travelled back to renew their supplies and smuggled them in, sometimes getting caught by the customs men, who would lie in wait for them and make them pay if they caught them. These traders also smuggled by using a local canoe transport company. The owner hired young men from the villages. The traders paid his charges and he paid his workers. But these young paddlers would also earn money on the side by smuggling the traders' goods, for which they were paid secretly. When the traders had a big shipment, they would take a small quantity of the goods across the river legally and pay customs duties at the Banza-Ndouga post, which was not on the river bank. Then they would select a paddler they trusted to smuggle the rest. The goods were delivered to the Congo-Kinshasa side: the paddler would bring them across at night when the customs officials were not watching the river, and would keep them in his house. After two or three days, he would deliver the goods to the traders.*

For goods sent to their destination by air, personal connections with customs officials are one way of avoiding duty.

---

[23]Since the early years of independence, smuggling has been intense across this border as the two capital cities supply each other with their surplus goods. The traffic has been so intense that one area, Kingabwa, is known as 'Hong Kong' (Gondola, 1997a: 401). Such labelling shows us the reality of globalization at the local level.

Eloise (Chapter 2, p.45) *buys goods in France and air-freights them to Congo under the name of a customs officer in Brazzaville, who is allowed to import for himself without paying duty. Eloise pays him some money later, but much less than she would pay in customs duty. The normal charge per 100 kilos is 300,000 CFAF. On one lot of 300 kilos of babies' clothes, blouses and women's sandals, for example, she paid only 75,000 CFAF to the customs officer, instead of the 900,000 CFAF she would have paid in duty.*

As visa restrictions have tightened up, it has become more and more difficult for Africans to get into Europe, and they have had to devise various strategies for getting to the countries to which they want to go. Most commonly, they seek political asylum, as we explained in Chapter 2. But there are other ways of getting into a country clandestinely. It is easier for nationals of certain African countries to get into some European ones. In Angola, for example, it was easy until recently to obtain an Angolan passport and with that a visa for Portugal, or even for Belgium, Spain or Italy. Until the last few years, migrants could then travel by train to the country of their first choice without having to go through border controls.

Nanette, from Congo-Kinshasa, managed to obtain a multiple entry visa for Belgium in 1989, before it became difficult to get one even for those from Belgium's ex-colony. She arrived, then stayed one day at a hotel in Brussels before taking the train to France, for which she had no visa. She had always intended to go to Paris because she had heard it was easier to get a job there. She was able to find work with an ethnic sister[24] who had residence papers and owned a café.

But this strategy is no longer an option because immigration controls have become much tighter.

Formerly, Africans and other non-European Community nationals needed visas for travelling to different countries within Europe. People got around this regulation by borrowing the papers of another African who was a French citizen, or by borrowing the papers of one who had a residence permit, and then getting themselves the necessary visa. Charles (p.83 above) borrowed the papers of his nephew, who is a French citizen, for getting a job and then later on for his travelling trade in Europe. Under the current law, with a visa for one country of the European Union, one can travel freely to the others.

A child born in France used automatically to be a French citizen, which conferred the right to a residence permit on the mother.[25] Some women

---

[24]People commonly refer to members of their ethnic group as '*soeur*' or '*frère*'.
[25]This law has been revoked and a child born in France of foreign parents is no longer automatically a citizen. Citizenship has to be requested when the child comes of age.

traders took deliberate advantage of this regulation to solve their visa problems.

> *Eloise* (p. 98 above) *traded between Zaïre and Congo, saving up money to buy her ticket.*[26] *When she became pregnant at the age of 20, she decided that that was the moment to go to France so that her child could be born there. Afterwards she did not need a visa to enter the country. She started trading between France and Congo when her baby was eight months old. In 1994, she had been travelling back and forth for three years. She bought babies' clothes, blouses, women's sandals at Tati and out at Auchan, and air-freighted them to Congo-Brazzaville, where she sold them to Senegalese wholesalers or to market retailers. Sometimes she goes to Amsterdam to buy jewellery (it is said to be the best place to buy it), such as large earrings. They cost 200 FF and she resells them in Brazzaville or Paris to people she knows for 500 FF.*

Exceeding the Bounds of Institutional Participation

In her study of the different dimensions of making ends meet in north-eastern Kentucky, Rhoda Halperin deals with livelihood processes that cross boundaries of different kinds, noting that they operate 'in at least two qualitatively different domains: spatial and institutional' (Halperin, 1990: 139). Members of Kentucky kin networks move through different kinds of economies, organized on different principles, different relations of production and different work schedules. In so doing, they are 'crossing spatial, institutional, and cultural boundaries' (Ibid.).

We have described the spatial boundary crossings of Central African traders. We now focus on the ways they stretch the boundaries of institutions. What these traders do adds an interesting variation to the kinds of institutional boundary crossings observed by Halperin. The traders have ingeniously devised opportunities to bend and stretch normal institutional participation to its limits in order to increase the profitability, or make possible the operation, of their trading enterprises. Case histories show how they expand their business opportunities by taking advantage of incidental benefits from their jobs, exploiting the bonds created by church membership, and activating ties of kinship, ethnicity and friendship.

Airlines allow free tickets and free baggage and freight to employees and their immediate family members, and tickets at a fraction of their regular cost to employees of some other airlines. The idea is to subsidize vacations

---

[26]In 1992, it was reported that traders selling goods in Brazzaville that had cost them 5 million zaïres in Kinshasa could realize 10–20 million zaïres on their return to Kinshasa by selling the CFAF they had received for the goods (*Le Soft du Finance*, 20 July 1992).

as a job benefit and to fill up empty seats on planes, but certainly not to facilitate and enable people to set up import–export trading enterprise. These traders cross over the intended boundaries of the use of these perks.

We have already learned of the importance for Josephine's trade of free airline tickets through her mother, and of free freight through flight attendants who are friends of her mother's (pp. 84–5 above). The following cases show other ways the traders use such connections.

> *Olivia's father worked for an airline in Congo, which enabled her to travel free to West Africa and to France to trade. She went to Cotonou in Benin and to Côte d'Ivoire and bought sandals. She sold them to the Senegalese traders in Brazzaville, effectively becoming their whole-saler. If she needed more, she had an ethnic brother in Abidjan who would buy for her and send them under her father's name so that she paid no freight or customs charges.*

The next history is of a woman who is in process of developing a worldwide trading enterprise by stretching the limits of normal institutional participation.

Beatrice was born in 1954; she has one child. Her family is solidly middle-class: her father was an army colonel (her mother, a housewife, died when she was very young); one of her brothers is a tax official, another a police commissioner, and her sister works in a tax office. She is a NiBoLek from Congo but is married to a trader from Congo-Kinshasa. She had two years of university education, during which she studied English. She has a job with an airline in Brazzaville, where she started working in the tariff department, but soon realized that she had reached the limits of progress in her career and had no chance of promotion. She took matters into her own hands and chose a different path by accepting a post in the baggage department at the airport, where she had more free time. In this position, she worked for several consecutive days and then got two days off, which allowed her time to start up a trading enterprise and go for quick trips to different countries. By working at the airport, she was able to oversee the despatch of her goods. She is a woman of great initiative and ability, willing to work hard, with an obvious talent for business and an instinctive feel for selecting people who will manage her affairs well. In her, one sees the capability and drive of a high-level executive of a big corporation. But that path is not open to her in her job: she is blocked from exercising her talents and increasing her rewards. So she has set up a trading business, but, she says, 'my trade is informal' (that is, unlicensed). To build up her business, she has creatively made the most of the opportunities available to her not only from the perks of her job, but also from her membership in a worldwide church organization and from her creative manipulation of the law.

Her business consists of importing exotic foods and some other products from countries all over the world, to sell in Paris, in Congo-Kinshasa and in

Congo-Brazzaville. She has been to Los Angeles for fish, to Hong Kong and Seoul for other foods, to Johannesburg for the hair extensions that it is the current fashion for women to braid into their hair. (She bought these wholesale and sold them to wholesalers in Paris for twice the purchase price.) In order to capitalize this trade, she has engaged in various clandestine trade operations: 'Since we have nothing to export [from Congo-Brazzaville] to earn foreign exchange, we have to find means to get it somehow'. She tried trading in various commodities: first in art with a friend, and then in gold and diamonds. In these last two ventures she was not successful and actually made losses. This she attributes to her failure to get into the right circuits. She is going to try again through her husband's family because they are in the business.

The airline she works for gives her free tickets when she travels. This has been the basis for building up her enterprise.[27]

> *Ticket costs vary for me. On this trip to Paris, I paid 15,000 CFAF (150 FF) return. I prefer to take complimentary tickets from airlines other than* [her airline], *in which case I pay 10 per cent of the fare and the tax. I had one from Brazzaville to New York via Brussels, and I paid only 7,500 CFAF plus taxes. But, if we work with another airline a lot, I can go to the boss and he will give me a free ticket. I went to Hong Kong and to New York on another trip on free tickets. It all depends on relations with the boss. My job thus covers the cost of my tickets.*

To deal with the problems of doing business and finding her way in strange countries, cities, languages and cultures, she takes advantage of her membership in the Association for the Reunification of the Christian World (also known as the Moon Church, after its founder the Reverend Moon from Korea).

> *This church is just about everywhere in the world. We all know each other and form a community; we marry within the church; we have the same way of thinking. I have a lot of connections through the church: I have Zaïrean brothers in Korea, the USA, Japan, Nigeria and elsewhere. We have facilities and are organized to help one another. When I arrive in a country, I go to our church community, to the sisters. I have often done it before and I know that I can have a little house with them. In return, I receive other members of the community when they pass through Congo. I am general secretary for the Federation of Women for World Peace and once I went to Seoul, one of their headquarters, for a meeting, and combined it with a trading trip.*

---

[27]This phenomenon is reported in other parts of the world. Not only airline personnel but also sailors and diplomats keep the markets of Bombay, Madras and Calcutta supplied with goods from the West, the Middle East, Hong Kong and Singapore (Appadurai, 1990: 12).

During my stay, I visited the market and found lots of goods very cheaply priced.

There was, however, a difficulty with all this:

I only have a holiday once a year. So what was I to do to stop my business suffering? I have two brothers still at school and I have adopted them. As my children, they can have free tickets until they are 25. The only problem is that getting visas from the French embassy is very complicated and they have to have them because they are students, even if they only go for two days. I shall have to get them trade passports so that they can go regularly to supply me. The first time they went on a trading trip, I took them to show them what to do.

She thus solves the problem with her ingenious manipulation of the law to make it work for her. On her trading trips, she also relies on personal relationships based on kinship, friendship and business contacts: they will be described in the next chapter.

Beatrice meets people and learns about trade and how to be a more effective businesswoman on her trips. She is actively planning how to expand her business, making full use of her acquired knowledge, and her access to free air freight and free airline travel:

In Hong Kong, I went with a West African colleague from Mali. They are better organized in West Africa than we are: a group subscribes to send someone, which reduces the cost. This person is delegated to take the money of all the rest, which amounts to a lot and enables them to negotiate directly with the factory because they can buy in such large quantities. In Hong Kong, I entrusted my money to this Malian trader and was thus able to buy at the factory price. In Central Africa, it is everyone for themselves. This makes it hard for us to compete with West Africans because their co-operative organization means that their costs are lower.[28]

Beatrice here shows herself very conscious of the value of organization and co-operation among those with common interests. She herself is aiming to gather a group of associates around her rather than taking on employees. Her idea is to organize a group of people with capital who can invest together in a container shipment of goods and by trading in bulk reduce their costs. But she is very particular in her choice of whom she works

---

[28]In his 1990 study of women in trade in Kinshasa's big market, Kanene reports that these women did organize themselves into groups of two, five or ten to purchase wholesale, thus reducing time and expense for long trips. Each group would support the expenses of the members who travelled to make purchases (Kanene, 1990: 305).

with as she begins to organize such a group, assessing ability as well as relying on personal connections.

> *I do not want to be associated with just anyone because there are plenty of dishonest people, and kinship doesn't prevent embezzlement, that is why I really get to know people. There is a girl here in Paris called Josephine (pp. 84–5 above), who works with me. She is very smart. Since I work at the airport in Brazzaville, I can send packages to her free. She goes to the airport and takes delivery, and she even goes out of Paris to make deliveries. She hires an unlicensed taxi driver to take her. I pay for this taxi and for her expenses, and I always add a package for her to sell on her own account. I do not pay her directly, but I give her something to make a bit of capital. She puts my money into an account.*
>
> *Josephine can be counted on, she will not take my money, because if she does she will lose in the long run. She knows that I aim high and have lots of ideas. We are related and she is also the daughter of a colleague whom I know well, who is a trader in Brazzaville and has built houses there. Not just anyone can succeed in trade, but Josephine is a fighter and is going to go far. I feel the same about my Nigerian sister-in-law, a Yoruba, who also has big traders in her family. I am going to adopt her too, and we are going to work together: I am going to export to Nigeria from Congo. It will give her the opportunity to expand her trade: I shall give her free tickets which will put her in a good competitive position among other traders there. These free tickets are our trump card. Those who work with me need money as I do: I give them free tickets and start them off by helping them to have some capital, then they work for themselves.*

Beatrice's plans to expand her worldwide trading enterprise, like all her undertakings so far, show great flair and boldness. She feels the Congo-Brazzaville market is too small and prefers to trade in Congo-Kinshasa, where the traders currently pay in dollars. She plans to develop her activities in Nigeria, where she has a family connection, because it is such a huge country.

Transgressing the Limits of Co-operative Behaviour

Christopher Steiner comments on traders in African art in West Africa: 'One might say that like players engaged in a game with agreed upon rules, traders modify and contest the boundaries of co-operative behaviour' (Steiner, 1994: 49). In Paris, Congolese involved in trade and its related activities may betray the norms of co-operation in order to make a windfall, thus breaking the unwritten rules and trust which are the basis of the personal relations organizing the trade. While some people lose out in this process, others gain and thus find *their* opportunity, which in this individualistic world is to be sought and seized anywhere it can be found. This is another form of boundary crossing for profit: there is a continual dynamic of uncertainty as to whether those one trusts can be counted on, because some people find their chances in breaking the norms and boundaries of co-operative behaviour and swindling others. Confidence and trust ('*confiance*') can be misplaced, no matter how close the relationship. Individuals seek always to find someone they can rely on absolutely; when they believe they have found such a person, they are sometimes right, sometimes mistaken. The sanctions of this Central African trade are very weak, as the next chapter will spell out; this weakness is a function of the nature and basis of the personal ties which organize it.

Material from our case histories supplies details of the betrayals of the boundaries of co-operative behaviour. Such betrayals contrast strongly with the behaviour of traders in the Islamic networks of West Africa we discussed in Chapter 1, with their extremely powerful religious sanctions to enforce compliance with the norms of co-operation.

Nanette was swindled of a large sum of money by a man she had good reason to trust. He could not resist the opportunity to make a windfall to support his trading enterprise, which was drug dealing. This experience has changed her attitude towards those with whom she works.

> Nanette saved up 15,000 FF to bring her brother over from Kinshasa. She entrusted this money in cash to a Congolese from there whom she knew well, who was older than she was, and who had taken money home several times to her parents for her. He owned a travel agency and had promised to arrange the ticket and visa for her brother. He embezzled the money. She has no hope of getting it back as he is now in prison for selling drugs.
>
> She emphasized to us the difficulties of the bureaucratic hassle and the expense of trying to open and run a legitimate enterprise. In 1994, she was running a nganda in a squat with a friend. She had taken precautions to safeguard herself from being swindled. She and her friend put down the money for the nganda together and they share the takings on a fifty–fifty basis daily. She emphasized the importance of doing this: 'Dans les affaires on ne fait pas confiance à 100 pour cent pour les autres' (in business one does not have 100 per cent trust in others).

Jerome, the wholesaler (pp. 1–2, p. 43), has prospered in his import wholesale business, but he has run into trouble in investing his profits in businesses run by family members back in Congo. The scale of his investments are an impressive measure of his success in trade. His brothers, however, have transgressed the bounds of co-operative behaviour and squandered his money on their own pleasures.

*Jerome has a commercial licence for his import trade. He also sells
from his house in an unlicensed enterprise. He imported manioc, salt
fish and smoked meat and quickly did well. He decided to invest his
profits in the transport and furniture manufacturing businesses of his
brothers in Brazzaville. He bought his older brother, who had already
obtained a small car, a larger vehicle and shipped it out for him to run
a transport business. But Jerome asserts that this brother is not a
serious businessman, he squanders his money on women: he has three
wives and eighteen children: 'Money must only be spent on business
and not on sleeping with women all over the place'. His other brother is
a carpenter and Jerome helped him by borrowing money to lend him to
buy machinery. This brother also has done nothing with it: 'When he
has money he goes to drink palm wine at Linzolo, and he also likes to
chase women'. The enterprise failed and he sold the machinery
without telling Jerome, who continues, however, to pay off the loan.
Jerome also bought three new cars and two buses to be used as taxis in
a family transport business managed by his brothers, and a Peugeot
505 for his mother's use. The money earned in this business was to be
divided into two: half was for his mother and the other half was to be
deposited in his own account. His mother received hers, but nothing
has ever been paid to him; his brothers have just made off with the
money. They are older than he is and he feels he has no recourse
against them; he believes in, and is afraid of, their magical powers.*

Beatrice (pp. 100–103 above) was also taken advantage of by the person
she trusted to manage the business in which she invested her profits. As in
the case of Jerome, her investments are an indication of the scale of her
enterprise.

*I bought all the equipment for a medical office, with a radio and
everything. The office started operations but the Congolese who was
managing it embezzled the money and we had to close down. I could
rent out the equipment but Congolese do not respect contracts and we
don't have a legal system that can enforce them, so I don't want to do
that. I can sell it all for 15 million CFAF to the General Hospital, where
I have good contacts.*

Another such case is Marie (pp. 85–7 above), who suffered badly back in
Brazzaville from being swindled and from problems resulting from the
political and economic situation. She owed the bank 3 million CFAF and
did a deal with a banker. She paid him the money but, instead of giving it
to the bank, he borrowed an additional 4 million from them. He bought
merchandise and divided it between his wives and Marie. He then lost his
job because of the political crisis. Marie was thus left with a debt of 7
million CFAF at the bank. Because she had operated without any formal
legal papers, she had no recourse to litigation and has to cope with this

huge loss. In five years, her debt plus interest amounted to 20 million CFAF.

Conclusion

Traders resist the constraints imposed on them by state regulations at local, national and global levels as they contest boundaries in the ways we have described. The rich and powerful also participate in international second-economy trade but they have privileged access by reason of their class position to the most profitable forms of such trade. Political office or contacts with the powerful enable them to evade state regulations and to cross legal and institutional boundaries with impunity. For all these reasons they trade on a greater scale and in more profitable commodities than are available to the traders of our study, such as large-scale trade in gold and diamonds and the unofficial export of cobalt and of planeloads of coffee. By accumulating enormous wealth in such extremely lucrative commerce, they maintain and consolidate their class position. They exploit their position in the state, or their contacts with those who have such a position, to trade in these informal markets.

They cannot, however, monopolize this activity or second-economy international trade in general, and many of the forms of this trade that the Paris traders in this study have discovered are not sufficiently large-scale and lucrative to be of any interest to those who have the opportunities offered by political power. The ease with which the powerful can operate and the resources they can command to facilitate their trading activities contrast substantially with the difficulties the traders of our study must surmount to organize and create their smaller-scale but nevertheless far-flung trading enterprises. How they carry out and organize their trade and their various other enterprises will be described in the next chapter.

5

**The Organization
of the Trade**

The Importance
of Personal Ties

In their home countries, Congolese traders face oppression or exclusion by the state and the social and economic disorder of violence, chaos and institutional disintegration resulting from the rise of the 'shadow state'. In addition to suffering from the depredations of the state, they feel they are subject to the witchcraft of kin back in the village, who are jealous of their wealth. In Europe, they face racial discrimination and police harassment, intensified by their visibility as black people in a white society. To cope with all these problems, they evade state regulation and oppression by operating outside, or on the margins of, the law, and they create their own form of order to cope with the prevalent disorder. In this chapter, we show how they construct the reliable social relations that are the basis of this order and how they make at least some areas of social organization work without the support of the state. We detail the ways they turn to personal relationships to organize their trade and then depend on the trust inherent in such relationships to back up their transactions in the absence of the support of formal contracts sanctioned by an established judicial system.

Personal ties remain powerful throughout Africa today for a variety of political, economic and environmental reasons. They help people cope with risky situations, which seem as prevalent now as they were in the past. These ties bring 'entitlements that buffer vulnerable people from the full force of natural as well as social calamity' and they have to be renewed, modified and remade with a stream of social transactions to keep them active (Krokfors, 1995: 57–8). Constructing and maintaining such personal ties constitutes an investment in 'social capital'. This capital of interpersonal relations is a particular kind of resource available to individuals that facilitates transactions in which trustworthiness is an essential feature (Coleman, 1988: S95–S101).[1] For particular individuals,

---

[1] 'Social capital' is the concept that James Coleman has used to reconcile two opposing explanations of social life, the one seeing the actor as constrained and governed by social context, the other seeing the actor as acting independently and maximizing self-interest. The concept of social capital reconciles these two explanations, since it involves the rational action of individual maximization and also reliance on social relationships.

such social resources consist of the number of people who want to help them, the resources they can directly mobilize, and the extent to which others can support them (De Graaf and Flap, 1988: 453). The kind of social capital available in any particular society and the way it is used differs with class level.[2] Case histories show how this social relations capital was created in the past and is maintained by the traders in Paris, who send money and other gifts to relatives back home. This capital can be drawn upon for support, assistance with trade, house room and care of dependants.

We find personal ties to be the basis for the organization of trade outside the law at all its different stages.[3] This chapter first explores the ways in which the trade works. It looks at the norms of reciprocity involved in the use of personal relations, shows how different kinds of reciprocity operate according to the degree and kind of relationships involved, and describes the different purposes to which personal relations are put. It shows how, in these activities on the margins of the law, where formal judicial sanctions are lacking, a sort of parallel system of justice operates against those who violate the trust of personal relationships. It continues with an account of the ways in which some of the ideas and values of traditional society operate as pressures for redistribution of the profits of trade among kin. It ends by reflecting on the wider global context of this second-economy international trade: on the intensification of the development of an inter-nationalization of kinship, and on the use of personal relations not just in underdeveloped economies, but also as an efficient way of operating in multinational companies and in the developed capitalist economies of some countries in the world today.

Personal Ties: the Norm of Reciprocity

The personal relations that are so especially important in activities unreg-ulated by formal institutions are sustained and even created by the recip-rocal exchange of favours. This often ambiguously used concept of reciprocity can be precisely defined as a series of transactions which need not maintain an exact equivalence but which are directed towards securing it (MacCormack, 1976: 90, 94).[4]

---

[2]De Graaf and Flap, for example, demonstrate the use of informal social resources to achieve occupational mobility in the United States and Europe.

[3]Stuart Henry and Gerald Mars's study of dealings in stolen goods in the UK shows that the sale of these goods involves open-ended personal obligations. Dealing is not impersonal as in commodity exchange but takes place between people linked by kinship, neighbourhood and other personal ties. These deals make little profit, payment is in kind as well as in money, is permeated by time lags, and transactions take place in series (Henry and Mars, 1978).

[4]For a useful survey on the literature see Gouldner (1960).

In 1925, Marcel Mauss identified the reciprocity governing gift exchange as the three obligations of gift giving: the obligation to give, the obligation to receive and the obligation to repay. Others have since elaborated on the way the norm of reciprocity morally obliges people to return benefits or favours to the giver, so that the recipient is in debt and remains so until repayment is made. Such outstanding obligations help to maintain social relationships; they constitute mechanisms which 'induce people to remain socially indebted to each other and which inhibit their complete repayment' (Gouldner, 1960: 175). Furthermore, the requirement of only rough equivalence in transactions induces a certain amount of ambiguity as to whether the indebtedness has been repaid, and generates uncertainty over whether one is in debt or not, leading to a situation of comparative indeterminacy. 'Being indeterminate, the norm can be applied to countless *ad hoc* transactions, thus providing a flexible moral sanction for transactions which might not otherwise be regulated by specific status obligations' (Ibid.: 175). In reciprocity networks in Chile, for example, social and economic equality requirements can never be exactly met, nor can the resources available to each party be the same, because there would no longer be any motivation for exchange (Lomnitz, 1988: 45). Continuation of any relationship depends on exchange, but it is not necessarily one that is immediate or identical in content. Material services may be reciprocated with non-material returns, such as esteem and social approval. Such non-material returns can help exchange relationships to persist and develop. Too rapid a material reciprocation terminates a relationship or confines it to specific activities, whereas non-material reciprocation provides a flexible basis for other types of exchange to develop (Roberts, 1973: 171).

According to Marshall Sahlins, people with strong personal relationships practise generalized, delayed reciprocity, while those with less strong personal relationships look for balanced, direct reciprocity (Sahlins, 1965: 148–58). The reciprocity in the different relationships of the Congolese traders in this study conforms to this pattern. We find that assistance and services rendered by kin, that is to say, by those in affective relationships, are not directly repaid nor is their value calculated: Sahlins's generalized reciprocity is the norm. A description of reciprocity within the urban middle class in Chile parallels exactly the way it works among the traders and their kin: 'the obligation is stored in a sort of savings account of future services to be rendered to various persons and drawn upon as the need arises' (Lomnitz, 1971: 94). On the other hand, those Paris traders who are operating within less close relationships say they feel obliged to make a direct, more calculated and balanced return – Sahlins's balanced reciprocity.

The next section documents via case histories the ways in which kinship relations and other kinds of personal ties function, and the uses to which they are put in organizing trade.

The Basis of Personal Ties and their Use in Trade

The traders rely on personal ties based on the bonds of kinship, ethnicity, friendship, religion, and nationality.

Kinship relations carry the strongest obligations to render assistance and the strongest right to ask for it. The obligations of such relationships 'are not legally enforceable, but depend for their enforcement on the values of the relationship itself' (Moore, 1978: 62). The particular importance attached to kinship ties is reflected in the great efforts made by individuals in our study to live up to kinship obligations and maintain relations by sending money home regularly. One trader belonged to a rotating credit association (*muziki*) which returned 30,000 FF to her every six months; she gave 10,000 FF each time to her mother in Congo-Brazzaville. Another, despite having a very marginal business, sent 500–1,000 FF monthly to help her sister, who had eight children, or to help her brother or her father's brother. Thus, even when circumstances are very straitened, people in general feel strongly obligated to maintain these relations.

Abner Cohen's classic studies of long-distance trade in West Africa showed that ethnic identity and religious ideology made it possible in pre-industrial social conditions to overcome problems concerning trust, regular credit arrangements, information about conditions of supply and demand, and the lack of an authority structure to enforce respect for contract (Cohen, 1969, 1971: 266–7). In modern conditions, in which private contracts are socially enforced, where there is ready access to adjudication, where there are moral and religious pressures for generalized honesty and where money is a social institution, the role of identity is reduced. Situations in which identity continues to be important, however, include transactions in which there is uncertainty about the quality of the objects exchanged or about the terms of the transaction, and those transactions which are not consummated instantaneously but involve obligations or consequences that extend over time (Ben-Porath, 1980: 7–13). For Congo traders in just such situations who do not always use money in their transactions and who operate on the margins of the law, ethnic identity, built on common culture, on similar ways of doing and thinking and on the same ethical values, provides a basis for trust.[5]

Friendship is a voluntary relationship, with no legal or moral component to maintain or enforce its obligations. It is a relationship of equality, and has culturally specific values that comprise a standard of behaviour appropriate for friends in a particular society (La Fontaine, 1975: 52–3). Friendship takes two forms: emotional friendships, in which the relation is

---

[5]Grabowski notes that in many countries where the state fails to fulfil its expected functions, ethnic ties also take on the function of conveying information, giving technical advice and providing access to credit, thus solving some of the dilemmas traders confront in such a situation (Grabowski, 1997: 399).

restricted to the two persons involved, and instrumental friendships, in which each person acts as a possible connecting link to others (Wolf, 1966: 12). Traders use friendship instrumentally in their trading activities to cope with situations of constraint and uncertainty. We find a parallel situation in Russia's oppressive state and failing economy. Here friends render services without expecting material rewards, and are helpers in facing the difficulties of daily existence and in 'beating the system' to procure necessary goods. 'To a considerable degree, the institution of friendship functions to protect the individual as far as possible, from the arbitrariness of state authorities' and provides the goods and services lacking in the state-run system (Shlapentokh, 1984: 218–38). Congolese traders use ties of friendship in just this way.

We shall examine the use of these personal ties in the organization of trade by exploring in turn the co-operation of family members in business, how traders acquire venture capital, how they attract and keep customers, how they assess who is creditworthy, and how they find the help they need when they arrive in a strange country.

Family Business

A crucial strategy for the successful operation of some enterprises is for the owners to work in conjunction with family members back home. By 'family' we mean forms of the extended family, not the nuclear or restricted family. In the cases under consideration here, 'family' refers to a loosely defined group of close kin who are not co-resident, and which minimally includes parents, parents' siblings, own siblings, children and siblings' children. It may also include affines considered to be close.

The following three histories are of people who import African foodstuffs to Paris through the help of family members living in Africa. The ways in which this help is organized vary with each case.

The first history is that of Jean and his wife. He is 35, she is 33. He has a degree in sociology from the University of Brazzaville and had continued his studies in international transport in Paris. His wife traded between Paris and Brazzaville, buying and selling and taking the goods back and forth herself. Then she decided to set up an import business, in which he joined. They are assisted in their retail business by what he calls their 'teams' back in Congo-Brazzaville. These teams purchase, prepare and ship foodstuffs to Paris for them.

> We have a team in Brazzaville and another in Pointe-Noire to supply us. We send money each week and receive packages every Thursday or Saturday. Our primary team is made up of family members: my wife's mother, father and brother, and father's sister. This small team activates our second team, the women who get the manioc: they are not family members and they are paid. These women are known to us and work for us. They sell to us wholesale, otherwise they sell retail in the market. Then we also buy saka-saka, which is pounded, prepared

and bagged in my father-in-law's house by our third team: a variable group which numbers about a dozen members of my wife's family. We occasionally pay them some money, say 1,000 CFAF, but they really do it for family solidarity. The team is not stable but is mobilized when needed. People volunteer: someone comes to visit, sees other women working and says, 'Listen, I'll come next week.' Another woman may have problems and fail to turn up. We have from three to fifteen people at a time. Other family members buy things for us in the market, such as eggplant and other vegetables, smoked fish and peanuts.

The profits of the business are not shared out with the members of the four primary support teams. Jean's account of how financial arrangements are handled vividly conveys the strength of family feeling and the delicacy and sensitivity necessary for successful family co-operation. In this case, the goodwill and support of close kin for their offspring or siblings are paramount: it is not just a business partnership. The social capital being amassed by the older generation in the form of such assistance to their children will be drawn on later for the needs of their old age.

If we send more purchase money than they spend, they keep it. But they may also add some if we do not send enough. My father-in-law may claim it back, but, since it is in the family, we do not feel we have to hurry to repay him. They feel the business belongs to us, their children, and they want to do things for us. We therefore owe a lot of money to my father-in-law, since he even gave us some to add to our capital. They are not working with us for profit, but on a family basis, in which money does not count for much. Sometimes we find ways to give them things. One time I went back to Congo with some jackets for sale. They had just appointed new police prefects there and I succeeded in selling the lot to a prefect of police, who gave me 20,000 CFAF for them. It was an unexpected windfall. Without saying anything about debts to my father-in-law, I gave him the money. He asked me what it was for and I told him that it was from a 'coup' and I was giving it to him so that he could eat. But I made no allusion to my debt to him.

Jean proceeds to detail the working of the norm that members of the family are not paid for their work. His precise account clearly delineates for us the nuances of interpretation of this behaviour pattern. He is talking about the women relatives, who do not have a fixed salary and work for the sake of family solidarity:

I think that with us there is some shame attached to taking money from the family. Although we do not yet operate with real business spirit, people who come to work do, in fact, want to be paid. These women want money, but they don't like to ask for it, because, since it is

in the family, it is not appropriate. From time to time, since we under-
stand this, we anticipate their wishes and give them some money, but
it is not discussed as a contract. When we can, we give what we can:
1,000, 2,000 or 3,000 CFAF. It all depends on how we feel and what is
available. But it is felt to be shameful to ask for pay from members of
the family. For example, I could not take a loan from my mother: I
know that for her to lend is to make a gift. Shame plays the same role
with all members of the family. But really it is hypocrisy. One feels
that, since the others don't want to ask for money, it is up to you to take
the initiative. For example, when a woman comes to work, she will
take a long time to finish and will stay all day. But she is really
waiting, saying to herself that in two hours you are going to ask her
what she is doing there, should she not have gone already? As soon as
you give her something, that is the moment she will leave. There is
also an exchange in kind, which is more honourable for women. One
gives them food or clothes. These women who work in the team are
more or less tied to us because they have several times received
presents (particularly when my wife traded back and forth between
Paris and Brazzaville): skirts, pagnes, T-shirts. They remain loyal to us
and do not like to ask for money because they know that they have
accepted these things.

Our second history is of Rachel and her husband who have a retail shop.
Rachel runs the shop because her husband has a job. This history shows
clearly the operation of family co-operation in business over time and
across continents. At first the giver of labour to her kin, Rachel now
receives help in buying the goods she needs from those who profited from
her services earlier. She is cashing in on the social capital she accumulated
as a girl.

Rachel is 40 years old. She comes from a large family, all of whom are
traders. She herself started when she was twelve years old by working
for her sister, who was already an international trader in clothes and
shoes and married to an importer of salt fish. Rachel gave her sister
unpaid help in her shop during the school holidays, even minding the
shop on her own sometimes. The business was a family one, profits
were invested in houses, hotels and trucks. After she married, Rachel
set up independently of the family with her own stall at the market.
But, when she moved to Paris, she relied on family again: she bought
shoes, blouses and other things, which she sent to her sister to sell for
her in Congo-Kinshasa. Her sister sent her back the profits. Later,
when Rachel worked as a street trader, she sent money to her sister
and brother for them to buy and ship to her the foodstuffs she sold.
Now that she has a shop, she continues to place orders for foodstuffs
with her sister, and sends the money to pay for them. In addition to the
foods Rachel imports, she buys canned and dry goods, and, in

> *between import arrivals, additional manioc and other vegetables from*
> *wholesalers in the Château Rouge neighbourhood.*

Rachel thus converts the social capital of relations into material advantage as she asks for her sister's help in shipping goods. Reciprocation for her earlier services is not in money but in services she needs in buying and shipping goods to supply her shop. She said that she always trusted her sister implicitly not to take money sent to pay for the goods shipped to Paris, because as a child she worked for her without pay, which she did because of her obligation to 'work for the family'. Rachel and her husband Paul regard the profits of the business as part of their joint marital wealth to be used for family expenses.

Jerome, the wholesaler of African foods (p.104), is 48 years old and works with his sister in Brazzaville. He depends on her to organize the purchase, processing, packing and shipping of the foods he sells, and to hire the necessary temporary workers (paid by piece work) to carry out these extensive activities. He imports manioc, *safu*, salt and smoked fish, smoked meat and *saka-saka*. His sister buys smoked fish at the market on Saturdays, freezes it, and on Tuesdays sends it off in a rented truck which delivers it to the freight company for shipping and customs formalities. Jerome also goes to Brazzaville himself twice a year. He described how he buys fish at the dock in Brazzaville and sends it all to the village to be smoked. His sister does not share in the profits of the business, but he gives her occasional presents.

The expectation of future return for working for close kin without pay is present here also.

> *Jerome says of his sister, who manages the purchase and shipping of*
> *foodstuffs from Brazzaville: 'I don't pay her a salary because she is*
> *family. I give her presents: a* pagne, shoes, make-up, *help for her*
> *doughnut-making enterprise. For her, the idea of working for the family*
> *is important' (i.e. it is the family who are going to profit from all this).*

In these cases, the help and participation of family members in business are clearly a crucial factor in the operation of the enterprise. Other businesses may only rely partly on kinship for their business connections.

It must be noted, however, that some people do not use this strategy and are wary of working with relatives at all. The interpersonal conflict, often expressed in witchcraft accusations (discussed below), that can be generated in such co-operation can result in swindling for which it is difficult to obtain redress. Conflict between family members co-operating in business is something that some people manage to cope with, that others do not cope with so well and consequently are under great stress, (like Jerome pp. 1–2) and that some refuse to try and cope with at all.

The following cases are of this last kind, of people who will have nothing to do with family members for the daily operation of their business. Chantal (p. 44) has a manager for her Paris shop who is not a relative and whom she pays. 'For me, family solidarity does not count for anything. Good sense decides me to pay someone: how can a person live on family solidarity? How can they support a family? It is better to be clear about it.' She does, however, have a brother and sister in Europe whom she describes as associates or 'shareholders' in her business. They have put in money and get a share of the profits (when there are any), but it is a smaller share than hers. They do not work with her in any way.

Another trader, Olivia (p. 100), was pressed to invest in a family enterprise. When her father retired from working with an airline, he opened a hotel-restaurant and passed it on to his sister's son. It went well for a while, then began to decline. She was asked to invest in it, but refused because she did not want to have anything to do with a business owned by a family member.

Some people employ family members in their enterprise, which may, or may not, work out well. Marie (pp. 85–6) has her son working in the shops and her nephews working in the bakery she owns in Brazzaville. However, Jean (pp. 111–13 above) started out employing a member of his wife's family as an assistant in their shop. This did not last long because the young man started running his own business in the shop and even taking goods to sell on his own account elsewhere.

For family who remain in Africa, a crucial survival strategy may be to have some member overseas. Marianne Schmink points out that complex patterns of migration can be viewed as a mechanism by which the disadvantaged are able to draw on diverse economic sectors to sustain themselves. Such strategizing indicates an active rather than passive role for those concerned, though she is uncertain to what extent such migration patterns imply conscious rationalization or, as is more likely, are a label applied to the results of this behaviour (Schmink, 1984: 88–9, 95). A comment by one of the women money-changers who dominate Kinshasa's parallel money market, known as *'Le Beach'*, shows that she conceives of placing family members overseas as a quite deliberate strategy. This woman obtained hard currency for her money-changing operations from both her sons. The elder was a diamond trafficker between Kinshasa and Angola and brought her dollars; the other son was in Europe and sent her a monthly sum of money. She stated: *'Chez nous, on le sait, chaque parent se bat pour envoyer un enfant en Europe. En retour c'est ce genre de service qu'on s'attend'* (Here, as everyone knows, every parent struggles to send a child to Europe. In return, one expects this kind of assistance) (*La Référence Plus*, 15 February 1993).[6] Obviously, this is not a strategy available to the poor, however, since it requires money and contacts. We

---

[6]In Sierra Leone, families try to place different members in various overseas countries as a deliberate strategy (Carol MacCormack, personal communication, November 1996) and the same phenomenon is reported in Ghana (Clark, 1998).

can see that sending money back to the family is not the same as investing in a business; rather, it reinforces the sender's position in the family. It is thus an investment in social capital.

Access to foreign exchange and business contacts from family members in other countries has long benefited entrepreneurs of ethnic diasporas, as, for example, with the Lebanese in Sierra Leone, whose family co-operation and access to foreign exchange have been crucial for their business success (Reno, 1995: 118). The internationalization of the family we see here is a means to the same end.

In order to get started in any kind of business, traders must accumulate venture capital. Here also family ties are drawn upon, but so are other kinds of personal ties. Such resources may also be combined with savings and bank loans.

Venture Capital: Help Through Personal Ties

Since it is extremely difficult for Congolese from either Congo-Kinshasa or Congo-Brazzaville to get loans from the bank, as reported in Chapter 4, people are more likely to rely on personal relationships for accumulating venture capital. Among the traders we studied, money to start up in trade or other enterprises came from relatives, from spouses or lovers, as well as from savings from wages or petty trading, or from illegal activities such as theft or drug dealing, or from some combination of any of these.

For some women, it was their father who provided the venture capital. Olivia's father in Brazzaville gave each of his children 2,000 CFAF to put to further education or to start up in trade. Eloise's father in Kinshasa shared the family allowance from the state among his children, three boys and three girls. It amounted to 4,000 CFAF (88 FF) each per month. At the age of fifteen she used it to start trading soap and powdered milk in Congo. Rachel's original start-up capital for trade between Kinshasa and Brazzaville came from her husband. Véronique, also in Kinshasa, was given 30 zaïres by a lover when she was twenty, a reasonable amount of money at that time. It was intended as a gift to buy a *pagne*, but she wanted to trade and increase the money rather than buy something with it. She was under no obligation to return it and turned the custom of gift-giving in a relationship to her economic advantage.[7] She bought manioc and traded it upriver by boat towards Bandundu.

Prior to having a shop, Rachel, the retailer (p. 113 above), was one of the first to sell food on the street. She did it for five years, standing outside in all weathers, summer and winter, in wind and rain. A fellow vender got a

---

[7]Carmen Dinan, writing of young professional women in Ghana, explains similar circumstances: 'Traditionally, it would seem that the sexual act was regarded as a service and sexual ethics seem to have operated according to the same ethical principles that regulated other services: they were based on reciprocity. In the traditional courtship system a man exchanged valued gifts in return for sexual services' (Dinan, 1983: 353).

shop and Rachel was very envious. Her husband, Paul, helped with savings from his wages to put up the capital they needed to obtain the shop she dreamed of, and Rachel contributed profits from her street trading and her import–export trade to Congo-Kinshasa.

Some traders start with very little capital. For instance, the *sapeurs* come to Paris with very little money. They may get some money from kin but are more likely to steal clothing in department stores and then sell it in the cafés and streets of Château Rouge. With the proceeds, they buy the fashionable designer-name clothes they want to wear, as well as clothing to export to Kinshasa or Brazzaville to finance their lifestyle. They can sell clothes back home for twice or more what they pay for them. Personal contacts with customs officials or the personnel of shipping companies are important for keeping down costs in this trade. The contact person may be paid some money, though much less than the customs duties; he may be done a favour, or the trader may do a favour which is owed by the contact person to someone else. *Sapeurs* may start up in trade in this way, accumulate capital and then continue as traders. Some get their initial capital by pulling off a coup in the drug trade. After a few years of trading, some *sapeurs* return home with the money they have acquired and settle down. In 1992, one such young man was managing a garage in Brazzaville and owned three taxis.

The example of the *sapeurs*, however, shows that social capital is more important for traders than monetary capital. Once an enterprise is started, networks of personal ties are essential for obtaining and keeping customers and getting an edge in the competition with others in the same line of business. Here, however, the traders primarily draw on ties other than kinship.

Getting Customers and Beating the Competition
The connections which help one to get customers are primarily based on bonds of nationality, of religion and of acquaintance and friendship forged in neighbourhood or workplace or at social events.

Rachel (p. 113–14 above) sells a lot of the fish and vegetables in her shop to street traders. She has connections with them from previously working among them, and they are loyal customers. The shop is small and it is hard for her to survive in competition with larger, Asian-owned shops, which stock a wider range of goods. The shelves of Rachel's shop are stacked with tins of pilchards, corned beef, peas, tomato paste and tomatoes; peanut butter; sodas, beer and mineral water; palm oil (canned and bottled), peanut and sunflower oil; rice, manioc flour and dried beans. There are bins below the shelves for manioc and salt and smoked fish. She also has crates of African vegetables, such as manioc leaves, hot peppers and okra; kola nuts imported from Côte d'Ivoire; long packets of stalks and leaves for making an aromatic tea; and plastic bags of dried caterpillars or ground peanuts. She has a large freezer, a cash till, a weighing machine, a calculator and a table-model pay telephone, which is in use much of the time.

The shop is often crowded with people, who come in not just to buy but to gossip, exchange news and generally socialize with others whom they know. The couple belong to the Kimbanguist Church[8] and Rachel emphasized that being a Kimbanguist helped her to get customers, because, as she put it, she is *'dans un milieu'*. She said: 'When Kimbanguists are in a foreign country and know that one of them has opened a shop, they all come.' A Congolese owner of a similar shop down the street spoke with envy of Rachel's Kimbanguist clientele. Rachel's husband, however, downplayed the importance of their Kimbanguist customers and emphasized the importance of their compatriots from Congo-Kinshasa. But he did mention the importance for them of non-Congolese Kimbanguists as customers, specifically from Angola, France, Gabon and the Central African Republic. When they moved in, they got help from fellow Kimbanguists, who helped Paul to build the new shelves for the canned and dry goods. Were it not for customers who come faithfully because of personal connections, Rachel and Paul's shop would not be able to survive.

Annette, owner of a beauty salon in Matongue, Brussels, has a steady clientele of customers, who are like friends. They drop in and, if they have money, they buy and, if not, they sometimes take things and pay later. 'The better you know your customers, the more you can sell.' She will ask a slightly lower rate from her regular customers when she does their hair (250 BF rather than 350 BF).[9] Her loyal customers will pass by other shops selling the same things and come straight to her. When they came for the first time, she would show them things and explain the prices. Finding her sympathetic and helpful, they returned and she would welcome them and show she was pleased to see them. 'Your customers get attached to you as a person,' she says. 'If they don't find you in the shop and then meet you in the street, they will say they went to find you, but because you weren't there they did not think of buying.'

When Véronique took up unlicensed import trade in Paris in 1992, her customers were made up of her acquaintances. She sold shoes, hats and *pagnes* at the houses of people she knew in the city. Charles, however, who also does such trade, sells from his house, advertising his goods by word of mouth: 'I can make appointments at home and thus avoid the police.' He also buys on commission, taking orders before he goes on buying trips to Italy, Holland or Spain. When he returns, he telephones and the customer comes to his house. If they do not like what he has bought, they are not obligated to buy. He then sells the goods by hawking them around the cafés, bars and stores of the Château Rouge neighbourhood.

---

[8]The church founded by Simon Kimbangu, the prophet, a Baptist catechist who broke away from the mission church in the colonial period. The Kimbanguist Church is now a member of the World Council of Churches and the fastest-growing Christian church in Africa.
[9]The rate of exchange in 1994 was 34.29 Belgian francs (BF) = US$ 1.00.

African solidarity does not seem to be a factor in attracting customers. A Congolese shopkeeper, in Lille, selling African foodstuffs thought when she opened her shop that all the local Africans would come to her rather than to the Chinese-owned shop down the street, out of a sense of pan-African solidarity. But they do not do so; some Congolese do come and are her loyal customers, but some, along with other Africans, continue to go to the Chinese.

Participation in social events, such as end of mourning ceremonies, parties, weddings and attendance at the stadiums, are an important means of establishing and maintaining the personal contacts on which these traders are dependent for finding their customers. Such social events are also places where one's presence is a form of the ostentatious behaviour we discuss in the next chapter: it is necessary to be there to prove that you are a part of the social world as well as to make business connections.

For the end of mourning ceremony, a requiem mass is held in church twenty-five days after the funeral, followed by a meal in the church hall for as many as 250 people or more. The church permits this gathering to be held on church premises though it is not primarily a religious event. In this way, the church plays a part in structuring the social life of these immigrants.

Printed invitations are sent out in the names of the group of brothers and sisters of the deceased and of their spouses. Many invitations are issued and people are invited to bring friends; this event is a more public one than other parties and celebrations. The women of the family put on an elaborate meal, each helping to prepare different dishes. It will include grilled chicken, salt fish, fritters (making them involves a great deal of work) and an abundance of beer and whisky. The whole family contributes money: the minimal cost of such an occasion is likely to be 5,000 FF.[10]

The people who put on such events in Paris will be middle-class with good jobs and residence status. Prestige is bestowed by guests who are well placed socially, but those sent formal invitations will include some of the *gens des circuits*, the young adventurers. These young traders will attend but are expected to conform to the appropriate dress and behaviour. At these events, they meet people, renew acquaintances and publicize the services they can supply.

---

[10]These ceremonies recall the celebrations in rural traditional society called *malaki*, which reinforced relations of kinship and alliance. They were held during the dry season, typically set in motion by the end of mourning for an important person. Written invitations were issued (Balandier, 1963: 347–8). In the past, people did not change their clothes during the mourning period. At the end of it, they would wash, dress in clean clothes and return to the activities of everyday life. These *malaki* ceremonies displayed wealth through elaborate feasts and competitive gift-giving (Ibid.: 511). Many urban dwellers would return to the village to take part in this event. In Paris today, written invitations are likewise issued. People will dress elaborately for the occasion, and women will buy new outfits specially for it, an urban consumption element that has been added to the traditional ones.

In dealing with their customers, traders find that they have to give credit: it is too difficult for them to sell their goods without doing so. Yet they are always wary about giving it because of the problem of default. It is difficult to get people to pay and trying to collect debts can waste a lot of time. This problem raises the whole issue of trust.

Credit: 'Who Can be Trusted?'
'Familiarity is an unavoidable fact of life; trust is a solution for specific problems of risk' (Luhmann, 1988: 95). Abner Cohen's study of Hausa traders first showed the importance of trust in trade. Keith Hart shows how it works in his description of Frafra migrants in Accra who are 'faced with the need to build economic relations from scratch in a world lacking both orderly state regulation and the segmentary political structure of their customary society' (Hart, 1988: 178). In such situations, he points out, economic life depends heavily on finding complementary or shared interests which can make short- and medium-term commercial agreements self-reinforcing and which depend on trust generated by shared experience and mutual knowledge in relationships entered into by choice rather than by status obligation. Trust 'is located in the no man's land between status and contract' (Ibid.: 185, 188).

For these Congolese, for whom problems of risk are acute in the operations of second-economy trade, the concept of trust is expressed in the word *'confiance'*. It is comparable to *'confianza'*, as described by Larissa Lomnitz in Mexico.

> Ego feels *confianza* in alter to the extent that he perceives alter as willing and able to enter (or continue) a sustained relationship of reciprocal exchange. *Confianza* is not a static category like genealogical distance: it evolves in time according to the variable intensity of the flow of goods and services between the partners (Lomnitz, 1977: 200).

Congolese traders are obligated to give credit to those with whom they have relations of *confiance*. Paul, Rachel's husband, said emphatically that they depended on people with whom they had such *'relations'*. By this he meant people with whom they had developed a reciprocal relationship of loyalty and solidarity to render help in different ways as needed.

Shopkeepers have ways of sizing up the creditworthiness of their customers: 'A good customer is one who has a job,' says one; another says he only gives credit to privileged customers, 'responsible people' he knows well and to whom he will provide this service from time to time. (He is doing it less and less, however, because his notebook is filling up with unpaid debts.) He will also take cheques only from certain similarly favoured people. Thérèse, owner of a *nganda* and a trader, makes the same sort of assessment of clientele in whom she has *confiance*. Those 'who are responsible' are allowed credit. Véronique, when trading through the villages in Congo, said that traders assessed creditworthy customers by their age: they could count on older people not to let them down. Such customers would give orders for merchandise from Kinshasa and would gradually become regulars, who could be trusted to go without paying for as long as two weeks. When they had trouble with younger customers who would not pay two or three times running, they just abandoned collection of the debt.

But the problem can be insoluble. Later in her career, Véronique was forced to abandon her import trade to Paris from other European cities because she could not get people to pay what they owed her. Although she sold on credit only to customers whom she knew, going to their houses with her goods and picking up the money after fifteen days, she found they always had all sorts of excuses not to pay up: they had not received their allowance or had a sick child, or could only pay a little at a time. Her enterprise was not able to survive. *Confiance* can be misplaced.

But, for the *sapeurs* in particular, giving credit constitutes a kind of forced saving: they feel that if they do not have the money in hand they will not be tempted to spend it on ostentatious living. Ultimately, feelings about the cash that the traders have in hand are different from those they have about money they are owed. If they can recover a debt, they think of it as an unexpected profit: if one can get it, that is good, if not, then it's just too bad. This attitude contrasts strongly with feelings about credit in the official economy.

Some traders travel worldwide to buy the goods they sell. Here too they rely on personal connections for assistance in finding a place to stay, getting help with the language and acquiring the goods they need.

Itinerant Trade: Help in Foreign Lands
As the traders go boldly to strange countries, they need hospitality and help in buying their goods. They say: 'It is difficult when you don't know anyone: we need to help each other; we are helped and in our turn we help others.' For this help, they rely on personal connections, sometimes based on family ties, but more often on ties of ethnicity, nationality, religion and friendship from locality or workplace. In such cases, some form of balanced reciprocity is felt to be appropriate. Details from three histories of traders from Congo-Brazzaville and a fourth from Congo-Kinshasa show what this help consists of and what is given in return.

Our first case continues the history of Charles, whom we have already met in Chapters 3 and 4 and above.

> *Charles, in the process of trying to surmount the visa difficulties of getting to France from Congo-Kinshasa, goes to Cabinda in a truck. 'I was received by some Congolese who were living in a hotel. They were not friends, but they were Lari [his ethnic group], so it was easy to get to know them. They were from Pointe Noire and because we spoke the same language, they helped me to get to Luanda (in Angola). I did not*

know anyone there, but that's life. When one embarks on an adventure, one does not know what is ahead of one. I had heard there was a market in the town, where there were lots of Congolese, so I asked how to get there and found a Zaïrean woman whom I had known in Congo. She put me up for two weeks.'

Charles eventually made it to Paris and arrived in the Gare du Nord, where he had been told by a Zaïrean he would find plenty of Congolese; after a while he found some friends, one of whom put him up for a month. But he had no money to contribute to expenses and had to leave at the end of that time.

After he had been in Paris for a while, Charles began to travel to different European countries and bring back goods to sell to Central Africans in Paris, financing these trips by selling squats. His girlfriend's sister was in this trade and said that if he could find 6,000 FF she would take him to Italy and arrange everything for him. Subsequently, he expanded his trade to Spain and Holland. 'When I go to Italy or Holland, I go to people I know; in Spain I know no one and pay for a hotel. In Italy, in some towns, for example Turin, Florence and Milan, I don't pay for a hotel. In Turin, I have an aunt of one of my children's mothers [Charles is not married but has several children by different women]. I don't pay, but I take her African food obtainable in France but not in Italy. In Florence, I have a Zaïrean friend whom I got to know on a bus in Italy because he thought I was a Zaïrean. He had lived in the Bacongo area of Brazzaville. I take food to him also. I first went to Spain with a friend from my neighbourhood in Brazzaville, who told me it was profitable. In exchange I shall perhaps show him how to go to Italy.'

But, when Charles finds a close relative, he does not have to worry about any direct return for the help he receives:

In Holland, I go to my mother's brother, who is a diplomat and lives in Amsterdam. I don't give him anything because he understands that I am trying to make my living honestly, without stealing, selling drugs or being violent. I am not obliged to give things to him, it is just up to me. Sometimes I call and ask what they would like me to bring and they say they don't want anything; I just go and stay with them.

The second case gives more details from Marie's life story (pp. 85–7):

When Marie traded with West Africa, she went to Lomé and Cotonou with her sister, who had a contact in Lomé: she knew a Congolese who was living there with her brother-in-law. This woman housed them for free for two nights till they found a place to stay, for which they paid. They spoke the same language as their contact and her help was given because of ethnic solidarity. Marie and her sister remained friends with this woman and saw her on subsequent trips, giving her small gifts or an occasional meal in a restaurant, nothing specific: 'It is up to you how you reciprocate,' says Marie.

Beatrice, the airline employee (pp. 100–103), explains the difficulties of finding appropriate ways to reciprocate for help and favours.

Beatrice, on a trading trip to Los Angeles, goes to the brother of a friend she had known in Abidjan. 'The first time I went, I relied on his help, and thereafter I found a cheap hotel. In Seoul, I have two brothers-in-law. They know the language and the country; with their help I am able to buy at good prices. When I am with someone, I try to contribute. It is complicated because sometimes giving things annoys people. I sometimes bring food and leave it with people, or I propose buying some petrol. If people say not to worry, then one must find some other way to pay them back.'

The fourth case, of Véronique from Kinshasa (p. 97), specifically contrasts the balanced reciprocity appropriate to relationships that are not close with the generalized reciprocity of close ones.

Véronique, in Paris, took up trading by travelling to buy goods in London and Brussels. In London, she stayed with 'brothers' from her neighbourhood in Kinshasa, who are working in London. One of them showed her how to shop for summer shoes, pagnes and hats wholesale. She brought them African foods, which were difficult to get locally, in return for this help. In Brussels, she stayed with her sister and bought super-wax cloth. 'I brought the family some food, but in fact she was obligated to lodge me because we have the same mother and father, and this relationship has much greater value than any goods given in return for help.'

Jerome, the wholesaler from Congo-Brazzaville (p.114 above), has been able to establish personal connections with airline flight attendants, so that he does not have to travel himself to get some of his goods. He has offered various services to set up personal relations with these attendants, creating obligations that enable him to ask them to bring in the foodstuffs he imports in their baggage allowance. He told us that he had been a trader in Paris for eighteen years, knows almost all the Congolese in the city, and over this long period has established many '*relations*' (personal connections) among them. He details how he does this:

'Some people whom one asks to do something demand money in return. For myself, when I do a service for someone, I demand nothing in return because sometime I shall have need of a return service.' The first flight attendant he got to know was called Vincent. Jerome met him through

someone he had put up in his house, who had problems and needed help. Vincent asked Jerome for various small services, such as getting spare parts for cars when he had no money, and paying for them only when they arrived. Through him, Jerome got to know other airline staff and gained a reputation for being very nice. Others among them would ask him for help. He would then confide mail and money to them for his family, who would then go to great lengths to make them welcome back in Brazzaville. These flight attendants included Congolese for whom Jerome had performed other services, such as inviting them to his home and having his wife cook Congo dishes for them, after which he would drive them home. This, he said, 'made them very happy'.

These case histories all show the variation and complexity of individual strategies and the range of personal ties that are drawn upon by the traders in their trading activities and enterprises. They are able to solve by these means many of the problems of trading outside or on the margins of the law, but there is one problem that they all confront that has no very satis-factory solution: the sanctions to back up transactions based on trust are weak in the absence of either the legal and institutional support of a func-tional and predictable official economic system or the norms of religion powerfully enforced by the bonds of religious community.

Sanctions: a Contrast to West African Trade

The situation we observe in Paris contrasts strongly with that described in the studies of long-distance traders from West Africa cited in Chapter 1. Religion imposes sanctions and strict rules for these Islamic traders from West Africa, whether they are in Africa or in other continents. Nonconformity brings exclusion from both the business and the religious communities because of the ties between the two. In contrast, West Central Africans in Paris are not members of a tight-knit religious community and the sanctions they have against breaking rules and betraying trust do not threaten an individual's whole existence as do those of the West African traders.

Sanctions to compel people to pay what they owe are very weak for West Central African traders and primarily operate to damage an individual's reputation in the traders' milieu or among the immigrant population in Paris. In traditional society in the past, betrayal of trust was penalized by being shamed in the village community or by the action of the family or local group. But in urban society this is not so easily the case. Traders say resignedly that losses are all part of their occupational risks, and they make the mark-up on their goods high enough to enable them to absorb small ones.

In fact, the debtor in this system is seen to be in the stronger position and the slightest pretext will serve to put off repayment: pressure of some sort has to be exerted or the loan will go unrepaid. The moral obligation to repay debt is there but it is not strongly felt. However, a sort of parallel system of justice does exist in this milieu, operating outside or on the margins of the law, as reported by our informants and by Vangu Ngimbi (1996), in which there are explicit rules about repayment of debts and means for sanctions to enforce them.

In this parallel system, a strict rule in the collection of debt is that creditors must not exercise any kind of physical force themselves: if they do so, the debt is considered to be cancelled.[11] The first strategy to enforce repayment of a debt is a non-violent one, known as *'faire une cérémonie de deuil pour son argent'* (putting on a mourning ceremony for one's money). It consists of going to the debtor's residence and making a fuss, and complaining in public about the debt you are owed, so that everyone hears about it. An extension of this strategy is to speak of it also to people who know the person involved. This invokes the sanction of damaging an individual's reputation and honour.[12]

If this strategy fails in Paris, creditors may purchase violent enforcement, even though they may not use it themselves. The next step is to enlist the help of a 'strongman' within their group of associates or friends. Such a one can use force and beat up the debtor without its resulting in cancellation of the debt. He must, however, be paid for this service and will therefore only be called upon in cases of debts of 400–500 FF or more. The strongman has his reputation to preserve and always manages somehow to get the money back. Sometimes, if the creditor is very angry he will motivate the strongman by telling him that when he gets the money he can keep it. The strongman employs various approaches: he may fight with the debtor every time he sees him, he may harass him at his home every day (though for this he needs to live nearby), or he may telephone him continually, even using the ruse of getting a friend to do it for him, and then picking up the receiver himself.

Vangu Ngimbi reports that, if the debtor cannot pay when confronted by the strongman, he must hand over goods of the equivalent value to the money he owes, such as furniture, jewellery, television, hi-fi or other appliances (Vangu Ngimbi, 1996: 132). One *nganda* owner that we visited had a large television set that she had acquired as compensation for an unpaid debt.

Nganda owners threaten that, if people do not pay for their drinks, they will not serve them again. One owner, Thérèse, says that she has rules and principles that customers must respect. She has no regular bouncers, but one of her frequent customers is a big, tough fellow and he will sometimes threaten to beat up people who do not pay. She tries to avoid altercations,

---

[11]This is an interesting contrast to the forceful debt collection by loan sharks in the United States!
[12]In Congo-Brazzaville, women in particular actually weep and cry loudly outside a debtor's house.

however: 'Why ruin an evening because of one person? I have losses that I have to make up for. Commerce is like that and the other customers understand.' There is not much she can do, and she is philosophical about it.

To sum up, we can concur that:

> When people are not tied by multiple ties and do not engage together in many activities, the range and certainty of exchanges are reduced. The value of esteem and the force of social approval are the greater when they are visible to others and when they occur in situations in which the members are to some degree constantly involved. (Roberts, 1973: 172)

The latter is the case in the Islamic religious communities of West African traders, but the former in the milieu of West Central African traders.

Pressures for Redistribution

Concepts from the cosmology and ways of thinking of some of the different ethnic groups of these two Congolese nations work powerfully today to redistribute wealth within the extended families of these traders. One of these concepts is *lusolo*, namely the idea that success in commerce is a gift that is inherited in the family and that the wealth it brings belongs to the family and should be shared among them. Another is the belief in witchcraft (*kundu* in Congo-Brazzaville, or *ndoki* in Kikongo and Lingala in both countries) and the fear of misfortune caused by the witchcraft exercised by close kin who are jealous of one's success in life and of any perceived accumulation of wealth.

Lusolo *and the Obligations of Kinship*
We first learned about *lusolo* when a Kongo woman introduced her account of how she got into trade by explaining that the ability to be successful in commerce was a gift that was inherited, called *lusolo*. Thereafter, we always asked people what this term meant to them. Among the Bangala, one explained, *lusolo* is thought of as '*bongo ya famille*' (family money). Another trader from Kinshasa, whose ethnic group was the Mbunza of Upper Zaïre, called it *bokumu*. Agreement was general that the money accumulated through this gift was family money and should be used to take care of the family. One even described it as a family asset: it was the gift of being good at business, and the money earned as a result counted as part of the family's wealth. This belief seemed to be widespread; it was not, however, universal. Some people had never heard of it; others did not know of the term but agreed with the idea; others clearly thought when we asked about it that we were referring to the use of magical objects and witchcraft and said firmly they did not subscribe to such ideas.

The beliefs surrounding the concept of *lusolo* appear to serve as a sanction to ensure the redistribution of wealth within the family. A description by a young male trader provides the details of how this works.

> *My mother and sister have* lusolo. *It is a gift of the family, passed on by a senior member. If the gift is properly used, it brings wealth: a person who has it can rapidly sell whatever goods he has. The wealth earned is for the individual because they are investing their own money, but it is also necessary to please the family, concern yourself with their needs, give them food. If I do not give in this way, the* lusolo *will leave me, because it is a gift from the family. It must be preserved and managed well. Otherwise, it will move through the family until it finds someone who can use it or exploit it better. But it can also stay away altogether.*

One who has *lusolo* but works for her/himself and keeps the profits away from the family offends the ancestors. One of the traders in the histories given below did this and it was said to have caused her to become ill.

Lusolo is inherited. It is a substance similar to *kundu*, the substance found in the abdomen of witches. It is not, however, the same thing as *kundu*, which gives witches the power to harm. Instead it brings happiness and wealth.[13] It also brings the power to dominate people, either through politics or through success in commerce. Among the Vili of Loango in Congo-Kinshasa, *lusolo* is thought to take the form of an actual substance like a precious stone. Those who have the gift of four eyes (who can see things in the other world, which is in Kongo thought the world of the dead, of the ancestors) can see *lusolo* in others.

Proof that one has this gift is to be successful in commerce. When the gift is inherited it may jump a generation, remaining meantime in the grave of the original holder. Traditionally, the term referred to the wealth of the matrilineage, which was controlled by the head of the lineage, the maternal uncle, and passed down in the matrilineal line. The conflict inherent in matrilineal systems, arising from the claims upon a man of his sister's children versus those of his own, is reflected in an account given to us concerning a particular instance of the inheritance of *lusolo*. The complex pathway of this particular example was related in the tale of Jerome, the wholesaler in the interview in the hotel lobby described at the beginning of the book (Figure 5.1 shows the relationships involved).

---

[13]Wyatt MacGaffey informs us that the *lu* prefix is appropriate to an abstraction, as for 'gift' or 'talent', for example. Such a talent would be at least similar to a 'money *kundu*', i.e. a witchcraft capacity for making money. *Lusolo* is also the word for a long red glass bead employed in some *minkisi* (charms). This explanation fits with some of our informants' reactions to *lusolo* as implying witchcraft.

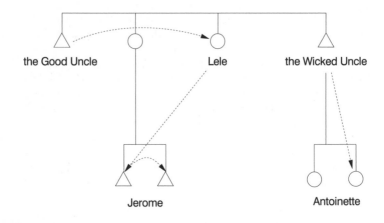

Figure 5.1   Disputed paths for inheritance of *lusolo*

How Lusolo Came to Jerome the Wholesaler. '*Everywhere I go, people tell me that I have* lusolo. *If you like, you can call it luck. My maternal uncle* [henceforth referred to as the Good Uncle] *had money, but jealous people bewitched him because he had too much of it* [i.e. he was working too much for himself]. *One day he left for Kinshasa in a canoe to sell his goods and buy others to bring back to sell in Brazzaville; the canoe capsized and, of the four people in it, my uncle's body was never found. According to tradition this meant that the witches were keeping him in their grotto, telling him that he was too proud and boastful and was now in their power. Maybe that is indeed what happened. We have another uncle* [hereafter referred to as the Wicked Uncle], *who died in 1972. He had* kundu. *He did not want us, his matrilineal heirs, to be able to benefit from his* lusolo, *even though our Good Uncle had told him he should not give it to his children but to his sister's sons. However, the Good Uncle* [he had drowned but in Kongo cosmology the dead continue to intervene in the affairs of the living] *wanted it to pass down the maternal line. A* nganga [ritual expert] *came to my elder brother and said: "You have this luck hanging over you, can't you do something?" – "But what can I do?" – "You have* lusolo *in your family. Is there someone older than you?" My brother mentioned his mother's younger sister* [Lele], *who was a strong and courageous woman. They all left for Makana, where the* nganga *asked for a demijohn of water. He wanted to get back the* lusolo, *which had gone with the Wicked Uncle when he died, and he made a little hole in the earth with his hand and asked us to pour the contents of the demijohn into it. The water all disappeared. The Good*

Uncle asked from the other side "Who is there?" The nganga *told my aunt to answer and she said her name, Lele. "Good," said the uncle, "I thought that it was Antoinette (the Wicked Uncle's daughter) and I couldn't give it to her because it is the luck of the matrilineage and belongs to your oldest nephew, so take it." The* nganga *drew back his hand, in which there was a little coin with a hole in it. It was an old coin, known as* meya *or* ndichu.' *This coin was given to Jerome's brother: he was told to buy a* nbangu *(calabash) and cover it with a* nkampa *(the red scarf that was the badge of office of a traditional chief). But he was not a serious businessman and his transport enterprise failed, despite help from Jerome. 'At this moment, the gift (the* lusolo*) came to me, because it was seen that I helped people and that I made money.'*

In another case, two *mpangi* (term for brother, sister or maternal or paternal classificatory sibling of the same generation) named Monique and Marie had fallen out. Marie (pp. 85–7) said that Monique refused to work with her in a trading partnership because she felt there could not be two with the gift of *lusolo* in one generation of a family (see Figure 5.2).

Marie's maternal grandmother was in trade, selling palm oil to the European oil companies. Marie's mother was not a trader but the gift reappeared in Marie. Her mpangi, *Monique, who was older than she was, took up trade also. 'Thereafter, she said, there were two of us with* lusolo *in the same family and we were in competition.' Monique took up the travelling trade between Brazzaville and Lomé in Togo and*

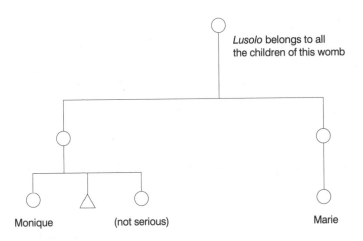

Figure 5.2 Dispute over *lusolo*

Cotonou in Benin, buying pagnes and selling them wholesale back in Brazzaville. After Marie went to France, Monique no longer felt she was in competition for lusolo, but she became proud and distant and paid no attention to the needs of the family. 'The ancestors became angry', said Marie, 'because when one receives lusolo one must always think of the family and help them'. Monique's friends entered the trade and she lost her monopoly. Her affairs no longer prospered and she fell sick.

Kongo beliefs about *lusolo* thus motivate redistribution of personal wealth within the family, an obligation that is sanctioned by fears of witchcraft. These beliefs work to support the obligations of kinship and to sustain the dispersed kin networks of today's global economy.

Witchcraft: 'People Have Died From Sending Parcels Only to Their Mothers'
This statement was part of Charles's explanation of why he does not send money or goods home to his mother:

'When our parents receive things from us, they tell everyone and we are exposed to the jealousies of the others.' Charles knows his mother needs money, but he says that if he does not also send it to his mother's sister there will be a problem: he fears her witchcraft against him. She does not have any children in France and would be jealous. 'I could only send to my mother if my mother's sister also has someone who is sending her money.' Charles's fear of death from illness caused by the witchcraft of jealous relatives, however, is directed at the generation above him, since he does send parcels, clothes and money home for his children.

Some scholars are pointing out how, as nation states have Africanized throughout the continent, the old association between power and the occult is being re-established (Rowlands and Warnier, 1988; Fisiy and Geschiere, 1991). But it seems that beliefs in witchcraft operate not only as a resource for the powerful but also as a weapon of the weak against new forms of inequality (Geschiere, 1995: 24–5).[14] This new inequality is perceived to come about as successful kin become wealthy and middle-class, but fail to share and redistribute their wealth. The levelling implications of sorcery are often balanced by its accumulative implications and the same discourse serves also to protect or to reinforce the accumulation of wealth and power.

---

[14]In Cameroon, Geschiere observed that local government officials regularly launched long and furious attacks on witchcraft, particularly if it seemed to be directed against government projects or members of the elite (Geschiere, 1986: 328).

It is high time that anthropologists began to show ... that the stereotype of sorcery discourses as 'traditional' residues, by definition opposed to change, is highly one-sided and blocks real insight into the impact of these discourses on politico-economic development. (Fisiy and Geschiere, 1991: 253)

Sorcery discourses can also be seen as the way people construe a link between what happens at local and global levels. These discourses are, in many parts of Africa, an idiom in which people try to comprehend the articulation between what goes on in the household and developments taking place in a wider context (Ibid.: 271).

Among the Kongo, those living in the village are believed to be closer to the powers of the other world: they are near the cemetery and the graves of the lineage ancestors, which gives them power over those in town. Jean La Fontaine found that in 1962 in Léopoldville (now Kinshasa) village kin were often suspected of witchcraft, reflecting the existence of new tensions with urbanization. Rural kin were said to be jealous of the wealth they assumed their kin in town were amassing, and their ill-will caused misfortune. In one typical case, a woman was so worried by this hostility that she did not dare to carry out plans to expand her business (La Fontaine, 1970: 185).[15] Those living in the country are likewise seen as more powerful in this respect than those far away in France.

As Charles's comment shows, the jealous feelings directed at those kin who have attained wealth and other good fortune are greatly feared. Witchcraft in Kongo society is indubitably '*le côté noir de la parenté*' (the dark side of kinship) (Geschiere, 1995: 18), though this is by no means universal, since some societies do not believe kin can bewitch each other.

In Brazzaville, accusations of witchcraft seem to reflect an attempt to combat inequalities. With the economic crisis, many people are unable to find work in the city. Witchcraft accusations there do not seem to be diminishing but rather to be on the increase. Those outside the norm, such as the rich, are particularly susceptible to accusations. A study of small businesses in Brazzaville in the period 1968–71 found that any entrepreneur who was particularly intelligent, wealthy or successful was likely to be subject to accusations of witchcraft. In the majority of cases, entrepreneurs considered themselves to have been bewitched by their maternal kin (Devauges, 1977: 114, 132). In the mid-1980s, suspected witches were sometimes burnt to death; in the 1990s, they are stabbed.

---

[15]A study of the evolution of traditional solidarity among the Ntomba and Basengele of Lake Mai-Ndombe in rural and urban areas in Kwilu, east of Kinshasa, details the way the fear of witchcraft and cursing by the mother, father and maternal uncle motivates sharing of material wealth and income from productive activities, including salaries. '*La crainte des sanctions est un moteur puissant qui pousse chaque member de la société à justifier sa conduite et à la rendre irréprochable*' (The fear of these sanctions is a powerful motor pushing each member of the society to justify his conduct and make it irreproachable) (Mpase Nselenge Mpeti, 1974: 34).

In the 1990s, the elders of urban neighbourhoods are becoming more feared for their powers of witchcraft than are lineage elders in the village. They supposedly bewitch people by means of witchcraft mosquitoes, which they are said to excrete. If we regard witchcraft as a discourse, the subject-matter of which changes over time, it appears, in this instance, to be a way of talking about the decline of the state, since in recent years there has been a noticeable increase in mosquitoes because preventive eradication measures are no longer carried out.

In the following case history, fear of witchcraft by kin jealous of his success back in Congo-Brazzaville afflicts Jerome, the wholesaler in Paris.

> *Jerome has four children of his own and takes care of two of the children of his older brothers. 'I have done it because traditionally, if you provide only for your own children and they succeed in school, others are jealous. Thus I have been obliged to take on the two children of my brothers.'*[16] *Although his brothers wasted the money he gave them that was intended for investment in the family business and for sharing the proceeds, he says, 'There is no way to get the money back. If I complained, in traditional fashion they would wish me ill. I am thus obliged to submit. When one has dealings in the family, it is necessary to be on the lookout, otherwise one will be struck down by* kundu. *I suffer with my right hand and have trouble with my kidneys because I am no longer on good terms with my family. You see why it is that I feel compelled to return home to help them?'*

Jerome's brothers are older than he is, which makes them mystically more powerful. In addition, they live in Brazzaville and are thus closer to the village and the ancestors and so to the powers of the other world. He therefore feels that he dare not express his anger against them or accuse them of causing his illness. Here fear of witchcraft is acting as a pressure for the redistribution of his wealth.

Resentment of success is evident again in witchcraft accusations levelled against Beatrice, the trader who uses incidental benefits from her airline job to build up her international trading enterprise.

> *Beatrice has an older sister who is not doing well. She works in the tax office of the Ministry of Finance in Brazzaville, but she failed at school and has not managed to get together the money to buy a building plot in town: both things considered to be indications of social failure. Beatrice, the sophisticated traveller and international trader, exhibits all the signs of success in her life. The sister's jealousy of Beatrice is*

---

[16]Balandier reports that a son in town with a good income was expected to take charge progressively of each of his younger brothers (Balandier, 1985: 127). Here Jerome feels this obligation extends to his brothers' children.

expressed in accusations of witchcraft, specifically that she eats human flesh. This sister levels the same accusation against their older brother, a successful professional man with a job as a director in the tax office.

These and other case histories in this chapter show that these traders are indeed pushed to redistribute their wealth, but equally some histories show that their kin are pushed to help them accumulate it. This is a culturally determined way of functioning in today's economic situation, a feature of background and context that is a significant factor in the forms of capitalism arising in Africa today.

We shall end this chapter by setting the traders' activities in the wider context of the global culture and economy. Their family networks have become a global cultural phenomenon as they have developed and taken on a new form with the revolution in transportation and communications; their reliance on personal ties has interesting parallels historically as well as in some highly developed sectors of the world economy today.

Global Culture: the Internationalization of the Family and Personal Relations in Economic Transactions

Anthropologists emphasize the need today to study the transnational socio-cultural systems created by globalization. The traders' use of family ties is evidence of the new developments in kinship discussed in the recent literature. Dispersed kin networks in different countries are not new, but today's global system allows primary kin who are dispersed across vast distances to be in closer communication and to have the possibility of travelling back and forth much more rapidly and frequently than in the past. Given these circumstances, the most meaningful social ties may not be those of the local kin group but rather those of the geographically dispersed networks that have brought about what is being called 'the internationalization of the family' (Sutton, 1987; Ho, 1993).

The classic studies of Meyer Fortes (1949) and Jack Goody (1962) have shown the variations in household structure over time according to the developmental cycle of the domestic group (a more precise term than 'family'). A new dimension is added to the alternatives available at the different stages of development of such groups with this internationalization of close kin. Tracing the location of close kin dispersed across continents to see how the networks of ties between them are activated, in what circumstances and for what purposes is as likely to reflect the realities of kinship in the global system as constructing household studies of the co-resident domestic units drawing on a common resource pool that are conventionally favoured as units of analysis.

Studies from all over the world support this view. For example, Christine Ho describes the way Caribbean women are 'embedded in networks of exchange and mutual support based on kinship, as kinship is organized along the network principle rather than nucleated corporate groups, in contrast to household forms like the nuclear family with stable boundaries' (Ho, 1993: 34). Lilian Trager emphasizes that, in the Philippines, women's migration and urban economic activities need to be seen in terms of family strategies that cross geographical boundaries (Trager, 1984: 1265). In the United States, Rhoda Halperin finds in north-eastern Kentucky that the unit of economic activity is a family network dispersed over the whole region (Halperin, 1990: 21).

The traders of our study have the same expectations of kin overseas as they have of them back home. The history of migration commonly shows the progression of an initial move from rural to urban areas, and then migration to other countries and other continents. Throughout Africa, urban kin have provided support and assistance for rural migrants, who expect to be received by a relative or co-villager and to be able to stay with them on arrival in town (Gugler, 1975: 296–7). In Congo-Kinshasa, dispersed kin united rural and urban areas into single social fields before and after independence, within which the scale of contributions from urban to rural kin was massive (Lux, 1971, 1972; MacGaffey, 1983; Balandier, 1985). The same obligations hold among kin dispersed overseas. In many parts of the world, the remittances of overseas migrants have been a source of support for family remaining behind in the home country. In these ways, people are using family forms of insurance and support to cope with the costs of economic changes (Guyer, 1988: 161). More recently, the process has intensified; what is new is that making use of kin overseas is becoming an essential strategy for survival and improving life for some populations. This internationalization of the family is a cultural form emerging as the globalization process intensifies. These international networks of close kin function as economic units. Their dispersal enables them not only to survive but sometimes also to improve individual chances for social mobility that would be unattainable by remaining concentrated in one locality.

Pnina Werbner comments that expressing relations through gifting and hosting objectifies morally binding relations and highlights the ethnic distinctiveness of a group. It also allows for transactions to be initiated beyond culturally established boundaries.

> The interhousehold domain in which such gifting occurs is, in a sense, the stronghold of ethnic consciousness since it embraces almost every member of the group. This domain is perpetuated and reproduced through the extension of personal gifts and services, and through hosting and feasting on domestically important occasions. (Werbner, 1990: 283)

To turn now to personal relations, the case histories of this chapter show that they serve to create order in a situation of disorder, making international trade a possibility for these Congolese traders. As has been shown in studies of ethnic trading systems, the social norms of particularistic exchange relations operate as the equivalent of contract law for deterring traders from breach of contract; they function as institutions of private ordering (Landa, 1994: 28–9). 'Under conditions of contract uncertainty, kinship/ethnic status ... is a valuable intangible asset for a potential trading partner', as the code of ethics of such relations functions to deter breach of contract (Ibid.: 107–8). However, the general view that such relations are only of significance in underdeveloped economies where a legal framework is lacking, that particularistic networks based on mutual trust will eventually be replaced by impersonal exchange based on contract (Ibid.: 112–13), or that trade diasporas will inevitably work themselves out of business (Curtin, 1984: 4) is open to challenge.

James Carrier has pointed out that the commodity system has never been as impersonal as we tend to think: in the West people bought and sold well into the twentieth century in the context of enduring personal relationships of trust. Furthermore, commodity relations do not dominate in the West to the extent that is usually assumed. To represent them as doing so 'is essentialistic and is likely to hide as much as it reveals'. Carrier, after a discussion of Edward Said's Orientalism (Western images of the Orient) and then of Occidentalism (images of the West by Westerners), and their essentialistic renderings, asserts that such a categorization of Western capitalist society is inaccurate and thus cannot realistically be contrasted with societies which have similarly been essentialized by Mauss as having the gift as the focus of all their institutions (Carrier, 1992: 200–2).

Francis Fukuyama writes of the decline of trust and sociability in the United States, and its important implications for the economy. He considers that this liberal democracy is not entirely 'modern' and that:

> If the institutions of democracy and capitalism are to work properly, they must coexist with certain premodern cultural habits that ensure their proper functioning. Law, contract, and economic rationality provide a necessary but not sufficient basis for both the stability and prosperity of postindustrial societies; they must as well be leavened with reciprocity, moral obligation, duty toward community, and trust, which are based in habit rather than rational calculation. The latter are not anachronisms in a modern society but rather the sine qua non of the latter's success. (Fukuyama, 1995: 11)

Several studies have also shown the importance of the trust engendered by personal relations in other countries of the developed world. For example, kinship and marriage, and social club membership ties, formed the basis of personal networks in the operation of the financial institutions of the City of London (Lupton and Wilson, 1959). Also we find that there are many instances in which large Western companies engage in international trade transactions that do not involve money. Particularly in trade between the West and Eastern Europe and the developing countries, trading relations may be formed between several countries to carry out transactions in which very little money changes hands. Instead, goods and services are bartered according to a variety of reciprocal arrangements. Barter specialists exist to initiate and broker such arrangements (Weigand, 1977). The brokers' capital consists essentially of their networks of communication channels (Boissevain, 1974: 158). Barter in the 1990s is on the increase: it is estimated to amount to $12 billion in the United States alone. Internationally it is a response to the increasing barriers to international trade and finance, and it links the exchange of commodities between very different social, technological and institutional circumstances (Appadurai, 1986: 10).

Then again, we learn that moralized trading relationships of mutual goodwill were prevalent in Japan's modern economy, where manufacturing firms and their suppliers often considered themselves to be bound by durable obligations. Goodwill implies feelings of friendship and a diffuse personal obligation between those carrying out recurring contractual economic exchanges. Large Japanese enterprise groups formed networks of preferential, stable, obligated, bilateral trading relationships, that is, networks of relational contracting. These networks, in fact, promoted efficiency and may have been a reason why Japan experienced a better growth for a while than the rest of the world. The loss of allocative efficiency in relational contracting is more than outweighed by countervailing forces which enhance the ability to plan and programme: the security of these relations encourages investment in supplier firms; trust makes for a more rapid flow of information; and an emphasis on quality is a by-product of a sense of mutual obligation (Dore, 1983: 463–75). The Japanese are not unique: relational contracting can also be found in the United States, in Britain (Ibid.: 476–8) and in France, where personal relations are stressed in informal networks of subcontracting in some industries, and partnership entails a set of normative rules determining which behaviour is permissible and which violates trust (Lorenz, 1988: 206–8).

Thus the traders' reliance on personal relations as they struggle to overcome the problems of institutional decay and state oppression is not unique to them for participation in the modern global economy. The use of personal relations also features in the operation of some large capitalist enterprises and in trading relations between certain nation states. This apparently increasingly widespread usage seems to be another emergent global cultural form.

6

**To Survive
& Shine**

Two Oppositional
Cultures

> Cultural meanings are not free-floating and disembodied, but are
> implicated in systems of power relations. (Kondo, 1990: 231)

In the preceding three chapters, we have examined the trade and its
commodities and their uses; the contesting of boundaries of different
kinds in order to find opportunities for profit; and the ways in which this
extra-legal international commerce is organized. The traders whose life
histories have revealed the details of these processes come from the ranks
of the socially marginalized. They are people who refuse to accept
passively the constraints imposed on their lives, but instead actively
engage with them through activities outside the law, thus resisting their
exclusion from the opportunity to fulfil their ambition or to better their
lives. In this chapter, we focus primarily on a specific sub-category of such
people, the *sapeurs*, and on their particular form of resistance through the
creation of an oppositional, counter-hegemonic culture. Within this
culture, they assert their identity and compete for status according to their
own system of values. In this process, they exclude those who are part of
the system that has excluded them.

We shall begin with a description of *la Sape* and how it has developed,
and then of *nganda*, one of the principal arenas for the ostentatious
display and competition of the *sapeurs*. We find that their trade and their
lifestyle, with their performances in *nganda*, provide a new example of
the 'tournaments of value' identified by Arjun Appadurai (1986) as spectacular events of ostentatious display used in certain societies to construct
individual reputation and status. We find the ideas of James Scott (1985,
1990) on everyday resistance to authority rather than opposing it through
organized rebellion, and on the hidden transcripts the dominated oppose
to the official transcripts of the powerful, to be illuminating for the
analysis of our traders' life histories. The chapter ends with the traders'

aims and aspirations for investing the wealth they accumulate as they resist an oppressive system that would forbid them opportunity to improve their lives. Data from the case histories indicate, however, that the odds against fulfilling their hopes and dreams are substantial in the present political and economic conjuncture.

La Sape

'Forget that commodities are good for eating, clothing, and shelter; forget their usefulness and try instead the idea that commodities are good for thinking; treat them as a nonverbal medium for the human creative faculty' (Douglas and Isherwood, 1979: 62). This idea applies particularly well to the phenomenon known as *la Sape*.

La Sape[1] stands for the *Société des Ambianceurs et Personnes Elégantes* (The Society of Ambiance Creators and Elegant People). *Se saper* means to dress elegantly in French. The form of *la Sape* has changed in every decade since it began. The cult of elegance originated in the 1950s, when a number of youth clubs appeared in Brazzaville, primarily in the Bacongo quarter, which was dominated by the Kongo people. The identity of these young people was tied to Western films and the images of Paris life diffused through the media and café life. These groups came to be known as *existentialistes* or *existos* because of their identification with the dominant lifestyle, mood and clothes fashions of postwar Paris. The clubs competed for status through their clothing, but they declined in the 1960s. In 1968, the Kongo were displaced when the Mbochi seized power in a military coup (Gandoulou, 1984: 32–9; Friedman, 1990: 113–15).

In the late 1960s and early 1970s, another wave of fashionable dressing occurred among groups from Bacongo, which became *la Sape*. This movement emerged among unemployed young people who had been displaced politically and ideologically, and who formed themselves into clubs (Gandoulou, 1984: 39–52). They contrasted with the *existos*, who had been employed, married men. These young people competed through the wearing of French designer brand-name clothing to achieve the position of a *Grand* or Great Man. This practice led them to migrate to France in order to acquire these clothes, which they then paraded ostentatiously in Paris and Brazzaville.

Few of the youth in Brazzaville who began this popular movement had enough money to support its lifestyle, so at first they mostly borrowed the clothes from those wealthy enough to own them, rather than purchasing them themselves. They called this practice *la lutte* (the struggle). Struggling (*lutter*) described the social energy expended in all that one had

---

[1]This section draws on Justin-Daniel Gandoulou, 1984, *passim*; Jean-Daniel Gandoulou, 1989a and b; and Friedman, 1992, *passim*. See also Bazenguissa-Ganga, 1997: 327–32.

to do to borrow a luxury clothing item. This activity was called *la mine* or *miner* (to mine), meaning to search for a precious good. Here again we find the concepts of the gold and diamond diggers, for whom migration is the equivalent of *casser la pierre* (breaking rocks) in order to find gold or diamonds. Unlike purchases, *la mine* requires the actors to activate a network of acquaintances, in which social relationships are reinforced by these continual loans. *La mine* was thus the most common means of temporarily changing one's appearance by wearing designer clothing in the home country. The *lutteurs* were only interested in clothes imported from Europe, and especially from France. They were bought in the shops of downtown Brazzaville, particularly at Tissu KM, where only the '*grands messieurs*' ('great men' who are high-ranking civil servants or executives of private enterprises) shopped for clothes.

The first *lutteurs* to migrate to Paris to acquire these designer-name clothes themselves did so in the mid-1960s. To emphasize the significance of their journey, these young people called it *partir à l'aventure*. They got together in Paris at the *Maison des Etudiants Congolais* (the Congolese Students House), known as MEC. The homonym with the sacred city of Islam (Mecca is *Mecque* in French) is significant because, for the *lutteurs*, this journey to Paris is like a sacred pilgrimage. They consider Paris to be the centre of the world, because it is the fashion capital. This cult of appearance is so emotionally charged that it is analogous to a religious practice (Gondola, 1993: 156, n. 5), and was actually called the 'religion of *kitendi*' (a scrap or end of cloth) by Zaïreans when they adopted the practice of *la Sape*.

Once in Paris, these young people took up trade, which they financed in various ways. They borrowed the residence papers of a friend and found work in a variety of unskilled jobs, or they engaged in activities outside the law: theft, forging papers to sell to other Africans, or selling drugs, which they bought from dealers and sold retail (Gandoulou, 1984: 91–134). When they had accumulated enough money, they would go to Italy and buy the clothes they wanted more cheaply than they could in France, then sell them in Paris or send them with someone to sell for them in Brazzaville.

At the beginning of the 1980s, the movement took the name of *la Sape*. The *sapeurs* created a new physical appearance known as 'the Look'. It consisted, on the one hand, of acquiring a wardrobe of designer clothes called *la gamme*, i.e. the scale of great names in clothing (copies rated low on the scale), and, on the other, of a transformation of the body. They achieved this transformation by means of a special diet, which gave them large stomachs and buttocks and chubby cheeks, by lightening their skin colour in order to have what was called the 'papaya yellow' tint, and by simulating the early stages of baldness with a particular hairstyle. They called this 'the look of a well-to-do man' (Gandoulou, 1984: 145–8; Friedman, 1990: 116–19).

In this context, luxury clothes are transformed; the clothes themselves become secondary because it is the designer label that counts. The young people's emphasis on the labels shows that they do not respect the Parisian or international rules which usually govern the wearing of designer clothes. The *sapeurs* display these clothes at particular sites in Paris, which change regularly. They include the fifteen metres of pavement marked off by chains linking the twelve posts in front of the Tati store in the 11th *arrondissement*; the space in front of certain cafés in the 18th *arrondissement*; and the concourse of the Gare du Nord. These are all areas where there is constant movement, which is symbolic of the flux characterizing this world.

Thus, despite living in France clandestinely without residence permits, the *sapeurs* do not hide. Rather, they flaunt themselves through ostentatious practices, which are necessary to confirm the new status that they will claim and make use of in their home country. This status is constructed by means of success in their trading activities and is manifested in the possession of luxury clothing. It is the monetary value of the clothes that confers social value on the individual, not the clothes themselves. The success achieved in commerce must be confirmed in stages of self-transformation in different arenas: in *nganda*, in sports stadiums, in the streets and in cafés in the 18th *arrondissement*. Each time, self-esteem is increased by parading a spectacular new appearance that visibly transforms the self.

The display of these clothes conforms to specific practices, including the 'dance of designer labels' and the issuing of 'challenges'. The first entails showing off the labels of the clothes one is wearing by means of gestures. The second occurs when an argument arises between two *sapeurs* and their friends put an end to it by proposing that the two protagonists present themselves the next day at an appointed place, superbly dressed. These friends (also very well dressed) make up the jury, which passes judgement on which of the two is better turned out, pronouncing on the merit of his clothes, according to price, quality, etc. and deciding whose are the best: *'Ngue affaire za fua, yandi za ka zebi'* ('you're out, he's in') (Gandoulou, 1984: 126). The challenge is thus taken up in a symbolic conflict in which the weapons are clothes. It functions as a means of controlling any tendency to violence in the milieu. It was explained to Justin-Daniel Gandoulou (author of the most detailed accounts of *la Sape*) in the 1980s that there was no fighting in *la Sape*, because of the criticism it would attract from all the other *Parisiens*.

Challenges used to take place regularly. Nowadays they are rarer but we have witnessed several instances (at *nganda*, parties, sports stadiums, etc.) when the disapproval of a spectator has provoked a violent reaction from the person judged. In one example, an argument broke out in an *nganda;* it turned out to be because someone had taken the girlfriend of another and they had been in a state of hostility for a long time. Friends intervened to put an end to it, but the two have not spoken to each other since. Every time they meet, however, they each criticize the way the other is dressed. One will say that the other does not own the clothes he is wearing. The latter responds angrily: 'Why pick on me? I am quite able to buy my clothes', and asks for confirmation from those around him that his clothes are his own. They agree and the argument ends.

In another instance at a Papa Wemba concert, traders from a *nganda* vied with each other in giving money to the musician, whom they adored. This is often the way they 'prove who they are,' especially when they are in competition over a lover. The amounts given are announced by someone at the microphone. Everyone is very well dressed on these occasions. Friends know why these women are bidding against each other. On another occasion, one of the competing traders saw a girl who was going out with her boyfriend about to give a 500 FF note. A few minutes later, the trader came up and handed over a blank check. This was to show that she was 'more capable' than her rival. Challenges are currently not so formal as they used to be. Everyone knows with whom they have a problem and when they must settle it.

These situations now often provoke violence, which, at parties, brings the event to an end. But, even if the evaluations are not presented as challenges every time, such encounters continue to be like tournaments, where each person demonstrates their prowess by means of their clothes and their wealth. We shall take up this analogy in more detail later in this chapter.

Since 1985, another kind of presentation has been initiated in Brazzaville: *le réveillon*, all-night parties in a rented bar, to which people come to see and be seen in their fine clothes. Two kinds of activities take place. One is called *la Boude* (from the French *bouder*, to sulk). It consists of verbal contests directed at an adversary and calculated to humiliate him but not to the point of provoking a violent reaction. He will not be addressed directly but those present will have their attention called to him with such comments as: 'Who does he take himself for? What does this idiot want? He doesn't know what he's up against ...' (Bazenguissa-Ganga, 1997: 329, n. 231). The other practice, known as '*Théorie*' (theory), involves an expert speaker with a microphone who rouses his audience with a discourse on *la Sape*, drawing on many sources for inspiration: politics, sayings or proverbs, the dictionary, etc.

These *aventuriers* return to Brazzaville for vacations in possession of many clothes with designer labels. They are acclaimed; their visit is called '*la descente*' (the descent); and they receive the status of *Parisien*.[2] After each *descente*, these young people return to France. After a certain number of successful trips, they are able to stop and are accorded the status of *yaya* or '*Grand*' (Great Man).[3]

Life in Paris, where the *sapeurs* most often live clandestinely, stirs up the imaginary world of *la Sape*, which has become the sign of success in

---

[2]Devisch notes that in Congo-Kinshasa moving between village and city was seen as a vertical progression in the ascent of the social scale: *monter en ville* or *descendre au village* (up to town or down to the village), the former the precondition for social climbing (Devisch, 1995: 603).

[3]In Kongo society, *yaya* is a term of deference towards one who has proved his worth, a senior relative or person of experience or expertise (Wyatt MacGaffey, personal communication).

France. People from other quarters of Brazzaville and from other African cities, particularly Kinshasa, have joined this movement. In the mid-1980s, the phenomenon became visible to the French and to Parisians, especially since famous musicians from Congo-Kinshasa, such as Papa Wemba, declared themselves '*les rois de la Sape*' ('the kings of *la Sape*'). It is here that the symbolic world of the Zaïrean digger meets that of *l'aventure*.[4]

We see in the phenomenon of *la Sape* a common response to the dominant 'other', which takes the form of a combination of idealization and hatred (Scott, 1990: 40). Idealization takes the form of emulation, with the use of skin lighteners and hair straighteners, and the value put on French designer-name clothing. It exists alongside intense anger against the powerful, and the contravening of their laws as a means of resisting their domination.

Nganda are important arenas for the competitive displays of *la Sape*. We turn now to details of how they are run, organized and owned.

The World of *Nganda*

Nganda are unlicensed bars, which serve African food as well as drinks. They exist in Paris as well as in Brazzaville and Kinshasa, and are run and generally owned by women. Men make up the majority of the clientele and tend be of the same nationality as the owner. In Paris, *nganda* are mostly found towards the outskirts of the city limits, but a few are either close to the centre or far out in the suburbs. According to the estimate of one owner, there are at least sixty of them in Paris: fifty owners are from Congo-Kinshasa, ten from Congo-Brazzaville.[5] Some traders sell their goods in these bars and make contacts for their trade there, and some wealthy women traders own *nganda* back home as well as in Paris. Since they are unlicensed and cannot advertise as bars, customers come by invitation of the owner, as friends or friends of friends; strangers are unaware of their existence.

Nganda are generally open all night and do not start up until at least 11 p.m. People may tour around several in the course of one night. In these bars, African popular music plays loud and non-stop from a CD or cassette player. The latest news from home is discussed, arguments rage about politics, and gossip is exchanged. People dance in the cramped space and celebrate birthdays or anniversaries by buying whisky, champagne or sparkling wine. They may buy rounds of drinks for acquaintances short on cash, counting on reciprocity when they are similarly unlucky. Occasionally the bar owners give free drinks to patrons.

---

[4]For an account of the connection of *la Sape* to politics, see Bazenguissa-Ganga, 1997: 187–90.
[5]In the course of our fieldwork, we visited ten *nganda* whose owners were from Congo-Kinshasa, and eight whose owners were from Congo-Brazzaville.

The presence of women who are 'available' is an essential feature of *nganda*. This does not mean for prostitution (though some of these bars do have such a reputation). This need for the presence of women means that these bars are generally owned by women, who will work with, or employ, two or three others. The occasional male owner will have a woman run his bar for him. A steady clientele is ensured by a woman who projects a sparkling personality, by the way she dresses and adorns herself, by her gaiety and warmth, and in the way she talks to customers and circulates among them, chatting and joking as she serves drinks. One owner said: 'Men go to *nganda* to drink and to see women; a man knows he can always come here and laugh with me.' Back home women customarily animate occasions of pleasure and relaxation in the same way.

Nganda developed in both Congos both as a clandestine activity, reflecting people's relations with the state, and as an arena for ostentatious expenditure to express social power. Owning bars has been a means of opportunity for women since independence. In Kinshasa, in the 1960s, many bars offering food and dancing were owned by women; it was the most profitable of the few activities open to them (Comhaire-Sylvain, 1968: 182, 226). During the colonial period, women in cities experienced a decline in the economic and social power they had enjoyed in rural society, resulting in an accentuation of their domestic and sexual roles. Single women in the city were known as *ndumba*, literally meaning 'young girl', but it came to have the connotation of courtesan, or *la femme scandaleuse*. The relative wealth, independence and lavish lifestyle that these women achieved made them appear as symbols of success and paragons of beauty (La Fontaine, 1974; Biaya, 1994: 93–5). A number of them, at the end of the 1950s, formed associations for mutual aid, solidarity and recreation. After this time, the presence of *ndumba* became an essential element in the functioning of a bar. They presided as the mistresses of scenes in which the other actors were conscious of transgressing the rules of urban life (Gondola, 1993: 163).

In Congo-Kinshasa, *nganda* have existed in a variety of forms since the colonial period. They first came into being when people sold drinks to their friends in their own houses. In 1972, they became unofficial bars, when closing hours were imposed on regular bars after Mobutu's 1971 policy of *authenticité* (supposedly a return to traditional cultural ways). In response to this decree, unlicensed bars in people's courtyards or living rooms proliferated. In 1974, after the Zaïreanization (indigenization) of businesses, the managers of big companies began to open very expensive, luxury *nganda* run by their mistresses (*'deuxième bureau'*), to which they took their professional clientele, using the bars to make contacts and to do business. Later, when opposition parties were allowed to form, certain *nganda* were frequented by members of networks based on political or religious affiliations.[6]

---

[6]The source of this history is a personal communication from Professor Pius Ngandu, April 1994.

In Congo-Brazzaville, *nganda* started at the end of the 1970s, also as a response to the imposition of closing hours, in this case following the assassination of President Ngouabi.

Nganda designate the 'semi-clandestine sale of drinks and, metaphorically, a place where one can "live it up"' (Ossebi, 1988a: 70). They differ from bars because they are not so noisy, lights are dim and they are not advertised by signs. Since they want to avoid detection, people can only learn about them by word of mouth. Also, in *nganda* the barrier between public and private space is blurred or abolished: while a bar is self-contained and may occupy an entire lot, *nganda* exist in inner courtyards or living-rooms. Consumption patterns are also different: people just drink in bars; in *nganda*, food is served as well.

After the socialist government in France relaxed restrictions on immigration in 1981, *nganda* appeared in Paris as many Zaïreans moved there from Brussels. At first, they were just bars, but then they began serving food: *brochettes*, grilled chicken, roasted peanuts and eventually African dishes.

The majority of customers go to these bars for reasons other than drinking and eating: to meet friends and acquaintances and have a good time, to make useful contacts and get information, and to receive news from home. Women traders bringing wax-print cloth from Brussels, for example, came to one particular *nganda* to meet their customers. In this way, *nganda* assist women traders by putting people from different groups and of different status in contact with one another, and providing a milieu in which these traders can conduct their affairs. Another function of *nganda* is to serve as a place where people may spend the night: sometimes because they want to avoid the police and dare not return home, sometimes because they may have no other place to go, sometimes because they are doubling up in a small apartment and if they have no regular job they must take the day shift to sleep and then find some other place to spend the night hours.

There is a hierarchy among Paris *nganda*, as there is in Brazzaville and Kinshasa. The simplest is a very small curtained-off room with stools and a table at the back of a licensed and legally rented shop. Then there are others consisting of one or more rooms of varying sizes in the owner's home, which is often a squat. Sometimes they exist in illegally sub-rented premises, such as the basement of a café. *Nganda* are so important socially that even licensed establishments take on their form and are known as *nganda* in order to boost business. Two of these constitute the most prestigious of these establishments in the Paris hierarchy. One is a café in the city, the other a nightclub in the suburbs. But they both have unlicensed activities in addition to being licensed bars.

The café is located in a neighbourhood in which there are many shops selling African foods, wax-prints and beauty products. It is larger than the usual *nganda*, with an (unlicensed) larger room in the basement. There will be 30–50 people at a time upstairs, crowded together at very small tables.

Downstairs the setting is more intimate, with the room divided into blocks around small tables and with more comfortable seating for around 30 people. This is the largest of the *nganda*. Small coloured lights and tinsel hang on the walls. The atmosphere is more like a party, more crowded and noisier than in the comparable setting of an average English pub. People exchange greetings and conversation across the room; music plays continuously; there is much coming and going. The clientele are mostly men; there will be few women, other than the owner and the waitresses. Women will only go to specific *nganda* occasionally in order to make business contacts.

The nightclub is owned by a European whose wife is from Congo-Kinshasa. It has the usual features of a nightclub: a dance floor, space for a live band, flashing strobe lights and high-volume music. It qualifies as a *nganda* because upstairs there is an unlicensed restaurant, run by another woman from Congo-Kinshasa, which serves African food. This woman is also a big trader and sells merchandise which she imports from Africa.[7] Entry to the club is free but drinks cost twice as much as they do in other *nganda*.[8] People who come plan the weekend around one or two evenings here. In contrast to *nganda*, the numbers of men and women are almost equal in the nightclub and they dress elaborately. The night begins at around 1 or 2 a.m. and does not end until 6 a.m.

Varieties of Nganda: Some Examples. In a café near the Gare du Nord, if one is in the know, one descends a narrow staircase to a *nganda* run by three women. They have paid the café proprietor 30,000 FF down as well as the monthly rent. But to buy a licence would cost even more than this huge sum. This *nganda* seats 40–50 people on chairs set around tables or on padded banquettes around the walls. We were there early before the crowd arrived. The ceiling has varnished stone arches and the entire end wall consists of a mirror. There is a kitchen off to one side; we are served *brochettes* and salt fish with manioc. Loud music comes from a big speaker, and the room is decorated with tinsel and flashing lights. The three women are well turned out in African dress with scarves or poncho added, earrings and other jewellery, and elaborate make-up and hairstyles.

On another occasion, to make the initial contact with the owner, we visited a *nganda* in the afternoon in a squat in an HLM building in which 60 Congo families were living. The owner supplemented her income by looking after children while their parents were at work. That day, she was dandling two babies on her knee and there were several young children running around the apartment. There was no sign of any provision of things for them to do or of anyone to supervise or do things with them. Two men and a young woman were drinking and watching violent American

---

[7] Despite good contacts and introductions and the setting up of several appointments, this woman would never talk to us.

[8] Bottles of whisky or champagne are 500 FF compared with 250 FF; 33 cl beers or soft drinks are 30 FF compared with 66 cl bottles at this price in *nganda*.

movies on a huge TV. The large living-room was sparsely furnished with a table and four chairs and a five-person sofa. There was also a large freezer, the essential item for setting up a *nganda*.

In the 20th *arrondissement*, there is a *nganda* in a tiny room up a shabby dark staircase and at the end of a dark passage. It is furnished with a sofa, white plastic chairs, stools, two small tables and a square freezer. When we arrive, the owner is washing glasses in a bowl of soapy water on the freezer, drying them and stacking them on a shelf on the wall above. She wears a wax-print cloth skirt and a frilly black blouse, large costume-jewellery earrings, elaborate sandals and a wig of straight bronzed hair. Two women and six men are present when we come in at 11.30 p.m., which, with the three of us and the owner, makes twelve people crowded into a very small space. It is very noisy, with music and conversation that gets louder and louder as people drink. Our assistant treated us to *brochettes* with our drinks to celebrate his approaching birthday. There is another *nganda* on the floor above. The neighbours apparently are able to tolerate the noise.

We had a dish of mutton, *chikwanga* (manioc pudding) and onions with peppers, cokes and beer in another *nganda*, which consisted of a large carpeted room with a sofa and freezer at one end, and stools around a low table in the middle. Music played continually and a young woman cooked and served food from a kitchen in an adjoining room. An older woman, who was keeping the *nganda* for the owner, who had just opened a restaurant elsewhere serving African food, presided on the sofa with her husband.

Nganda are expensive. To have a good time it is necessary to spend a lot of money. These young Congolese are likely to lay out 200 FF a night. Yet, despite such high costs, *nganda* are primarily frequented by the unemployed and those who work only spasmodically. People with jobs do not really belong in this milieu, because they cannot afford it with the minimum wage at 4,800 FF a month. Those who move out of the clandestine life to get jobs can no longer go to these bars: their entire salary could easily be spent in a few visits, and being up all night makes it hard to get to work on time in the morning. Nor is this the world of the wealthier professional African middle class in Paris. They frequent the bars and cafés of mainstream society.

Given the clandestine nature of these bars, it is extremely difficult to obtain any precise information on costs, expenditures or profits, or on how often people attend them or spend ostentatiously. However, details of individual expenditures were made available to us by one owner, who gave us her accounts for two short periods. They provided evidence of the high expenditures in *nganda*. Her *nganda* was located in the basement of a store selling ethnic foods in central Paris. The owner was a young woman from Brazzaville and the 26 regular customers, whose names were noted in the accounts shown in Table 6.1, came from there as well, with the exception of four Haitians (three of them connected with the Haitian landlord) and two Ivoirians, one of whom worked in the *nganda*, while the other was a friend of hers.

Table 6.1
Examples of Individual Expenditures in a *Nganda* in 1994
(in French Francs)

Regular Customers	Thur 1/27	Fri 1/28	Sat 1/29	Sun 1/30	Wed 2/16	Thur 2/17	Fri 2/18
1	50*	50*					485*
2	30*		50*				20
3		70*					
4		150*					
5		90*					
6		40				30	
7			70				
8			70				50
9			90				
10			20**				
11			260*		20	115	200*
12			150				145*
13			210	200		30	270*
14			70			170*	60
15				310			
16					360*		130*
17					225*		120
18					120*		
19						245*	
20							240
21							130*
22							90
23							30
24							50
25							60
26						30	
Other Customers No. of people: amt. spent	8:830	0	1:15	0	1:225	2:180	3:235
TOTAL RECEIPTS	910	400	985	510	950	800	2,315
TOTAL NO. OF PEOPLE	10	5	10	2	5	8	18

*includes food; **bill not paid

These were the only takings recorded for this two-week period, but, as far as we could see, her accounting was not very comprehensive and some nights were simply not recorded. The highest individual expenditures ranged from 200 to 485 FF in one night, the lowest was 20 FF in a night; the largest number of people present on any one of these seven occasions was 18; and the total gross takings for all seven nights was 6,870 FF ($1,209). Of the four largest spenders:

no. 1 spent 585 FF ($95) in three nights
no. 11 spent 595 FF ($104) in four nights
no. 13 spent 710 FF ($125) in four nights
no. 16 spent 490 FF ($86) in two nights.

How can the clientele of *nganda* afford to spend so much money on drinks and food, quite apart from what they spend on clothing, and why do they do so? The majority make money in '*les circuits*' or '*bizness*'. They may make a lot of money in this way, which they spend in *nganda* and on the expensive clothes needed for *la Sape*, but they do so erratically. Those who make a 'coup' in *les circuits* will show off their wealth in the fine clothes they wear and by ostentatious spending when they buy rounds of drinks for all present in a *nganda*. Drug dealers, in particular, will also buy as many as three bottles of whisky, which they do not even drink. They will spend as much as 1,500–2,000 FF in a night, far more than the customers listed in Table 6.1. This conspicuous consumption is competitive and reinforces status: it ensures a certain prestige in the eyes of others and establishes one's reputation. Frequenters of *nganda* are the only public available for these displays; the clientele are simultaneously spectators and actors. The traders pull off a coup, which brings renown, and then, by lavish spending, ensure recognition for what they have done, thus confirming their status. However, such extremely lavish outlays can occur only rarely for particular individuals: in between they do not spend on such a scale. Experiencing such intense moments is what matters most to them and remains vividly in the minds of these young people, as described in Chapter 1. Biaya suggests that braving the danger and violence of crime, diamond smuggling and immigration, and the ostentation which then celebrates the triumphant return from adversity, can be likened to an initiation (Biaya, 1996: 11).

But how do we explain why drinks and food are so costly in *nganda*? In this clandestine world, prestige comes from making a coup in drug dealing, theft and other activities in trade outside the law. A woman who sets up a *nganda* and makes a success of it has pulled off a coup: she has demonstrated that she has the necessary looks and personality to attract a steady clientele, and she has managed to set up, and keep in operation, an enterprise outside the law. It is for this created social value that people pay when they spend so much more money in *nganda* for drinks and food than they do in regular bars. This feature of *nganda* resolves the seeming paradox that, whereas one might expect them to be cheaper than regular bars, since their overheads are certainly lower, they are actually more expensive: drinks cost more than they do in a licensed establishment and the food served is relatively expensive.

In Paris in 1994, women could make far more money running a *nganda* than they could make in the sort of minimum-wage job for which they were qualified and in which they were likely to work if they managed to obtain residence papers. One advantage of *nganda* is that they require little start-up capital: 200 FF will buy the two cases of beer that make it possible to set up such an enterprise in one's apartment. Two women who ran *nganda* in their own apartments each said that in a good week they cleared 4,000 FF, that is up to 16,000 FF a month, nearly four times the minimum monthly wage of 4,800 FF. In one *nganda* owned by three women, a good week brought in from 6,000 to 10,000 FF: they each put in 500 FF initially and then shared the takings at the end of the week.

If we take a range of sizes of *nganda* from our histories, we find that Nanette's small room will hold only twelve, that Thérèse has 26 regular customers, that the bar near the Gare du Nord has seats for 50; so we could take 30 as a reasonable number of regular customers for a typical *nganda*. One of the *nganda* owners mentioned above clears 4,000 FF a week. Since the gross takings must have been considerably more, a rough calculation gives an average expenditure for each of 30 men over a month of at least 685 FF. This indicates expenditures on a considerable scale by individuals who are doing well.

But the men's expenditure patterns have an interesting consequence. By spending money ostentatiously in *nganda*, the young men of this closed clandestine world establish their social identity and status. But it is the women who own and run these establishments who collect and benefit from a considerable percentage of the money the young men accumulate in their trade and other extra-legal activities. Life is not easy or secure for these women. Case histories of individuals show us the reasons why this is so.

The Fluctuating Fortunes of Nganda *Owners*

Some women become very wealthy from owning *nganda*. We heard of several who had bought two or three second-hand cars with the money they had accumulated, and then shipped them home to set up taxi businesses. But others fail or do badly: running these bars is, in fact, a risky and uncertain enterprise, often beset by problems. The following case history of a successful *nganda* owner reveals the nature of these problems and the ups and downs that are typical for this occupation.

When we knew her in 1994, Thérèse had residence papers (she is the mother of children born in France) and a substantial amount of money in her bank account. The income from her *nganda* enabled her regularly to feed a household of eight people (herself, her twin daughters, her brother and his wife, her half-sister, two men who are to some extent her protectors and who are dependent on her, and sometimes others in addition).

> *Thérèse, in her mid-thirties, is from Brazzaville. She was raised in a military camp as her father was a gendarme, but trade was in the family as her mother's mother was a successful palm oil seller. Thérèse thought she had inherited this success in trade because of the profits she made selling alcohol. After the attempted coup of 1970, her father fled to Kinshasa, so this family is an example of one disrupted by politics. Thérèse became a sapeur and in 1975 had an affair with the singer Bozi Boziana. She was mentioned in one of his songs, which was recorded, and this made her reputation. In 1979, she went to France, with the help of her elder brother, who worked for Pan Am. She trained as an accountant and took up with a trader of clothes between Paris*

*and Brazzaville, by whom she had twins. Thérèse soon separated from
the trader and began selling drinks at the stadiums, in which she was
helped by the reputation that came with her from home. Her success
took her into the bar business in 1989, when she joined in owning a
nganda with two women from Kinshasa. They put in 500 FF each and
shared the weekly takings. In a good week, which included selling
bottles of whisky and champagne, they took in 6,000–10,000 FF.
Thérèse built up her own network of customers, but the nganda was
closed down when one of her associates was caught selling drugs.*

*In her next venture, Thérèse was employed by an East African
woman, who owned a restaurant that was doing so badly she could
barely pay the rent. Thérèse, who brought with her the large clientele
she had acquired in her previous nganda, was paid 2,000 FF a week,
with 100 FF more if she sold a bottle of champagne. She was so
successful in increasing the number of customers that sometimes she
took in 7,000–8,000 FF a night; all the owner paid as bonus for this
success, however, was 500 FF. So Thérèse soon left and joined two
others whose nganda was fading in popularity. But the three of them
could not work well together so again she left. She next worked with
two women from Brazzaville with a nganda in a squat. Thérèse did the
cooking. One woman left after two months, and four months later
Thérèse moved off and rented the basement of a licensed café for
1,000 FF a week for her own nganda. She was not, however, allowed to
do any cooking, and on drinks alone she could not make a profit.*

*In 1994, she had set up her own nganda in two rooms of her
apartment, the ground floor of a squat. She did her shopping on
Tuesdays, spending at least 1,500 FF weekly. She could make a weekly
profit of 4,000 FF if people came to eat, if not, between 2,500 and
3,000 FF. She worked with family helpers (sisters-in-law and sisters).
At the end of the week, they chose payment in cash or kind. She also
paid a West Indian, who had worked with her before, 1,200 FF a week
or, if things were not going well, 600 FF. But this enterprise crowded
her living quarters for her daughters and she decided to find new
premises.*

*This time, she found herself at the mercy of an unscrupulous
landlord. He agreed to rent her a basement for 2,000 FF a month, with
the use of a kitchen upstairs. She made up a printed card and handed
it around to friends and all her old clientele, inviting them to the
opening of her new 'nganda/café'. She set it up like a café, with tables
with pink paper tablecloths and chairs down each side of the room,
blue and red strip lighting, and videos and music playing all the time.
Posters of well-known African singers decorated the walls, and also
one of Thérèse herself dancing. After a few days she installed a new
red, flocked, moquette wall-covering. Things went well: in the first
week she took in over 6,000 FF (from this she had to pay out 1,411 FF
for supplies and her helpers' wages of 150 FF a night, in addition to*

the rent). Then the blow fell: the landlord, seeing her obvious success from the number of customers crowding in, put up the rent to 5,000 FF a month, and demanded, in addition, that she pay the electricity bill. Thérèse tried to cope by working seven days a week. She also sold a delivery of manioc to her nganda *customers, and then stolen electronic goods given her by a boyfriend, as she tried to make ends meet. But she had to abandon this attempt and returned to the basement and open-air courtyard of her house, where she was still operating in 1998.*

Thérèse, the *sapeur*, is successful, despite the many vicissitudes she has been through: she pulls off owning a *nganda*, her name is enshrined in a recording by a famous singer, and she has a faithful clientele, who follow her from one *nganda* to another. Very pretty, with a smile that lights up the room, she dresses in a series of eye-catching outfits, creating a stir when she walks down the street; she is a star. Her clandestine occupation, for all its uncertainty, offers her the opportunity to 'be someone', and a more exciting existence with greater money-making potential than any low-level, low-paid, accounting job would offer her. Her history shows that, although it is women who frequently reap the wealth earned by men in clandestine activities, their success is, nevertheless, precarious.

In general, women find both advantages and disadvantages from their gender in the world of trade. The trader Eloise, whose history was given in Chapter 2, used motherhood to her advantage when she employed it as a deliberate strategy to acquire residence papers. On the other hand, among our case histories, both Josephine and Véronique had to give up trading or career opportunities because they became pregnant. Josephine had trained as a flight attendant and had obtained a job, but then could not show up for work when called because she was pregnant. Véronique had to leave school at 17 for the same reason. When she was 20 and trading successfully between Kinshasa and Bandundu, she had to give this up after only nine months because she was pregnant again, and could only manage petty trade from a kiosk in front of her house. Fatherhood does not similarly disadvantage young men, and, moreover, they often take little responsibility for their children, as we saw in the case of Charles.[9]

It is difficult for women to combine running *nganda* with looking after the children that the men they were involved with left them to raise. The following case history shows the kind of problems they have.

Nanette, from Congo-Kinshasa, whom we encountered before (p. 89), having trouble asserting her right to live in a squat, ran her nganda *in one small room. She worries about the inadequacy of her*

---

[9]Benoît Verhaegen gives many examples in his book on women in Kisangani, Congo-Kinshasa (Verhaegen, 1990).

accommodation for her seven-year-old son, the fact that she cannot supervise his schoolwork, and the problems she has getting schooling for him because she has no residence papers. For the first six months, he did not go to school at all. Now he goes to a school from an address in a good neighbourhood that is a 45-minute metro ride away. His mother bought a studio apartment in this neigh-bourhood from a customer who was the brother of her associate. This man cheated her by taking her money but then letting someone else have the apartment. However, before doing so he had enrolled her son in school from his address. She provides the boy with good clothing: when we saw him one winter's day, he was warmly and well dressed. Nanette complains about her hard life: she works all night and often does not sleep until 9 a.m., and she wonders about the effect on her health of drinking so much, since customers often buy her drinks, which are usually hard liquor. 'Perhaps I will get cirrhosis of the liver,' she says. At night she is gay and lively serving food and drinks, but the gaiety fades in the cold light of day as she relates the difficulties of her existence and of trying to raise a child. Sadly, in 1997, we heard she was in prison for selling drugs.

An earlier study shows that the second economy has offered women the means of escaping from male domination in the oppressively patriarchal society of Congo-Kinshasa (MacGaffey, 1988). The international trade of this economy has provided the women of our case studies with opportunities which they have turned to their advantage with extraordinary creativity and intermittent success. As we have seen, their gender has sometimes been an advantage, sometimes a disadvantage. Another avenue for the advancement of women has occurred with the success of Congo popular music. *Nganda* have played a specific role in this process.

Popular Music and Nganda: *Helping the Cause of Women*
In *nganda*, women, music and beer are associated, because hearing Congo popular music is as essential as the presence of women for the success of these bars. Since the end of the Second World War, when bands began to proliferate rapidly,[10] this association has greatly helped in the popular-ization of this now world-famous music, originating in Congo-Kinshasa (Gondola, 1993: 161).

The choice of music for the young is noisy compared with the prefer-ences of the Great Men: those who aspire to be in this category like it to be quiet enough for conversation; the young want to be in places where they can dance. Women have been important in the promotion of music, since

---

[10]There were twenty in Kinshasa by 1963, and they had increased to 180–200 by 1984. In Brazzaville, on the other hand, socialism proved discouraging: in the 1980s, there were only about thirty (Gondola, 1997a: 272, n. 19).

they select what is played and are a source of inspiration for songs (Gondola, 1993: 163). They are 'the central figure around which revolves the creation, production and spread of popular music' (Gondola, 1997a: 255). Initially, popular music was a male preserve in Congo-Kinshasa, in keeping with colonial ideas of the time. However, music remained outside colonial control, which was not the case with other recreational activities, such as sport (Ibid.: 233), and this made entry easier for women. Musicians sang in Lingala, not French (in which women were not fluent because they lacked education), performed in informal situations, violated curfews and incorporated criticism of the colonial system. Today, men and women are musical artists in relatively equal numbers, and women are a powerful source of inspiration for songs. For women, music has 'served as a terrain of gender struggle and provided opportunities for social and economic advancement' (Gondola, 1997b: 71–81).

Amorous adventures with women, listening to music and drinking beer in *nganda* combine to create what Congolese call 'ambience' or 'movement'. Metaphorically, this atmosphere reproduces the world of the traders, who live in transit circulating between Africa and Europe. It also symbolically reflects their existence outside the law because it celebrates their expenditure of energy and the realization of their hidden capabilities. The cult of ambience represents a flight from colonial violence and oppression through the release of living *la dolce vita* (Biaya, 1994: 89). Within this lifestyle, the traders construct their own competitive status system, for which *nganda* serve as arenas. We shall now explore the issue of the enhancement of value and the intense competition for prestige of the high spenders in these establishments.

Competing for Prestige: Tournaments of Value

Arjun Appadurai reminds us that, although economic exchange creates value and value is embodied in the commodities that are exchanged, it is not, as Simmel emphasizes, an inherent property of objects but a judgement made about them by people (Appadurai, 1986: 3). As commodities move between the official and the second, unofficial, economy, judgements about them change. Diversion of commodities from their usual circuits often enhances their value.

In Paris, goods acquire additional value when they are obtained in the course of pulling off a coup outside the law. Theft is a diversion of commodities from their usual circuits. Among these traders, stolen goods that are subsequently sold are not sold for less than they are in the stores: they have acquired greater value because they have been stolen and there has been triumph over risk. They are also assumed to be of good quality and costly because the assumption is that the thief would not have thought it worth his while to risk jail for something of little value. However, it is possible to pull off a double coup by manipulating these assumptions. In one instance, a stolen pair of men's trousers was sold to a buyer for 500 FF: he thought they must be of expensive quality but subsequently discovered that they cost only 250 FF in the shops!

Such diversion underlies the plunder of valuables in warfare; the purchase and display of tools and artefacts of non-Western peoples in Western homes; and the framing of 'found' objects. 'In all these examples, diversions of things combine the aesthetic impulse, the entrepreneurial link, and the touch of the mortally shocking' (Appadurai, 1986: 28). Appadurai further observes that, although in theory human actors encode things with significance, from a methodological viewpoint the human and social context is best illuminated by things in motion (Ibid.: 3–5). The enhancement in value of goods through their diversion from their usual circuits into the second economy is an example.

We have observed how the construction of identity for these overseas African immigrants creates a market for the commodities the traders supply. The studies of Philip Curtin (1984) and Eric Wolf (1982) show the importance of commodity flows throughout history, and not only recently with the development of global capitalism. However, as Appadurai points out, they show little interest in 'the question of demand and the related problem of the cultural construction of value' (Appadurai, 1986: 35), which are our particular concern here. Appadurai takes up Baudrillard's idea of the emergence of the 'object' as a thing that is no longer just a product or commodity, but 'essentially a sign in a system of signs of status' (Ibid.: 45). The drinks and clothes bought and ostentatiously consumed or displayed by *sapeurs* and traders who frequent *nganda* signify their progress in an intense competition for reputation and prestige in the status system they have created. Today, they acquire many of these clothes through second-economy trade: they may be stolen or fraudulently imported through the use of false or borrowed visas and passports, and they are sold without the vending licences required by law. This daring trade and the *sapeurs*' ostentatious displays recall both the *kula* trade of the Trobriand Islanders, with its exchange of shell valuables between trading partners in the pursuit of reputation and distinction and involving dangerous ocean voyages, and the lavish competitive giving to assert chiefly status in the potlatch of the peoples of the north-west coast of North America. Both exhibit an intense 'knock 'em dead' competitive fervour.[11] Appadurai has called these and other such forms of trade that construct fame and reputation for individuals 'tournaments of value'. They take place in specially created arenas (Ibid.: 50).

These Paris traders, the commodities they trade and use in their ostentatious lifestyle and their displays in the specialized arenas constituted by *nganda* and other sites provide us with a Central African example of such

---

[11]Our thanks to Keith Hart for this vivid simile and comparison.

tournaments. They are also found in this region among the diamond diggers, the *Bana Lunda*, young urbanites from all over Bandundu, Congo-Kinshasa, who come to the Angolan province of Lunda Norte to make their fortunes in diamonds. The money they make (in dollars, which are now the currency of the area), after months of suffering and risk-taking, is squandered on women, beer, jewellery, clothes and transistor radios, in ostentatious, potlatch-like behaviour.

> Diamonds and dollars offer the possibility of negotiation and recomposition of identity in a process, not only of self-realization ... and promotion of social status (through excessive expenditure and consumerism, for example), but also of 'self-making' ... as the process of capturing and 'fixing' the nonsteady state of selfhood and of one's own identify in different cultural situations. (De Boeck, 1998: 780)

But there are other comparisons to be made besides those involving the competitive construction of fame and reputation.

Oppositional Cultures of the Socially Marginalized

Besides *la Sape*, another example of the use of clothing to create a counter-hegemonic style in Africa is that of the Baay Fàl, members of an unorthodox Muslim sect in Senegal. Like the *sapeurs*, they frame their collective identities via their costumes in opposition to the dominant sectors of their society. These costumes include voluminous patchwork pantaloons made from scraps of brightly coloured cloth. The Baay Fàl let their hair grow and carry large studded clubs for self-flagellation in religious ceremonies. Their young people identify with Jamaican Rastafarians and their music, and twist their long hair into dreadlocks, thus entering into a transnational traffic in counter-hegemonic styles via the commodification and distribution worldwide of reggae music (Heath, 1992: 27–8). The dominant sectors of society in the Senegambia express hierarchy and identity through the elegant dress style of the women known as *sanse*, practised on certain public ritual occasions, in which cost indicates status. It is accompanied by gift-giving and display. This practice reproduces structures of inequality through the display of material wealth (Ibid.: 20–3).

We can find other examples of oppositional counter-hegemonic cultures outside Africa. In Britain, violence has a purpose for soccer thugs. During the week these fans are nobody, but when they come to the soccer match all that changes as they explode into an orgy of drunkenness, fighting and destruction of property. They say of this behaviour: 'It makes us somebody', or of a particular match, 'That was a once-in-a-lifetime experience' (Buford, 1990: 117–18). They flout the codes of civilized conduct, breaking and destroying anything in their way, existing intensely in 'exalted experiences that by their intensity, their risk, their threat of self-immolation exclude the possibility of all other thought except the experience itself' (Ibid.: 193). These comments seem to echo the reactions of Congolese traders to the thrill and excitement of the coups they pull off in drug dealing, theft and other anti-social law-breaking behaviour, when they say in triumphant moments of recall: 'We have lived!' And, just as frequenters of *nganda* spend a lot of money, so do football supporters: leaders will spend £335 a week (Ibid.: 30).

Parallels appear again in a study of working-class boys in an industrial city secondary school in the British Midlands, where exhilaration and excitement are found in violence and fighting and their ensuing highs, and in other anti-social practices such as theft, a source of excitement as much as of money because it puts one at risk. 'Violence and the judgment of violence is the most basic axis of the "lads"' ascendance over the conformists, almost in the way that knowledge is for teachers' (Willis, 1977: 34–40).

In the United States, the high-spending binge behaviour of Puerto Rican crack dealers in East Harlem, in which they spend large amounts of money on their personal drug addiction, notwithstanding its inevitably self-destructive effects, brings them something they are otherwise denied: it offers an alternative forum for autonomous personal dignity. This money was, in the words of one addict, 'Something only I could control. No-one could tell me what to do with it' (Bourgois, 1995: 118). Workers in the crack economy average slightly less than twice the minimum wage, but there are plenty of nights when they make ten times as much, and these are the nights they celebrate and remember (Ibid.: 92). The cultural assault faced by the young people of El Barrio when they venture out of their neighbourhood has spawned an 'inner-city street culture', which has emerged in opposition to their exclusion from mainstream society. They are trapped in a factory-based economy in New York city, which is being replaced by a service industry, causing unemployment and income reduction, and weakening unions. Entry-level employment in the service industry brings these youths into disastrous cultural confrontation with lower-middle-class whites: their lack of the appropriate cultural skills puts them at a hopeless disadvantage. Most are soon fired from such jobs. They 'treated their return to the world of street dealing as a triumph of free will and resistance on their part', even though at heart they still wished for steady legal employment (Ibid.: 114–15). Thus they refuse to accept their social structural victimization, seeking an alternative by immersing themselves in the underground drug economy and proudly embracing street culture (Ibid.: 143).

But Bourgois emphasizes that violence, substance abuse and their own rage mean that the street culture of resistance in Harlem 'is predicated on the destruction of its participants and their community' (Ibid.: 8). The oppositional culture of the *sapeurs* and the owners and clientele of *nganda* also has a self-destructive potential. With their excessive drinking and ostentatious living, they are at constant risk of prison terms for the theft, drug dealing and fraudulent trade and other activities that finance this lifestyle, and also of the potential ill effects of substance abuse. Likewise, Willis (1997) shows that working-class schoolchildren in Britain create an oppositional culture that involves rejection of all efforts to attain the educational credentials that would qualify them for upward mobility and thus contributes to their reproducing themselves as a working class. As Bourgois sees it, 'through the cultural practices of opposition, individuals shape the oppression that larger forces impose upon them' (1995: 17). But we would argue that the dominant reality is, in fact, that their marginality and oppressed situation are ensured by their structural position in society and by the mechanisms that put, and keep, these structures in place rather than by the oppositional culture they create in response. This structural position gives them little, if any, chance to move out of where they are; it is a given of their existence. Bourgois's study documents this most clearly in his accounts of doomed individual efforts to participate in the regular economy.

Yet all of these oppositional cultures have in common the fact that it is possible for their members to shine in intense satisfaction, to be somebody, to have the thrill of memorable moments, to make life worthwhile. They have 'fomented an especially explosive cultural creativity that is in defiance of racism and economic marginalization' (Ibid.: 8). For the young Congolese who are *sapeurs* and who take part in the tournaments of value in *nganda*, this is the only way they can shine out from an existence in which other options are frustrating, dreary or simply not viable. They have created their own world with its own status and value system and its own scale of achievement and satisfaction, and they have rejected the values of a system that has excluded and marginalized them.

But do any of the activities of the traders of our study mount any opposition to the power structure or constitute any sort of resistance to its oppression and exclusion? They certainly do not if we look for organized political resistance, but the answer is in the affirmative if we follow recent scholarship, which sees a silent, hidden, non-violent revolution taking place through everyday forms of resistance by the powerless, through what has been called the 'weapons of the weak'.

New Weapons in Everyday Resistance to Domination

James Scott has shown that Malay peasants, rather than resorting to violent revolution and open organized protest, whittle away at the control imposed from above by means of massive evasion of regulations and taxes. These peasants refuse to conform in a multitude of small actions in their daily lives, such as pilfering, poaching, flight, dissimulation and foot-dragging, in hidden, not overt, resistance to authority. Focus on such small acts, the 'weapons of the weak', leads to the discovery of resistance and protest in unlikely places (Scott, 1985). Scott and others[12] who take this approach of investigating 'the view from below' rather than adopting the more usual state-orientated perspective, argue that subordinated social actors are neither passive nor powerless and broaden the definition of resistance beyond formalized, organized actions (Kondo, 1990: 219).

The second-economy trade and other activities we document occur among urban traders rather than among rural peasants, so we add a new dimension to Scott's forms of everyday resistance. The traders refuse to abide by laws and regulations governing trade and commerce as they contest the boundaries of the law, the rules for crossing the frontiers of nation states, and the usual expectations for institutional participation. They mount no organized resistance to authority and its rules, they simply evade them in the creative and ingenious ways that we have documented.

Non-violent, unorganized, resistance to a predatory dominant class takes diverse forms. Margaret Levi believes that one of the most important of Scott's 'weapons of the weak' is the withdrawal of compliance (Levi, 1990: 414). In an analysis of the logic of institutional change, she focuses on the undermining of 'contingent consent'. By this she means that institutions (characterized by socially constructed rules that reflect a particular distribution of power resources) cannot depend only on coercion to implement their policies successfully; the costs of enforcing them would be insupportably high. Moral principles and behavioural norms also induce compliance. The norm of fairness offers a rule for when one should comply, and generates this contingent consent. If current arrangements represent an acceptable bargain and others are upholding it, the institution will be thought of as fair; if not, then contingent consent will be withdrawn.[13] From this point of view, institutions represent a social bargain. When those who possess institutional power abuse it, they break the social bargain, and people will then in turn reject their side of it (Levi, 1990: 406–10). In our two Congolese Republics, people are acutely aware of, and very explicit about, the betrayal of the social bargain by their leaders. This has led to the widespread withdrawal of contingent consent, evident in the massive scale of refusal to comply with the law after *la débrouillardise* was adopted as the solution to the problems of everyday living in Congo-Kinshasa's long political and economic crisis. Aili Tripp writes about the same phenomenon in Tanzania, calling it 'quiet strategies of resistance in the form of economic noncompliance' (Tripp, 1997: 8).

---

[12]See especially Bayart, 1981; Scott, 1985, 1987, 1990; De Soto, 1989; Isaacman, 1990; Singerman, 1995; Tripp, 1997.

[13]We could also note here Max Weber and domination by virtue of the belief in the validity of legal stature and in the functional competence of those who govern, based on rules that are rationally created. Obedience to these statutory obligations is expected (Gerth and Mills, 1946: 79). In Congo-Kinshasa and Congo-Brazzaville such belief no longer exists and obedience cannot be expected.

In his later book, *Domination and the Arts of Resistance*, Scott emphasizes that he privileges the issues of dignity and autonomy, which are generally given second place to a focus on material exploitation (Scott, 1990: xi). Specifically, the difference from his earlier work, *Weapons of the Weak* (1985), lies in his focus on language and ideology. He argues that the 'hidden transcript' of a subordinate group engenders a subculture which opposes its own form of social domination to that of the dominant class (Scott, 1990: 4, 14, 27). We have in the *sapeurs* and *nganda* frequenters of our study an example of such a subculture, with its own form of social domination. We see this domination exercised against those who participate in the wage earning of the formal economy, as in the case of Charles, who is forced to cease living with his friends who are occupied in clandestine activities, and again as the set-up, values and costs of *nganda* similarly exclude from participation those who are in regular jobs.

De Certeau's analysis in 1980 of the resistance of the Indians of South America to their Spanish conquerors makes the point, powerfully relevant to the *sapeurs*, that these Indians subverted the laws, rituals and representations imposed on them, not by rejecting or altering them, but by using them with respect to ends and references foreign to the system they were forced to accept.

> They were *other* within the very colonization that outwardly assimilated them; their use of the dominant social order deflected its power, which they lacked the means to challenge; they escaped it without leaving it. (De Certeau, 1984: xiii)

Besides the *sapeurs*, we have noted other such subcultures among soccer thugs, among the working-class lads of Willis's study and in the 'street culture of resistance' of East Harlem. We find among them all, including the traders, what Bourgois notes for the drug dealers: that resistance is not a conscious political opposition, but a 'spontaneous set of rebellious practices that in the long term have emerged as an oppositional style' (Bourgois, 1995: 8).

In Scott's 'hidden transcripts', public defiance is prudently avoided, rebellion and protest are not public, there is 'a wide variety of low-profile forms of resistance that dare not speak in their own name', which Scott calls the infrapolitics of subordinate groups (Scott, 1990: 19). Such politics are evident in *la Sape* and *nganda*, and in the whole range of second-economy practices we have described, although, as we have emphasized, with the *sapeurs* there is a continuing tension between the need to hide transgressions of the law from the authorities and the need for ostentatious display of the wealth acquired in the course of such transgressions in order to gain status and recognition. These practices do, however, take place in their own arenas and off-stage from the centre stage of the powers that be. But they present an interesting variant on Scott's notion of hidden resistance: this form is less low-profile than generally seems to be the case in his examples of infrapolitics.

Throughout this book, we have included the language usage specific to the traders and particularly to those among them who are *sapeurs*. These data provide rich illustration of Scott's thesis. The biting slang, euphemisms, vivid analogies and humour in the speech of the unofficial culture of the traders make up a hidden transcript expressing the opposition to the dominant reflected in their way of life.[14] We can identify other forms of hidden transcripts in which these traders and others participate. As we have shown, popular music is one of them. Another is the transformation of the names represented by acronyms in Brazzaville, giving them new meanings to represent political opposition, as reported by Bazenguissa-Ganga (1997: 310–15). Johannes Fabian sees popular painting as a 'complex expression of political and historical consciousness among the masses' (Fabian, 1978: 319). Middle-class city dwellers commonly hang these paintings in their houses. We can also add *radio trottoir* (street radio), the gossip, rumour and unofficial channels for transmitting information in the two Congos. Malays call such unofficial channels 'news on the wind'. Such communication is the most 'familiar and elementary form of disguised popular aggression' (Scott, 1990: 142). One scholar from Congo-Kinshasa refers to *radio trottoir* as 'hidden discourse' *(le discours en camouflage)* (Yoka, 1984). Another considers it to be popular political action, the equivalent of a free press under an oppressive regime, which expresses the antagonism between the governed and those who govern and constitutes a clandestine, latent form of political resistance (Ipaka Lokokwa, 1988).[15]

How effective is such resistance and what rewards are reaped by those who participate in it? The second economy has been effective in supplying these two countries with goods and services otherwise unobtainable because of the demise of the production and distribution system of the official economy.[16] The traders who organize importing and exporting in second-economy trade thus play a significant part in enabling their countries to survive. There are opportunities for accumulating considerable wealth in this process. What have the traders of this study done, and what do they plan to do, with the wealth they have acquired? How successful have they been, and how do they see their futures?

---

[14]A vocabulary particular to the *cambistes*, the unofficial money-changers of the parallel money market, exists in Kinshasa (De Herdt and Marysse, 1996c), and also for the diamond diggers from Bandundu, Congo-Kinshasa, in the Angolan province of Lunda Norte (De Boeck, 1998: 782n).

[15]Included among favourite themes in the information circulated are the embezzlement of public funds by those in power, deaths of public figures, supposedly by poisoning or other unnatural causes, and the dangers threatening from military intervention (Sabakinu Kivulu, 1988: 182–3).

[16]For details of Congo-Kinshasa, see MacGaffey et al., 1991; MacGaffey, 1992, 1994a and b, 1998; De Herdt and Marysse, 1996a,b and c.

Aims and Aspirations for Investment

This study of international second-economy traders has shown that both women and men certainly find extraordinary opportunities to acquire wealth but that they may rapidly lose it again. These opportunities are precarious, beset with danger and uncertainty, and long-term prospects for investment are fraught with political structural difficulties. The *sapeurs*, on the other hand, have turned their backs on the system and created another, in which they spend their wealth, when they have it, in ostentatious living.

The following case histories include both kinds of traders and show the sorts of aspirations they have and how some of them have fared, and why, as they have tried to implement them.

Our first case continues the fortunes of Marie, whom we left in Chapter 4 struggling with a huge debt to the bank incurred for her by a swindler. She had previously lost all her early investment in her taxi service in Brazzaville when her two cars were both in accidents on the same day. She had no insurance but had enough money to repair one of them. This disaster illustrates the precariousness of investing wealth back home in the current political and economic climate of both countries: there is no reliable insurance company, no supportive legal system and no protection against the many hazards.[17]

> *For four years, Marie said, she was paralysed and did not do anything besides her job. She married, got divorced and moved to France with her four children, getting a residence permit through a contact at the embassy. Her training as a nurse enabled her to get a job in a retirement home. Conditions at work were poor, however, and she left the job. She had remarried and decided to return to trading. Leaving her husband and children in Paris, she returned home in 1985 and took up trading with her sister between Congo and West Africa, selling a house lot she owned in Brazzaville to raise the capital. 'We went to Lomé where my sister used to rent a house. We bought* pagnes *always from the same market traders, took them home and sold them on credit to those we knew. I took out an importing licence and paid customs duties. We soon dealt in large enough quantities to become wholesalers. In six months, I had earned CFAF 7 million, most of which I sent to my husband and children.' These two sisters exemplify the high profits that can be made in the cloth trade, primarily carried out by women.[18]*

---

[17]Hernando de Soto has shown how informal businesses in Peru suffer from the absence of a legal system that guarantees their property rights and contracts and helps to promote their economic efficiency (De Soto, 1989: 153–8).

[18]A study in Kinshasa showed that, out of ten venders in the central market, cloth sellers, all of whom were women, made far higher revenues than women and men venders of other goods. Monthly earnings for cloth ranged from 5,226 to 152,000 zaïres, compared with earnings from other products ranging from 910 to 5,225 zaïres (Kanene, 1990: 304).

Marie now determined to open her own business and embarked upon an extraordinarily tenacious struggle to start up a bakery. She began in partnership with a Frenchman, but had to continue on her own when he backed out. She sold two more house lots, leaving only the one she lived on. Then she actually pulled down her house and reconstructed it as a bakery with just one room for her to live in. At last the bakery started up, though slowly at first. In five months it was thriving, and in one year she made enough profit to buy five house lots. She was able to pay off 8 million of her debt to the bank. Hearing that African foods sold well in Paris, she got a CFAF 40 million loan from the bank to expand her bakery business, but used it to start up a shop and a depot in Paris. This turned out to be a wise decision.

In 1994, because of political problems, lack of diesel fuel and the devaluation of the CFA franc, which doubled the costs of flour and transport, the bakery had to close down. The coup of 1997 and the resulting fighting and pillaging destroyed her bakery and razed to the ground the neighbourhood in which it was located. The shop was not doing well either, because a large part of her clientele were Congolese also affected by the political and economic situation back home; nevertheless it is the family's salvation. Marie combined it with running a nganda, but the shop was too crowded for her nganda clientele to pass easily through to get to the back-room bar. So, in 1998, she closed the nganda and opened a licensed restaurant nearby with a nganda in the basement. Her nganda clientele were brought in by her brother-in-law, who works in les circuits. She is not doing very well in this new enterprise, however: she is not young enough to make the nganda successful and the police are suspicious of so much drinking going on in what is supposed to be a restaurant. She continues to hang on grimly, summing it all up for us by saying: 'Life takes great endurance, will-power and patience.'

Our second case is of Beatrice, the worldwide trader who works for an airline. She is continually expanding and diversifying her enterprises. She also made an investment back in Congo-Brazzaville, which did not work out.

She bought equipment for a medical office with the profits of her trade. It went into operation, but was managed by a Congolese who embezzled the funds so that she had to close it down. She plans to sell the equipment to the General Hospital and has the necessary contacts there to do so. It would be possible to rent it out, but she does not intend to do so, because, she says, the Congolese do not respect contracts and there are no laws to enforce them. She plans to develop trade with Nigeria because it is a huge country and she has a family connection there. She already knows wholesalers eager to buy the

T-shirts she has seen in the United States. She also plans new lines of
business in Switzerland, where she has other connections.

Here we see the importance of the role of personal connections in trade:
these future plans are all predicated on them.

Beatrice's ultimate aim, however, is not continued expansion of her
trading enterprise, which she sees as merely a way to accumulate capital.
Her ambition is to set up small production units in Congo. She notes that,
although there is good land, apart from seasonal local products, almost
everything is imported. In 1994, she and some other women had obtained
a loan of CFAF 10 million from a rural credit organization to start soya flour
production. They had already purchased the equipment. One of the
women in the group is in the Chamber of Commerce, and has the
necessary influence and contacts. But the country's recent political strife
must have disrupted these plans.

Our fourth case is Josephine, the *sapeur*, who was so persistent and
successful in becoming a supplier for the Asian shopkeepers. She recounts
how she spent the wealth she acquired.

As soon as I left the Chinese's store, I went directly to a dress shop and
bought dresses for 3,000–4,000 FF. I lent money to my friends from
what was left, and by the end of the month it was all gone, except for
the 5,000 FF I kept back to buy goods in Zaïre and start again. All my
friends were ministers' daughters, I was part of their set. So, if one day
they wore a dress costing 5,000 FF, if I went to a party and wanted
people to notice me, I would wear a dress costing the same amount.
Every Saturday at our parties, we would have la Sape *and drink*
champagne. I was an ambianceur *and not a trader; each month I*
spent all my money. But one day I shall open a restaurant and a food
shop in Brazzaville with some other flight attendants.

The ambition of Thérèse, the *nganda* owner and *sapeur*, was also eventually to return to Brazzaville and to have a restaurant, nightclub and
grocery store on a plot of land she has bought there.

Both Marie and Beatrice aspired to set up productive enterprises
catering to the needs of the local economy in their own countries. Jean,
who owned the two shops with his wife in Paris, has likewise suffered
from the civil strife of Congo-Brazzaville because it has destroyed the shop
his wife owned there. The tax burden of their Paris shops became too
onerous thereafter and both had to be sold because of non-payment of
taxes. He has set up in a shipping business with a Malian. This was a
licensed enterprise but they had another unlicensed business on the side,
arranging the delivery of goods or money to Congo-Brazzaville.

We see here people struggling against tremendous odds: against political
upheaval and civil violence, against an unsupportive, unprotective legal
system, against oppressive regulation. They have resisted these odds with

creativity and innovation, persistence and sheer hard work. Their future does not look hopeful. Why are the odds against them so great? What are the implications of their histories and those of the *sapeurs*? The concluding chapter will attempt to provide some answers to these questions and to others that arise from the life histories of our informants.

7

Conclusion The Wider Context

We started this book with a vignette of the cultural mingling which is a commonplace of the traders' world and which has intensified with the transport and communications revolution. As we end our account, we want to highlight again the diversity and richness of this cultural process. Three of its features in particular have emerged in the course of our study: the combining of elements from African and European cultures as the means by which people are 'refashioning the West in their own terms' (De Boeck, 1998: 805); the mixed vocabulary of French and African words that graphically expresses this combination and the activities that are part of it; and the emphasis on appearance and performance. This latter is manifested in the wearing of wax-print cloth and the use of African beauty products; in the 'look' of the *sapeurs*, as they flaunt their designer-label clothes and engage in the competitive consumption of their 'tournaments of value'; and in the African popular music heard and performed so constantly in this culture.

We shall conclude with some reflections on how our study fits in with current developments in anthropology, as scholars confront the increasing complexity of the global scene. What of the wider political context of the traders' struggle? What implications does this trade have for understanding the working of the global economy and the relations between its local and global levels? The traders draw on diverse cultural elements as they construct multiple identities in their life trajectories through these levels, but is there a wider political and economic significance to their individual histories?

Chaos, Structure and Process

Recent trends in anthropological thinking have emphasized the dynamic but essentially chaotic nature of the global system that has come about through the intensification of worldwide social relations. Rather than seeking forms of social collectivity in this situation, some scholars think we should concentrate on individualized irregularities (Cheater, 1995: 124–7), while some find that structures disappear in the perception of a disjunctive global world, which lacks boundaries or regularities and has its cultural forms overlapping (Appadurai, 1990: 18–20). Others, however, point out that the idea of chaos rather than equilibrium in social systems is not new, but was already around forty years ago when Edmund Leach was questioning the equilibrium focus in anthropology in the early 1950s (Abrahams, 1990: 17). A different perspective for understanding this mingling of systems is that of John Law. He draws on the network philosophy of science, on structuralism and post-structuralism, and on actor-network theory, in which 'the vision is of many semiotic systems, many orderings, jostling together to generate the social', but he is more concerned with process than is most structuralist writing. He seeks to tell stories that have to do with the processes of ordering (Law, 1994: 18). The tale of Jerome the wholesaler, with which we began, vividly expresses the traders' instrumental ordering and incorporation of many semiotic systems in their lives as part of the cultural mingling of the world system.

But this ordering of juxtaposed systems, however chaotic they may seem, takes place in a world which still retains the political and economic structures of nation states, with their monopoly of the use of force to protect them and to enforce their laws. There are also multinational companies and other economic entities of the global economy, and the relations between them which reinforce their power, which must be taken into account. Questions concerning these aspects of society, which constitute the basis of relations and structures of power, are neglected in the views described above and, more generally, by postmodern anthropologists. In the focus on dynamism and agency, cultural mingling, global chaos and ramifying networks, we must not fail to take account of the political and economic structures that still retain their power and influence and constitute the context and framework of this chaotic mingling that we observe. In an overview of the history of anthropology and its current trends, William Roseberry asks: 'What has fallen out of favour in anthropology? In practice, it seems to be any work that is too ethnographic, too sociological, too structural, too political, too economic or too processual' (Roseberry, 1996: 21). We share this concern and emphasize that the traders of our study are marginalized by social structural constraints through which the rich and powerful of the dominant political class oppress them in the different countries in which they live.

Thus, although we have focused less on structures than on agency, showing by means of individual histories how those who are marginalized and excluded are actively engaged agents of their own lives and not just passive victims, we recognize that the balance between individual responsibility and structural constraints is a delicate one for ethnographic analysis. Van Velsen argued in the late 1960s for 'situational analysis' with its emphasis on process, because structural analysis laid too much emphasis on consistency, ignoring conflicting norms and the choice of action that resulted for individuals.

> Records of actual situations and particular behavior have found their way from the fieldworker's notebooks into his analytical descriptions, not as 'apt illustrations' ... of the author's abstract formulations but as a constituent part of the analysis. (Van Velsen, 1967: 137–43)

We have treated the traders' histories as constituent parts of our analysis, but, as we conclude, we emphasize also their location in the wider national and global context. What is lost in the current emphasis on the perspective of dynamic chaos, of international networks of individuals, of human agency, is the need to understand the relations and structures of power which are the context for, and impose constraints on, people's lives and on their individual actions. What do these structures consist of in the wider context of the global economy in which the traders operate?

Global Political and Economic Structures

World society is entering a new era in the relationship between power and the division of labour in the global context (Mittelman, 1996: 2). As part of the expansion of capital, the new international division of labour includes massive industrial relocation to the industrializing countries of the so-called 'Third World', the subdivision of manufacturing processes into multiple partial operations and major technological innovations. Firms are seeking new investment opportunities with cheap labour costs, but, though low-skilled labour tasks are transferred, most research and development are not. Thus manufacturing and sales are more globalized than technological development, research and financial control. In the 1980s the change was from an emphasis on mass production and mass consumption to a system of flexible production for specialized niche markets. Technological innovations enabled the newly developing countries to take up higher value-added operations. In this changing international division of labour, the gap between rich and poor has widened and upward mobility remains relatively limited (Ibid.: 15–16). Both the West Central African countries of our study are affected by this situation, and it constrains the alternatives and opportunities available to the traders.

The global system is routinely described in terms of global and local levels. But reality is more complex than this simple duality. What are the different levels in which the traders practise their international commerce? How are they affected by the political and economic structures of different levels?

We can demarcate these levels as follows. There is the overarching global level of international capitalism, controlled by multinational firms, by the governments of the advanced industrialized countries and by international financial institutions. Below this there is a nesting hierarchy of local levels, consisting of nation states, their component regions, cities and towns, urban neighbourhoods and rural communities, each level controlled by its own power structure and institutions. At each level and in the relations between them, there is a continuing dynamic of struggle between the dominant, who exercise power and control, and the dominated, who contest this power and the constraints it imposes on them.

In the details of their life histories, we move with the traders through these constituent levels of the global scene at different stages of their existence. At the local level, in village, town or city, they find themselves excluded and disadvantaged by their national political and economic system. As they seek greater opportunities in other continents, they find themselves disadvantaged again by the situation in the advanced industrialized nations of France and Belgium, where jobs and opportunities are dwindling because of the recent global economic developments we have just described, and where restrictions on immigration are becoming stricter. These forces in the local and the wider levels of the global economy have propelled the individuals of our study into participating in international second-economy trade. Our account has shown how they ingeniously find ways of exploiting institutions and organizations at the national and global level, seeking opportunities in creative and innovative ways to make their individual trading possible and profitable.

Moving Beyond State–Society Relations

In the past, the nation state and other organizations of a transnational kind have been emphasized as actors in the international arena.[1] But the increasing institutional dysfunction of African states has led to a move away from this focus on states and on state–society relations. Some recent studies provide more useful perspectives on the ruinous political and economic realities confronting the traders in their respective countries.

Jean-François Bayart's idea of the 'rhizome state' emphasizes the pervasive clientelistic networks of the complex and devious ramifications of state power so evident in these West Central African republics, which motivated some of the traders of our study to emigrate. This concept focuses on the interpenetration of state and society rather than on their separation (Bayart, 1993: 218–27). William Reno looks at the links between state and markets rather than analysing state versus society (Reno, 1995). He takes up Bayart's identification of political authority and its

---

[1]In Africa this has produced some classic studies of the state and of the relation between state and civil society, such as Callaghy, 1984; Young and Turner, 1985; Rothchild and Chazan, 1988; Harbeson et al., 1994.

conjunction with economic accumulation, *la politique du ventre* (the politics of the belly) (Bayart, 1993), and expands it in his seminal study of Sierra Leone, in which he shows that its rulers have drawn power from their abilities to control informal markets and their material rewards. As we detailed in Chapter 2, it is just such a situation which has been a major factor in the long decline and crisis of Congo-Kinshasa.

At the beginning of the book we raised the question: how can people live in the situations of disordered violence that we find in both these Central African countries and how do they react to such brutally predatory systems? The traders' life histories have provided us with some vividly graphic accounts of how they do so as they take up international second-economy trade.

Liminality as an Antistructural State

Through their trade, the traders resist and oppose the situation in which they find themselves. Victor Turner views liminality as an antistructural state and presents it as a creative response to disorder. The two types of liminality:

> consist of a confrontation between that domain which pertains to the person, that is, social structure and cultural order, and that which belongs to the individual, that is, the critical and potentially creative destructuration of that order. The intent of individuals in antistructural liminality is not to produce chaos but to realize a new and more effective integration of the components of experience for which there is no traditional precedent. This may look like chaos to the representatives of traditional order, but may in fact be a creative response to conditions that require societal reordering. (Turner, 1992: 148)

This view enables us to reconcile political and structural perspectives with the perceptions of global chaos discussed earlier. The conditions in the home countries of these traders and the exclusion they are subject to both at home and on moving to other countries certainly constitute conditions that require societal reordering. Their response, as has been evident in the life histories, is creative as they seek to provide their own order and predictability in the midst of disorder.

As well as the betwixt-and-between state of liminality, there are also states of outsiderhood and marginality. For Turner, marginals are members of two or more groups and include migrants of different kinds (Turner, 1974: 232–3). The individual who is excluded from the social matrix may become an innovator, an agent for the formulation of new moralities. But there is always the possibility that such formulations may be immoral or anti-moral (Turner, 1992: 160).

Ritual does not only refer to sacred ritual states: it has been described as an aspect of almost any kind of action (Leach, 1954: 13), and as 'an integral dimension of everyday existence' (Comaroff and Comaroff, 1993: xviii). Anthropologists and historians have been rethinking ritual, detaching it from the sacred to see it as 'an instrument of history in all human societies at all times'. It should not be reduced to ceremonial action isolated from the real world but seen for what it often is: 'a vital element in the processes that make and remake social facts and collective identities'. Jean and John Comaroff seek to discover the social events through which common people contest dominant discourses. They find that ritual, loosely defined as 'intentional communication' or 'signifying practice,' is especially productive for understanding unconventional subcultures (Ibid.: xvi–xvii), that is, people who might be considered liminal. This viewpoint is very different from the classical one, which sees ritual as essentially the means of ensuring social reproduction and cultural continuity, and of reinforcing political authority. It may be, and often is, instead 'a site and a means of experimental practice, of subversive poetics, of creative tension and transformative actions' (Ibid.: xxix). We can view from this perspective the ostentatious forms of dress and ritualized drinking patterns in *nganda* of traders celebrating successful ventures that are outside the law in various ways. In so doing, they are expressing their opposition to the dominant culture and simultaneously constructing and expressing their own collective identity.

Traders and the Process of Class Struggle

The background for the activities of the traders of our study includes the relations between classes at the local levels, the linkage of local levels into the broader system, and the shifting alliances and oppositions within levels, all of which are involved in the dynamic processes of class conflict in the global system. At issue are relations of domination and subordination and the dynamics of the struggle that challenges these relations. The traders' refusal to comply with regulations and their defiant reactions to exclusion from opportunity are a part of this struggle. They do not organize in any systematic way to further their class interests, and so do not constitute, in Marx's terms, a 'class for itself'. They are rather part of the unorganized broader category of a 'class in itself'. The networks in which they participate do not co-operate in organized opposition, they are activated to further the interests of individuals who are in competition with one another. But the histories of these traders and their language usage make evident their awareness of their class position and common class situation in opposition to those who dominate and oppress them. One specific form of resistance to domination has been the outbreaks of pillage and the enforced redistribution of wealth in Congo-Kinshasa, a form of collective action that is to some degree organized: things looted are things that can be sold; particular people or businesses are targeted (de

Villers, 1992: 135); *radio trottoir* is the means of communication and thus of organization.[2]

The multiple forms of everyday resistance identified by James Scott can constitute a significant element of class struggle. Scott argues that those who practise hidden defiance are an essential force in political break-throughs: 'charismatic acts gain their social force by virtue of their roots in the hidden transcript of a subordinate group' (Scott, 1990: 203). Though individual acts of hidden resistance amount to little, the aggregated effect of their acts can have considerable and significant effect.[3] Michel Foucault likewise believes that, even though power may take some institutionalized pyramidal form, its historical origin does not necessarily have to have come from an identifiable individual or group of individuals deciding to further their interests but may have come from 'tactics ... invented and organised from the starting points of local conditions and particular needs. They took shape in piecemeal fashion, prior to any class strategy designed to weld them into vast, coherent ensembles' (Foucault, 1972: 159). Resistance, like power, he says, is multiple, and we should not assume a massive binary structure of 'dominators' and 'dominated' but rather 'a multiform production of relations of domination' (Ibid.: 142).

In Congo-Kinshasa, the dominance of second-economy enterprise in housing construction, transportation and small retail and service enter-prises in Kinshasa and the dependence of the city's economic functioning on such enterprise have represented a change in the economic base of the subordinated classes in the last thirty years (MacGaffey, 1992, 1998). The huge scale of goods and services essential to the functioning of society that are provided by second-economy enterprise signifies a shift in the economic power base of the subordinated classes since independence that represents real change. As people take matters into their own hands and create a functioning alternative economy, and also functioning alternative social institutions (see MacGaffey, 1996), they are resisting and contesting the control and oppression imposed on them by the powerful. Laurent Kabila's easy takeover of Zaïre and overthrow of Mobutu in 1997 appear to be a classic illustration of Scott's view that charismatic acts have hidden roots.

Other studies have shown the role of networks of relationships and of non-violent action for bringing about political change both in Africa and in the Eastern bloc countries. In Tanzania, the government was forced to change its policies as the result of people's persistent daily resistance and

---

[2]One account in the press of the pillages of 1990 in Kinshasa was aware of this organization: 'Who ordered a demonstration throughout the city? No political organization or union can be suspected. Who decreed 10h00 for the commencement of hostilities? Who advised the frenzied participants to block all the main roads? Who?' (de Villers, 1992: 126)

[3]Criticism has been levelled at Scott's views on the grounds of their imprecision and lack of cultural particularity (Geschiere, 1986; Kondo, 1990: 219–21; Gal, 1995), but they seem to us very illuminating and to be borne out in our data from the traders' lives.

non-compliance (Tripp, 1997). In Cairo, the *sha'b*, the people of the subordinated classes, resist the state through pervasive and efficient networks that aggregate their interests and constitute a critical, though concealed, arena of political activity that 'does not directly oppose the state or its elite but lies between individual actions and organized, visible, legal collective, action within the context of Egyptian politics and society' (Singerman, 1995: 8). In Hungary, private producers have formed a new class of 'socialist entrepreneurs' in the socialist economy and forced concessions from bureaucrats in a 'silent revolution from below' (Szelenyi et al., 1988: 4–5). The dissent of 'citizens' initiatives' in Eastern Europe, as people oppose the alienating pressure of the system under 'post-totalitarian' communist states, constitute 'pre-political' events and processes (Havel et al., 1985: 50–67).

The traders in this study are part of such dissent. The cross-border and intercontinental trade that they and others like them engage in are critical for maintaining the economies of these two Central African countries, where the official economy has all but collapsed and the unofficial economy is sustained by its own system of import and export. The traders do not organize themselves into concerted political action but they are a part of this general dissent, which can result in, or provide support for, political change, in the way it has happened elsewhere.

Economically, the traders' activities are a part of a worldwide phenomenon. Taken singly, the contribution of these Central Africans to trade in the global economy through their international second-economy trade cannot be precisely calculated. Individual activities are small-scale, but, in the aggregate together with those of other such traders, they are very considerable because they are so widespread. They constitute an element in the functioning of the global economy that should not be ignored. Very little is known about such trade. This study of its organization, motivation, cultural connections, hazards and political and economic implications is intended to make a start on filling this gap in our knowledge.

BIBLIOGRAPHY

Abrahams, Ray. 1990. 'Chaos and Kachin', *Anthropology Today* 6 (3): 15–17.

Achikbache, Bahjat & Anglade, Francis. 1988. 'Les villes prises d'assaut: les migrations internes', *Politique Africaine* 31: 6–14.

Althabe, Gérard. 1963. 'Le chomage à Brazzaville en 1957. Etude psychologique (1ère partie)', *Cahiers Orstom* 1 (4), série sciences humaines.

Amin, Samir & Coquery-Vidrovitch, Catherine. 1969. *Histoire économique du Congo, 1880–1968. Du Congo Français à l'Union Douanière et Economique d'Afrique Centrale.* Paris and Dakar: IFAN, Anthropos.

Appadurai, Arjun, ed. 1986. *The Social Life of Things: Commodities in Cultural Perspective.* Cambridge: Cambridge University Press.

—— 1990. 'Disjuncture and Difference in the Global Cultural Economy', *Public Culture* 2 (2): 1–23.

Arditi, Claude. 1993. 'Commerce, Islam et Etat au Tchad (1900–1990)', in Grégoire & Labazée.

Balandier, Georges. 1963. *Sociologie actuelle de l'Afrique noire: Dynamique sociale en Afrique Centrale.* Paris: Presses Universitaires de France.

—— 1985. *Sociologie des Brazzaville noires.* 2nd edn. Paris: Presse de la Fondation Nationale de Sciences Politique.

Barou, Jacques. 1987. 'In the Aftermath of Colonization: Black African Immigrants in France', in *Migrants in Europe: the Role of Family, Labor, and Politics.* Eds. H. C. Buechler & J.-M. Buechler. New York: Greenwood Press.

Bayart, Jean-François. 1981. 'Le Politique par le bas en Afrique-noire' *Politique Africaine* 1: 53–83.

—— 1993. *The State in Africa: the Politics of the Belly.* New York: Longman.

Bazenguissa-Ganga, Rémy. 1992a. '"Belles maisons" contre S.A.P.E.: pratique de valorization symbolique au Congo', in *Etat et société dans le tiers-monde: de la modernisation à la démocratisation?* Eds. C. F. M. Haubert, F. Leimdorder, A. Marie & Nam Tran Nguyen Trong. Paris: Publications de la Sorbonne.

—— 1992b. 'La Sape et la politique au Congo', *Journal des Africanistes* 62 (1): 151–7.

—— 1996a. 'Milices et bandes armées à Brazzaville: enquête sur la violence politique et sociale des jeunes déclassés', *Les Etudes du Ceri* 13.

—— 1996b. 'Le role des médias dans la construction des identités de violence à Brazzaville', in *Identités et démocratie en Afrique et ailleurs*. Ed. P. Yengo. Paris: L'Harmattan.

—— 1997. *Les Voies du politique au Congo: essai de sociologie historique*. Paris: Karthala.

Bazenguissa-Ganga, Rémy, & MacGaffey, Janet. 1995. 'Vivre et briller: à Paris, des jeunes Congolais et Zairois en marge de la légalité économique', *Politique Africaine* 57: 124–33.

Becker, Howard. 1963. *Outsiders: Studies in the Sociology of Deviance*. New York: Free Press.

Bender, Wolfgang. 1991. *Sweet Mother: Modern African Music*. Chicago: University of Chicago Press.

Ben-Porath, Yoram. 1980. 'The F-Connection: Families, Friends, and Firms and the Organization of Exchange', *Population and Development Review* 6: 1–29.

Bertrand, Hughes. 1975. *Le Congo, formation sociale et mode de développement économique*. Paris: Maspero.

Biaya, T. K. 1985. 'La cuistrerie de Mbuji Mayi (Zaire)', *Génève-Afrique* 23: 62–85.

—— 1994. '*Mundele, ndumba* et ambiance: Le vrai "Bal blanc et noir(e)"', in *Belgique/Zaïre: une histoire en quête d'avenir*. Ed. G. de Villers. Cahiers Africains No. 9–10–11. Brussels: CEDAF; Paris: L'Harmattan.

—— 1996. 'S'inventer individu dans la modernité africaine (XIXè–XXès.). Une approche historique des pratiques et rationalités africaines à partir des cas *mwana dyamba, mwananyi* et *mwana mayi*'. Paper presented at 'L'argent, feuille morte? l'Afrique centrale avant et après le désenchantement de la modernité' Conference. Louvain, 21–22 June.

Boissevain, Jeremy. 1974. *Friends of Friends: Networks, Manipulators and Coalitions*. Oxford: Basil Blackwell.

Bolya, C. et al. 1994. 'Coopération, immigration: les "bons", les "brutes" et les "truands"', in *Belgique/Zaïre: une histoire en quête d'avenir*. Ed. G. de Villers. Cahiers Africains No. 9–10–11. Brussels: CEDAF; Paris: L'Harmattan.

Bourgois, Philippe. 1995. *In Search of Respect: Selling Crack in El Barrio*. Cambridge: Cambridge University Press.

Braeckman, Colette. 1992. *Le Dinosaure: le Zaïre de Mobutu*. Paris: Fayard.

Bredeloup, Sylvie. 1993. 'Les migrants du fleuve Sénégal: à quand la "Diamspora"?', *Revue Européenne des Migrations Internationales* 9 (1): 67–93.

Buford, Bill. 1990. *Among the Thugs*. London: Norton.

Callaghy, Thomas M. 1984. *The State–Society Struggle: Zaire in Comparative Perspective*. New York: Columbia University Press.

Carim, Xavier. 1995. 'Illegal Migration to South Africa', *Africa Insight* 25 (4): 221–30.

Carrier, James G. 1992. 'Occidentalism: the World Turned Upside-Down', *American Ethnologist* 19 (2): 195–212.

Cheater, Angela. 1995. 'Globalisation and the New Technologies of Knowing: Anthropological Calculus or Chaos?', in *Shifting Contexts: Transformations in Anthropological Knowledge*. Ed. M. Strathern. London and New York: Routledge.

Clark, Gracia. 1998. 'Après le Déluge? Commentary on Ghana from Kumasi Central Market'. Paper presented at the American Ethnological Society Annual Conference. 6–10 May, University of Toronto.

Clifford, James. 1983. 'On Ethnographic Authority', *Representations* 1 (2): 118–46.

Codou, Alain. 1987. 'Du vin de palme à la bière: changement de type de consommation et de mode de vie à Brazzaville', *Journées d'Etudes sur Brazzaville, actes du colloque*: 547–56. ORSTOM & AGECO.

Cohen, Abner. 1969. *Custom and Politics in Urban Africa: a Study of Hausa Migrants in Yoruba Towns*. London: Routledge and Kegan Paul.

—— 1971. 'Cultural Strategies in the Organization of Trading Diasporas', in Meillassoux.

Cohen, Ronald. 1978. 'Ethnicity: Problem and Focus in Anthropology', *Annual Review of Anthropology* 7: 379–403.

Coleman, James S. 1988. 'Social Capital in the Creation of Human Capital', *American Journal of Sociology* 94: S95–S120.

Comaroff, Jean & Comaroff, John. 1993. 'Introduction', in *Modernity and its Malcontents: Ritual and Power in Postcolonial Africa*. Eds. J. Comaroff & J. Comaroff. Chicago: University of Chicago Press.

Comhaire-Sylvain, Suzanne. 1968. *Femmes de Kinshasa: hier et aujour-d'hui*. Paris: Mouton & Co.

Cornelius, Wayne A. 1982. 'Interviewing Undocumented Immigrants: Methodological Reflections Based on Fieldwork in Mexico and the U.S.', *The International Migration Review (IMR)* 16: 378–411.

Curtin, Philip D. 1984. *Cross-Cultural Trade in World History*. Cambridge: Cambridge University Press.

De Boeck, Filip. 1998. 'Domesticating Diamonds and Dollars: Identity, Expenditure and Sharing in Southwestern Zaire (1984–1997)'. *Development and Change* 29 (4): 177–810.

de Certeau, Michel. 1984. *The Practice of Everyday Life*. Translation of *L'Invention du quotidien: arts de faire*, 1980, by Steven F. Rendall. Berkeley, CA: University of California Press.

De Graaf, Nan Dirk & Flap, Hendrik Derk. 1988. 'With a Little Help from my Friends', *Social Forces* 67: 452–72.

De Herdt, Tom & Marysse, Stefan. 1996a. *Comment survivent les Kinois? Quand l'état dépérit*. University of Antwerp, Centre for Development Studies.

—— 1996b. *L'Economie informelle au Zaïre: (sur)vie et pauvreté dans la période de transition*. Paris and Brussels: L'Harmattan and CEDAF.

—— 1996c. 'La réinvention du marché par le bas et la fin du monopole féminin dans le "cambisme" à Kinshasa'. Paper presented at 'L'argent, feuille morte? L'Afrique centrale avant et après le désenchantement de la modernité' Conference, Louvain, 21–22 June.

Desjarlais, Robert & Kleinman, Arthur. 1994. 'Violence and Demoralization in the New World Disorder', *Anthropology Today* 10 (5): 9–12.

De Soto, Hernando. 1989. *The Other Path: the Invisible Revolution in the Third World.* New York: Harper and Row.

Devauges, Roland. 1963. 'Etude du chômage à Brazzaville en 1967. Etude sociologique', *Cahiers Orstom* 1 (1), série sciences humaines.

—— 1977. *L'Oncle, le ndoki et l'entrepreneur: la petite entreprise congolaise à Brazzaville.* Paris: ORSTOM.

de Villers, Gauthier. 1992. *Zaïre 1990–1991: faits et dits de la société d'après de la presse.* Vol. 2, *Zaïre, années 90.* Brussels: CEDAF.

Devereux, Stephen & John Hoddinott, eds. 1993. *Fieldwork in Developing Countries.* Boulder, CO: Lynne Rienner.

Devisch, René. 1995. 'Frenzy, Violence, and Ethical Renewal in Kinshasa', *Public Culture* 7 (3): 593–629.

DIAL, Paris. 1997. *Les échanges transfrontaliers entre le Cameroun et le Nigéria depuis la dévaluation.* République de Cameroun, Ministère des Finances, Direction de la Statistique et de la Comptabilité Nationale.

Diata, Hervé. 1989. 'Ajustement structurel au Congo', *Revue Tiers-Monde* XXX (janv.–mars): 187–206.

Dinan, C. 1983. 'Sugar Daddies and Gold-Diggers: The White Collar Single Woman in Accra', in *Female and Male in West Africa.* Ed. C. Oppong. London: George Allen and Unwin.

Dodier, Nicolas. 1995. *Les Hommes et les machines: la conscience collective dans les sociétés technicisées.* Paris: Métailié.

Dore, Ronald. 1983. 'Goodwill and the Spirit of Market Capitalism', *The British Journal of Sociology* 34 (4): 459–82.

Dorier-Apprill, Elisabeth & Ziavoula, Robert. 1996. 'Géographie des ethnies, géographie des conflits à Brazzaville', in *Villes du Sud.* Ed. Emile Lebris. Paris: Orstom.

Douglas, Mary & Isherwood, Baron. 1979. *The World of Goods.* New York: Basic Books.

Ebin, Victoria. 1992. 'A la recherche de nouveaux "poissons": stratégies commerciales mourides par temps de crise', *Politique Africaine* 45: 86–99.

—— 1993. Les commerçants mourides à Marseille et à New York: regards sur les stratégies d'implantation', In Grégoire & Labazée.

Eliou, Marie. 1977. *La Formation de la conscience nationale en République Populaire du Congo.* Paris: Anthropos.

Ellis, Stephen & MacGaffey, Janet. 1996. 'Research on Sub-Saharan Africa's Unrecorded International Trade: Some Methodological and Conceptual Problems', *African Studies Review* 39 (2): 19–41.

Enquête collective du Département de Sociologie. 1986. 'Pour une sociologie des "bars" Congolais.' Conference, March 30, Marien Ngouabi University, Brazzaville.

Fabian, Johannes. 1978. 'Popular Culture in Africa: Findings and Conjectures', *Africa* 48 (4): 315–34.

Featherstone, Mike. 1990. 'Global Culture: an Introduction', in Featherstone.

Featherstone, Mike, ed. 1990. *Global Culture: Nationalism, Globalization and Modernity*. London: Sage.

Fidani, Geneviève. 1993. 'Les Zaïrois à l'assaut de Johannesburg', *Jeune Afrique* 1690: 52–4.

Fisiy, Cyprian F. & Geschiere, Peter. 1991. 'Sorcery, Witchcraft and Accumulation: Regional Variations in South and West Cameroon', *Critique of Anthropology* 11 (3): 251–71.

Fleisher, Michael. 1998. 'Cattle Raiding and Its Correlates: The Cultural–Ecological Consequences of Market-Oriented Cattle Raiding Among the Kuria of Tanzania', *Human Ecology* 26 (4): 547–72.

Flynn, Donna K. 1997. '"We Are the Border": Identity, Exchange and the State Along the Benin–Nigeria Border', *American Ethnologist* 24 (2): 311–30.

Fortes, Meyer. 1949. 'Time and Social Structure: an Ashanti Case Study', in *Social Structure*. Ed. M. Fortes. Oxford: Clarendon Press.

Fottorino, Eric. 1991. *La Piste blanche: l'Afrique sous l'emprise de la drogue*. Paris: Balland.

Foucault, Michel. 1972. *Power and Knowledge*. New York: Pantheon Books.

Francis, Elizabeth. 1993. 'Qualitative Research: Collecting Life Histories', in Devereux & Hoddinott.

Friedman, Jonathan. 1990. 'Being in the World: Globalization and Localization', in Featherstone.

—— 1992. 'The Political Economy of Elegance', *Culture and History* 7: 101–25.

Fukuyama, Francis. 1995. *Trust: the Social Virtues and the Creation of Prosperity*. London: The Free Press.

Gal, Susan. 1989. 'Language and Political Economy', *Annual Review of Anthropology* 18: 345–67.

—— 1995. 'Language and the "Arts of Resistance"', *Cultural Anthropology* 10 (3): 407–24.

Gandoulou, Justin-Daniel. 1984. *Entre Paris et Bacongo*. Paris: CCI-Centre Georges Pompidou. Reissued 1989 as *Au coeur de la Sape: moeurs et aventures de Congolais à Paris*. Paris: L'Harmattan.

—— 1989. Dandies à Bacongo: *Le Culte de l'élégance dans la société Congolaise contemporaine*. Paris: L'Harmattan.

Gambetta, D., ed. 1988. *Trust: Making and Breaking Co-operative Relations*. Oxford: Basil Blackwell.

Gerth, H. H. & Mills, C. Wright, eds. 1946. *From Max Weber: Essays in Sociology*. Oxford: Oxford University Press.

Geschiere, Peter. 1986. 'Hegemonic Regimes and Popular Protest – Bayart, Gramsci and the State in Cameroon', *Les Cahiers du CEDAF* (July): 309–47.

—— 1995. *Sorcellerie et politique: la viande des autres*. Paris: Karthala.

Giddens, Anthony. 1990. *The Consequences of Modernity*. Stanford, CA: Stanford University Press.

Gondola, Charles Didier. 1993. 'Musique moderne et identités citadines: le cas du Congo-Zaïre', *Afrique Contemporaine* 168: 155–68.

—— 1997a. *Villes miroirs: migrations et identités urbaines à Kinshasa et Brazzaville 1930–1970*. Paris: Harmattan.

—— 1997b. 'Popular Music, Urban Society, and Changing Gender Relations in Kinshasa, Zaïre (1950–1990)', in *Gendered Encounters: Challenging Cultural Boundaries and Social Hierarchies in Africa*. Eds. M. Grosz-Ngaté & O. H. Kokole. New York: Routledge.

Goody, Jack, ed. 1962. *The Developmental Cycle in Domestic Groups*. London: Cambridge University Press.

Gouldner, Alvin W. 1960. 'The Norm of Reciprocity: a Preliminary Statement', *American Sociological Review* 25 (2): 161–78.

Grabowski, Richard. 1997. 'Traders' Dilemmas and Development: A Variety of Solutions', *New Political Economy* 2 (3): 387–404.

Grégoire, Emmanuel. 1991. 'Les chemins de la contrebande: étude des réseaux commerciaux en pays Haoussa', *Cahiers d'Etudes Africaines* 31 (124): 509–32.

—— 1993. 'La Trilogie des réseaux marchands haoussas: un clientélisme social, religieux et étatique', in Grégoire & Labazée.

Grégoire, Emmanuel & Labazée, Pascal, eds. 1993. *Grands commerçants d'Afrique de l'Ouest: Logiques et pratiques d'un groupe d'hommes d'affaires contemporains*. Paris: Karthala.

Gruenais, Marc-Eric, Mouamda Mbambi, Florent & Tonda, Joseph. 1995. 'Messies, fêtiches et luttes de pouvoir entre les "grands hommes" du Congo démocratique', *Cahiers d'Etudes Africaines* 35 (1) 137: 163–94.

Gudeman, Stephen & Rivera, Alberto. 1989. 'Colombian Conversations', *Current Anthropology* 30 (3): 267–76.

—— 1990. *Conversations in Colombia: the Domestic Economy in Life and Text*. Cambridge: Cambridge University Press.

Gugler, Joseph. 1975. 'Migration and Ethnicity in Sub-Saharan Africa: Affinity, Rural Interests, and Urban Alignments', in *Migration and Development: Implications for Ethnic Identity and Political Conflict*. Eds. H. Safa & B. du Toit. The Hague: Mouton.

Guyer, Jane. 1988. 'Dynamic Approaches to Domestic Budgeting: Cases and Methods from Africa', in *A Home Divided: Women and Income in the Third World*. Eds. D. Dwyer & J. Bruce. Stanford, CA: Stanford University Press.

Halperin, Rhoda H. 1990. *The Livelihood of Kin: Making Ends Meet 'The Kentucky Way'*. Austin, TX: University of Texas Press.

Hannerz, Ulf. 1990. 'Cosmopolitans and Locals in World Culture', in Featherstone.

Harbeson, John, Rothchild, Donald & Chazan, Naomi, eds. 1994. *Civil Society and the State in Africa*. Boulder, CO: Lynne Rienner.

Hart, Keith. 1988. 'Kinship, Contract, and Trust: the Economic Organization of Migrants in an African City Slum', in *Trust: Making and Breaking Cooperative Relations*. Ed. D. Gambetta. Oxford: Basil Blackwell.

Havel, Vaclav et al. 1985. *The Power of the Powerless: Citizens Against the State in Central-Eastern Europe*. Armonk, NY: M. E. Sharpe.

Heath, Deborah. 1992. 'Fashion, Anti-Fashion, and Heteroglossia in Urban Senegal', *American Ethnologist* 19: 19–33.

Henry, Stuart & Mars, Gerald. 1978. 'Crime at Work: The Social Construction of Amateur Property Theft', *Sociology* 12: 245–63.

Herrera, Javier. 1992a. *Observatoire OCISCA impact des politiques différentielles et échanges transfrontaliers Cameroun-Nigeria*. Paris: OCISCA.

—— 1992b. *Bétail, naira et franc CFA: un flux transfrontalier entre Nigéria et Cameroun*. Paris: OCISCA.

Ho, Christine. 1993. 'The Internationalization of Kinship and the Feminization of Caribbean Migration: the Case of Afro-Trinidadian Immigrants in Los Angeles', *Human Organization* 52 (1): 32–40.

Igue, John O. & Soule, Bio G. 1992. *L'État-entrepôt au Bénin: commerce informel ou solution à la crise?* Paris: Karthala.

Institut National des Statistiques et des Etudes Economiques (INSEE). Results, no. 19. 1992. *Actualités Migrations*, no. 421: 16–31.

Ipaka Lokokwa, Nsambi. 1988. 'La radio-trottoir au Zaïre: une contribution à l'étude des modes populaires d'action politique', *Analyses Sociales* 5 (1): 57–62.

Irwin, John. 1972. 'Participant Observation of Criminals', in *Research on Deviance*. Ed. J. Douglas. New York: Random House.

Isaacman, Allen. 1990. 'Peasants and Rural Social Protest in Africa', *African Studies Review* 33 (2): 1–120.

Jarillo, J. Carlos. 1988. 'On Strategic Networks', *Strategic Management Journal* 9: 31–41.

Kanene, Mpali S. 1990. 'Les marchés de Kinshasa: structure, localization et leur role dans la distribution des biens et des services.' Ph.D. dissertation, Faculté des Sciences, University of Liège.

Kondo, Dorinne K. 1990. *Crafting Selves: Power, Gender, and Discourses of Identity in a Japanese Workplace*. Chicago: University of Chicago Press.

Kongo, Michel. 1987. 'Les Petits métiers crées à partir du trafic entre le Zaïre et le Congo', in *Journées d'étude sur Brazzaville*, actes du colloque, Brazzaville, 25–28 April, ORSTOM – AGECO: 411–26.

Kopytoff, Igor. 1986. 'The Cultural Biography of Things: Commoditization as Process', in Appadurai.

Krokfors, Christer. 1995. 'Poverty, Environmental Stress and Culture as Factors in African Migrations, in *The Migration Experience in Africa*. Eds. J. Baker & Tada Akin Aina. Uppsala: Nordiska Afrikainstitutet.

Labazée, Pascal. 1993. 'Les échanges entre le Mali, le Burkina Faso et le nord de la Côte-d'Ivoire', in Grégoire & Labazée.

La Fontaine, Jean. 1970. *City Politics: a Study of Leopoldville 1962–63.* Cambridge: Cambridge University Press.

—— 1974. 'The Free Women of Kinshasa', in *Choice and Change: Essays in Honor of Lucy Mair.* Ed. J. Davis. New York: Humanities Press.

—— 1975. 'Unstructured Social Relations: Patrons and Friends in Three African Societies', *West African Journal of Sociology and Political Science* 1 (1): 51–81.

Lambert, Agnes. 1993. 'Les commerçantes Maliennes du chemin de fer Dakar-Bamako', In Grégoire & Labazée.

Landa, Janet Tai. 1994. *Trust, Ethnicity, and Identity.* Ann Arbor, MI: University of Michigan Press.

Latour, Bruno. 1991. 'Technology is Society Made Durable', in *A Sociology of Monsters: Essays on Power, Technology and Domination.* Ed. J. Law. London: Routledge.

Law, John. 1992. 'Notes on the Theory of the Actor-Network: Ordering, Strategy, and Heterogeneity', *Systems Practice* 5 (4): 379–93.

—— 1994. *Organizing Modernity.* Oxford: Basil Blackwell.

Leach, Edmund. 1954. *Political Systems of Highland Burma.* Cambridge, MA: Harvard University Press.

Lebon, André. 1993. *Immigrations et présence étrangère en France.* Paris: Ministère des Affaires Sociales, de la Santé et de la Ville, Direction de la population et des migrations. November.

Leslie, Winsome J. 1987. *The World Bank and Structural Transformation in Developing Countries: the Case of Zaïre.* Boulder, CO: Lynne Rienner.

—— 1993. *Zaïre: Continuity and Political Change in an Oppressive State.* Boulder, CO: Westview.

Levi, Margaret. 1990. 'A Logic of Institutional Change', in *The Limits of Rationality.* Eds. K. Schweers Cook & M. Levi. Chicago: Chicago University Press.

Lockwood, Matthew. 1993. 'Facts or fictions? Fieldwork Relationships and the Nature of Data', in Devereux & Hoddinott.

Lomnitz, Larissa. 1971. 'Reciprocity of Favors in the Urban Middle Class of Chile', in *Studies in Economic Anthropology.* Ed. G. Dalton. Washington, DC: American Anthropological Association.

—— 1977. 'Survival and Reciprocity: the Case of Urban Marginality in Mexico', in *Extinction and Survival in Human Populations.* Ed. C. L. F. Brady. New York: Columbia University Press.

—— 1988. 'Informal Exchange Networks in Formal Systems: A Theoretical Model', *American Anthropologist* 90 (1): 42–55.

Lorenz, Edward H. 1988. 'Neither Friends nor Strangers: Informal Networks of Subcontracting in French Industry', in *Trust: Making and Breaking Cooperative Relations.* Ed. D. Gambetta. Oxford: Basil Blackwell.

Luhmann, Niklas. 1988. 'Familiarity, Confidence, Trust: Problems and Alternatives', in D. Gambetta.

Luiz, John M. 1997. 'The Political Economy of Zaïre: A Case of a Predatory State', *Africa Insight* 27, 4: 247–52.

Lupton, C. and Wilson, C. S. 1959. 'The Social Background and Connections of "Top Decision Makers"', *The Manchester School of Economic and Social Studies* 27: 30–51.

Lux, André. 1971. 'The Network of Visits between Yombe Rural Wage Earners and Their Kinsfolk in Westen Congo', *Africa* 41 (2): 109–28.

—— 1972. 'Gift Exchange and Income Redistribution between Yombe Rural Wage-Earners and their Kinsfolk in Western Zaïre', *Africa* 42 (3): 173–91.

MacCormack, Geoffrey. 1976. 'Reciprocity', *Man* 11: 89–103.

MacGaffey, Janet. 1983. 'The Effect of Rural–Urban Ties, Kinship and Marriage on Household Structure in a Kongo Village', *Canadian Journal of African Studies* 17 (1): 69–84.

—— 1987. *Entrepreneurs and Parasites*. Cambridge: Cambridge University Press.

—— 1988. 'Evading Male Control: Women in the Second Economy in Zaïre', in *Patriarchy and Class*. Eds. Sharon B. Stichter & Jane L. Parpart. Boulder, CO: Westview.

—— 1992. 'Initiatives From Below: Zaïre's Other Path to Social and Economic Restructuring'. in *Governance and Politics in Africa*. Eds. G. Hyden & M. Bratton. Boulder, CO: Lynne Rienner.

—— 1994a. 'State Deterioration and Capitalist Development: The Case of Zaïre', in *African Capitalists in African Development*. Eds. B. J. Burman & C. Leys. Boulder, CO: Lynne Rienner.

—— 1994b. 'Civil Society in Zaïre: Hidden Resistance and the Use of Personal Ties in Class Struggle', in Harbeson et al.

—— 1996. '"*On se débrouille*": the International Trade of Zaïre's Second Economy'. Paper presented at, 'L'argent, feuille morte? L'Afrique centrale avant et après le désenchantement de la modernité' Conference. Louvain, 21–22 June.

—— 1998. 'Creatively Coping with Crisis: Entrepreneurs in Zaïre's Second Economy', in *African Entrepreneurship: Themes and Realities*. Eds. B. McDade & A. Spring. Gainesville, FL: University Press of Florida.

MacGaffey, Janet, with Vwakyanakazi Mukohya, Rukarangira wa Nkera, Schoepf, Brooke Grundfest, Makwala ma Mavambu ye Beda, & Engundu, Walu. 1991. *The Real Economy of Zaïre: the Contribution of Smuggling and Other Unofficial Activities to National Wealth*. London and Philadelphia: James Currey and the University of Pennsylvania Press.

MacGaffey, Wyatt. 1997. 'Kongo Identity, 1483–1993', in *Nations, Identities, Cultures*. Ed. V. Y. Mudimbe. Durham, NC: Duke University Press.

Makonda, Antoine. 1988. 'Une école pour le "peuple?"', *Politique Africaine* 31: 39–50.

Makwala, ma Mavambu ye Beda. 1991. 'The Trade in Food Crops, Manufactured Goods and Mineral Products in the Frontier Zone of Luozi, Lower Zaïre', in MacGaffey et al.

Marchal, Roland. 1997. *Doubai: le développement d'une cité-entrepôt dans le Golfe*. Les Etudes du CERI, No. 28.

Marcus, George E. 1986. 'Contemporary Problems of Ethnography in the Modern World System', in *Writing Culture*. Eds. J. Clifford & G. E. Marcus. Berkeley and Los Angeles: University of California Press.

—— 1995. 'Ethnography in/of the World System: the Emergence of Multi-Sited Ethnography', *Annual Review of Anthropology* 24: 95–117.

Marcus, George E. & Fischer, Michael M. J. eds. 1986. *Anthropology as Cultural Critique: An Experimental Moment in the Human Sciences*. Chicago: University of Chicago Press.

Maton, Jef. 1993. 'Zaïre: Balance of Payments Problems 1992–93, Forthcoming Import Problems, Impact of Falling Exports on the Level of Commercialized GDP and Consumption'. University of Ghent (mimeo).

Mbembe, Achille. 1992. 'The Banality of Power and the Aesthetics of Vulgarity in the Postcolony', *Public Culture* 4 (2): 1–30.

McCracken, Grant. 1988. *Culture and Consumption: New Approaches to the Symbolic Character of Consumer Goods and Activities*. Bloomington, IN: Indiana University Press.

Meagher, Kate. 1990. 'The Hidden Economy: Informal and Parallel Trade in Northwestern Uganda', *Review of African Political Economy* 47: 64–83.

—— 1995. 'Parallel trade and powerless places: research on traditions and local realities in rural Northern Nigeria'. *Africa Development* xx, 2: 5–19.

Meillassoux, Claude, ed. 1971. *The Development of Indigenous Trade and Markets in West Africa*. Oxford: Oxford University Press for the International African Institute.

Mitchell, J. Clyde, ed. 1969. *Social Networks in Urban Situations*. Manchester: Manchester University Press.

Mittelman, James H., ed. 1996. *Globalization: Critical Reflections*. Boulder, CO: Lynne Rienner.

Moore, Sally Falk. 1978. *Law as Process*. Boston, MA: Routledge [reprinted 2000 by Lit Verlag, & James Currey for the International African Institute].

Mpase Nselenge Mpeti. 1974. *L'Évolution de la solidarité traditionelle en milieu rural et urbain du Zaïre: le cas des Ntomba et des Basengele du Lac Mai-Ndombe*. Kinshasa: Presses Universitaires du Zaïre.

Nair, Sami. 1992. *Le Regard des vainqueurs: les enjeux français de l'immigration*. Paris: Bernard Grasset.

Nugent, Paul. 1991. 'Educating Rawlings: the Evolution of Government Strategy Toward Smuggling', in *Ghana: the Political Economy of Recovery*. Ed. D. Rothchild. Boulder, CO: Lynne Rienner.

Omasombo, Jean Tshonda, ed. 1993. *Le Zaïre à l'épreuve de l'histoire immédiate*. Paris: Karthala.

Ossebi, Henri. 1982. 'Affirmation ethnique et discours idéologique au Congo: essai d'interpretation'. Thesis, 3rd cycle, University of Paris V.

—— 1988a. 'Un quotidien en trompe-l'œil: bars et "nganda" à Brazzaville', *Politique Africaine* 31: 61–72.

—— 1988b. 'Etat et ethnies au Congo: nouvelles situations, vieux démons', *Revue de l'Institut de Sociologie* 3–4: 211–17.

—— 1992. 'Production démocratique et transition post-totalitaire au Congo: portée et limites d'une expérience. Processus de démocratisation en Afrique: problèmes et perspectives,' Paper presented at 7th General Assembly, CODESRIA, Dakar, 10–14 February.

Politique Africaine. 1988. 'Le Congo, banlieue de Brazzaville' 31: 2–83.

Powell, Walter W. 1990. 'Neither Market nor Hierarchy; Network Forms of Organization', *Research in Organizational Behavior* 12: 295–336.

Reno, William. 1995. *Corruption and State Politics in Sierra Leone.* African Studies Series 83. Cambridge: Cambridge University Press.

Roberts, Bryan R. 1973. *Organizing Strangers: Poor Families in Guatemala City.* Austin, TX: University of Texas Press.

Roseberry, William. 1996. 'The Unbearable Lightness of Anthropology', *Radical History Review* 65: 5–25.

Rothchild, Donald & Chazan, Naomi, eds. 1988. *The Precarious Balance.* Boulder CO: Westview Press.

Rowlands, M. & Warnier, J.-P. 1988. 'Sorcery, Power and the Modern State in Cameroon', *Man (ns)* 23: 118–32.

Rukarangira, wa Nkera & Schoepf, Brooke Grundfest. 1991. 'Unrecorded Trade in Southeast Shaba and Across Zaïre's Southern Border', in MacGaffey et al.

Sabakinu Kivilu. 1988. 'La radio trottoir dans l'exercise du pouvoir politique au Zaïre', in *Dialoguer avec le Léopard.* Ed. B. Jewsiewicki & H. Moniot. Paris: L'Harmattan.

Sahlins, Marshall D. 1965. 'On the Sociology of Primitive Exchange', in *The Relevance of Models for Social Anthropology.* Ed. M. Banton. London: Tavistock.

Sanjek, Roger. 1978. 'A Network Method and Its Uses in Urban Ethnography', *Human Organization* 37 (3): 257–68.

Schatzberg, Michael G. 1988. *The Dialectics of Oppression in Zaïre.* Bloomington, IN: Indiana University Press.

Schmink, Marianne. 1984. 'Household Economic Strategies: Review and Research Agenda', *Latin American Research Review* 19 (3): 87–101.

Schoepf, Brooke Grundfest & Engundu, Walu. 1991. 'Women's Trade and Contributions to Household Budgets in Kinshasa', in MacGaffey et al.

Scott, James C. 1985. *Weapons of the Weak: Everyday Forms of Peasant Resistance.* New Haven, CT: Yale University Press.

—— 1987. 'Resistance without Protest and without Organization: Peasant Opposition to the Islamic Zakat and the Christian Tithe', *Comparative Studies in Society and History* 29 (3): 417–52.

—— 1990. *Domination and the Arts of Resistance: Hidden Transcripts.* New Haven, CT and London: Yale University Press.

Shipton, Parker. 1989. *Bitter Money.* Washington, DC: American Anthropological Association.

Shlapentokh, Vladimir. 1984. *Love, Marriage and Friendship in the Soviet Union.* New York: Praeger.

Singerman, Diane. 1995. *Avenues of Participation: Family, Politics, and Networks in Urban Quarters of Cairo*. Princeton, NJ: Princeton University Press.

Solomon, Hussein. 1997. 'From Zaïre to the Democratic Republic of the Congo: Towards Post-Mobutuism', *Africa Insight* 27 (2): 91–7.

Steiner, Christopher B. 1994. *African Art in Transit*. Cambridge: Cambridge University Press.

Sutton, Constance. 1987. 'The Caribbeanization of New York City and the Emergence of a Transnational Socio-Cultural System', in *Caribbean Life in New York City*. Ed. C. S. E. Chaney. New York: Center for Migration Studies.

Szelenyi, Ivan et al. 1988. *Socialist Entrepreneurs: Embourgeoisement in Rural Hungary*. Madison, WI: University of Wisconsin Press.

Thornton, Robert. 1996. 'The Potentials of Boundaries in South Africa: Towards a Theory of the Social Edge', in Werbner & Ranger.

Trager, Lilian. 1984. 'Family Strategies and the Migration of Women: Migrants to Dagupan City, Philippines', *International Migration Review* 18 (4): 1264–77.

Tripp, Aili Mari. 1997. *Changing the Rules: the Politics of Liberalization and the Urban Informal Economy in Tanzania*. Berkeley, CA: University of California Press.

Tsamouna Kitongo. 1990. 'Ethnies et urbanité dans la lutte politique au Congo après 1959', *Africa: Revista trimestrale di studi e documentazione dell'Instituto Italo-Africano*, XLV (4): 665–79.

Turner, Victor W. 1974. *Dramas, Fields and Metaphors: Symbolic Action in Human Society*. Ithaca, NY: Cornell University Press.

—— 1977. 'Frame, Flow and Reflection: Ritual and Drama as Public Liminality', in *Performance in Postmodern Culture*, Ed. M. B. C. Caramello. Milwaukee, WI: Center for 20th Century Studies, University of Wisconsin.

—— 1992. 'Morality and Liminality', in *Blazing the Trail: Way Marks in the Exploration of Symbols*. Ed. E. Turner. Tucson, AZ: University of Arizona Press.

Van Velsen, J. 1967. 'The Extended-case Method and Situational Analysis', in *The Craft of Social Anthropology*. Ed. A. L. Epstein. London: Tavistock Publications.

Vangu Ngimbi, Ivan. 1996. 'Les Zaïrois de France: sont-ils des immigrés?', *Sociétés Africaines et Diaspora* 4 (December): 129–33.

Vellut, Jean-Luc. 1991. 'Le communauté Portugaise du Congo Belge', in *Flandre et Portugal: au confluent de deux cultures*. Eds. J. Everaert & E. Stols. Antwerp: Fonds Mercator.

Verhaegen, Benoît. 1990. *Femmes Zaïroises de Kisangani: combats pour la survie*. Vol. 8, *Enquêtes et Documents d'Histoire Africaine*. Louvain-la-Neuve: University of Louvain and L' Harmattan.

Vwakyanakazi, Mukohya. 1982. 'African Traders in Butembo, Eastern Zaïre (1960–1980): a Case Study of Informal Entrepreneurship in a

Cultural Context of Central Africa.' Ph.D. Dissertation, University of Wisconsin-Madison, Madison, WI.

—— 1991. 'Import and Export in the Second Economy in North Kivu', in MacGaffey et al.

Weigand, Robert E. 1977. 'International Trade without Money', *Harvard Business Review*: 28–30, 34, 38, 42, 166.

Weissman, Fabrice. 1993. *Election presidentielles de 1992 au Congo: entreprise politique et mobilisation électorale*. IEP de Bordeaux, University of Bordeaux I, CEAN.

Werbner, Pnina. 1990. 'Economic Rationality and Hierarchical Gift Economies: Value and Ranking Among British Pakistanis', *Man (n.s.)* 25: 266–85.

Werbner, Richard. 1991. *Tears of the Dead: the Social Biography of an African Family*. Edinburgh: Edinburgh University Press for the International African Institute.

Werbner, Richard & Ranger, Terence. 1996. *Postcolonial Identities*. London: Zed Books.

Willame, Jean-Claude. 1991. 'L'Automne d'une monarchie', *Politique Africaine* 41: 10–21.

—— 1992. *L'Automne d'un despotisme: pouvoir, argent et obéissance dans le Zaïre des années quatre-vingt*. Paris: Karthala.

Willis, Paul. 1977. *Learning to Labor: How Working Class Kids Get Working Class Jobs*. New York: Columbia University Press.

—— 1990. *Common Culture*. Milton Keynes: Open University Press.

Wilson, Ken. 1993. 'Thinking About the Ethics of Fieldwork', in Devereux & Hoddinott.

Wolf, Eric R. 1966. 'Kinship, Friendship and Patron–Client Relations', in *The Social Anthropology of Complex Societies*. Ed. M. Banton. London: Tavistock.

—— 1982. *Europe and the People without History*. Berkeley, CA: University of California Press.

Yengo, Patrice. 1994. 'La démocratisation piégée'. Paper presented at 'Conférence national congolaise, entre contraintes économiques et fascination du passé. Démocratie et Développement' Conference. Forum de Delphes, Naupactos Monastery, Greece, 30 October–2 November.

Yoka Lye Mudaba. 1984. 'Radio-trottoir: le discours en camouflage', *Le Mois en Afrique* 225: 154–60.

Young, Crawford. 1994. 'Zaïre: the Shattered Illusion of the Integral State', *Journal of Modern African Studies* 32 (2): 247–63.

Young, Crawford, & Turner, Thomas. 1985. *The Rise and Decline of the Zairian State*. Madison, WI: University of Wisconsin Press.

INDEX